Drums Along The Antietam

by
John W. Schildt

McCLAIN PRINTING COMPANY
PARSONS, WEST VIRGINIA 26287

1972

Standard Book Number 87012-128-6
Library of Congress Card Number 72-84077
Printed in the United States of America
Copyright © 1972 by John W. Schildt
Chewsville, Maryland

This book is written in gratitude
for the life
and labors of
George Adam Geeting
Bishop John Russell
and
Fred Wilder Cross
with thanks
for the inspiration of Virginia

CONTENTS

ILLUSTRATIONS AND MAPS

Many of the pictures in this book have never before appeared in any publication. Most of them were taken by the Honorable Fred W. Cross, archivist for the state of Massachusetts, in the early 1920s. They were loaned to the author by John Winters.

The picture of President Franklin D. Roosevelt appears by special permission of United Press International.

PREFACE

On a hot evening, during the summer of July 1970 I started to wonder what happened to the eighteen thousand men who were wounded during the Battle of Antietam.

The answer took shape on New Year's Eve. A howling blizzard raged outside. But in the comfort of our home, I was thinking of a book which might give a comprehensive history of an area I dearly love. A title flashed into my mind, *Drums Along the Antietam*. Then came the idea to use phrases from "The Battle Hymn of the Republic" as chapter headings.

The writing of the book led to new persons and places. Some of the farms and homes in the Valley of the Antietam had been seen many times. But now came the search to find the original owners, as well as some of the events which had occurred at the property down through the years. The quest led to a study of the past and present, and the hope for preservation of the valley.

The search for material led to some exciting and wonderful new friends, and some new discoveries. Among the discoveries were the papers of the Honorable Fred Cross and Dr. James Oliver. Many wonderful hours were spent with the fine folks in the valley and with Colonel John Winters.

The book covers a relatively small area, approximately seven miles east and west, or from Keedysville to the Potomac, and about the same distance north and south, or from the Cecil Poffenberger farm to Antietam Furnace.

Yet the area is full of history, personal valor, hard work, stories of sacrifices and commitment to God and others. The *Drums Along the Antietam* led to world-shaking events. May the pages telling the story enrich and inspire your life as much as compiling the material has done for me.

John W. Schildt

March 25, 1972

ACKNOWLEDGMENTS

We acknowledge with gratitude the permission of the authors and publishing companies listed in the notes for permission to quote from their works.

Likewise we acknowledge the deep debt of gratitude owed to Dean McClanahan, superintendent of the Antietam National Battlefield Site, and Mrs. Betty Otto for their aid and encouragement. The author was given every possible help in his effort to uncover the unknown events transpiring at Antietam.

The Honorable Edward S. Delaplaine's writings and research were invaluable in the study of Lincoln at Antietam.

Miss Janet Brechbill, Mrs. Richard Rider, Mrs. Samuel Ford, Mrs. Harvey Leisinger, Mrs. Joseph Filsinger, and Mrs. Alan Weaver typed the manuscript.

The Wilmeyer Photography Studio in Hagerstown assisted greatly with the pictures as did A. K. McGraw.

John Winters and Thomas Kendrick shared the papers and pictures of Fred W. Cross and Dr. James Oliver.

To all who helped and shared in the production of this book we say thank you.

I

DRUMS

Down through the ages of history, the beat of the drum has been a symbol of action, adventure, danger, and sometimes death. Many drums have been heard along the meandering Antietam Creek as it winds from its source in the hills above Waynesboro, Pennsylvania, to the Potomac at Antietam Furnace.

The banks of the Antietam and adjacent fields have heard the beat of Catawba and Delaware Indian drums as they hunted, raided, and fought.

Next was heard the drums of the British Grenadiers under General Edward Braddock of the Coldstream Guards, marching in cadence on their way to disaster and death near Fort Necessity.

Then came the drums of "Yankee Doodle" and men from Sharpsburg and Shepherdstown marching off to fight in the War of Revolution for Independence and a new nation.

During this time a great awakening was sweeping America, and a new denomination came into being on the banks of the Little Antietam Creek, the Church of the United Brethren in Christ.

The years pass, and 1861 finds America at war again, two great sections of the country fighting for causes and principles in which they believe. In September of the following year, the Antietam heard the beat of the regimental drums of the Blue and the Gray as "Billy Yank" and "Johnny Reb" gathered near Sharpsburg to fight the greatest battle ever to occur on the American Continent.

On the night of the sixteenth, we might have heard the

1

drums beating out "Dixie," "Tenting Tonight," or "Just Before the Battle, Mother."

The next morning some would hear the drums for the last time. Before daybreak, the drummer boys called the men of the Blue and the Gray to battle.

In October 1862 the drums of the Army of the Potomac beat a welcome for the president of the United States, Abraham Lincoln. They beat again the next day as the army marched by in review. Through the years the drums would beat again as bands struck up "Ruffles and Flourishes," and "Hail to the Chief," as men occupying the highest office in the land came to visit Antietam battlefield.

September 17, 1867, found the drums beating for President Andrew Johnson who led a solemn procession to a hill at the east end of Sharpsburg. The occasion was the dedication of land set aside as the final bivouac for those who had given their "last full measure of devotion" at Antietam.

The drums have been heard along the Antietam on May 30 just about every year since 1868. Thousands have gathered to hear speeches by presidents, senators, congressmen, and men from the rank and file who have worked and prayed to make America great.

Upon conclusion of the speeches, three volleys of shots ring out across the hallowed fields, and from off in the distance there comes the haunting notes of taps. Then to the muffled beat of the drum, those present leave firmly resolving that those who rest on Antietam's soil shall not have died in vain.

Sadly, very few books exist on the history of Washington County, let alone the Valley of the Antietam. The earliest and most comprehensive is Thomas J. Scharff's *History of Western Maryland,* written in 1882. A very helpful little booklet is John P. Smith's *Reminiscences of Sharpsburg, from July 9, 1763 to January 1, 1912.* Mr. Smith lived in Sharpsburg and was well versed on local history. Thomas J. C. Williams followed with another county history and biographical record of select families in 1906. In 1910 Helen Ashe Hays wrote the famous *Antietam and Its Bridges.*

Beyond these four books, it is difficult to find much about the early history of the area.

This book, though far from complete, makes an attempt to describe some of the people and places who have made history in the Valley of the Antietam.

Indian Drums

Long before the eyes of white men ever beheld the beauty of the Valley of the Antietam, Indian drums were heard along the stream and in the dense forest. Canoe trips were made up and down the Antietam and the Potomac. Caves in the cliffs bordering the Potomac were used for shelter at night.

Years before Sharpsburg was laid out, or any homes erected in the area, the Delaware Indians and other tribes hunted and fished near the two streams which yet today bear Indian names, Potomac and Antietam. Campfires followed successful hunts, and the beat of the drum was the signal to dance for joy or in gratitude.

The mouth of the Antietam seems to have been a favorite camping and gathering spot. It must have been the place of rendezvous for hunting and war parties. Many Indian artifacts have been discovered in the area.

Indian war drums sounded in 1736. In that year, one of the biggest Indian battles fought in North America occurred between the Delawares and the Catawbas near Antietam Furnace.[1]

Indians traveling in the Valley of the Antietam created the trails that many settlers would follow and they handed down to the white men knowledge of good fording spots.

All Indian trails led to the Great Spring in Sharpsburg. The Indians came from the streams and the density of the woods to find rest and refreshment at the big spring which still flows today. Years later the settlers would drink of its life-giving water. And in 1862 soldiers and horses stood in line to get a cool drink. Ladies in the town carried water by the bucket to their homes to quench the thirst of the wounded.

Just a few years before the large land grants were made to those coming to the Valley of the Antietam, the Delaware

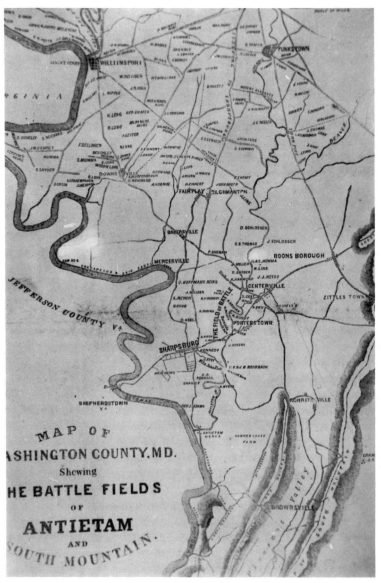

Washington County in the 1860s. This large map of the county appears in the October 11, 1862, edition of *Harper's Weekly*, the *Life Magazine* of that day.

4

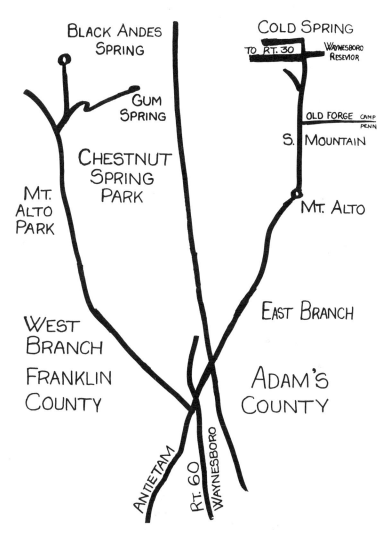

Source of the Antietam Creek.

Indians gained control of the area, ousting the Catawbas. This angered the Catawbas who had seen their prime hunting and fishing area invaded.

Once after a raid into the South, the Delawares stopped near the mouth of the Antietam for food and rest. While they were encamped, the Catawbas launched a surprise attack. For a while it looked as though they would be victorious. However, the Delawares rallied, and soon gained the upper hand. One by one the Catawbas went down, felled by the arrow or tomahawk. Finally only one Catawba was left.

The Delawares looked over the field of victory, and at the enemy scalps they had lifted. All but one of the Delawares had a fresh bloody scalp in his hands, or hanging from his belt. The lone Delaware knew what he must do. He had no scalp. Now he must leave his tribe and give chase to the one Catawba who had escaped. He would have to track him down like a bloodhound. After a chase of over a hundred miles to the north, the Delaware came upon the Catawba on the banks of the Susquehanna and killed him. He returned to the Delaware camp with his mission accomplished.[2]

Sharpsburg's Big Spring. This historic spring has given drink to Indians, early settlers, soldiers, animals, and wounded men.

The drums of the Indians were heard by a young French family living on Red Hill. The family of four including a son and daughter fled to South Mountain for shelter during the big fight at the mouth of the Antietam. The daughter was a slender, dark-eyed beauty by the name of Rosaline.

Not knowing what to expect from the hands of the red men, the white settlers apparently stayed in hiding for several days. During this period they suffered from hunger and cold. The mother and little boy fell ill and died, victims of life on the frontier.

Rosaline, tired, hungry, and cold was almost overcome with grief. For a time she stayed with some friends. Then according to the old story, she drank the healing waters of a nearby spring and rapidly regained her physical and emotional health. This spring was later to be known as "Belinda Springs."

Feeling better, Rosaline returned home to her father on Red Hill. However, she was to have an unpleasant appointment with fate or destiny. One day, a tall, handsome Catawba chieftain saw her, and promptly told Rosaline's father that he wanted to marry her.

The father's answer was, "No." Whereupon the Indian chief stomped angrily away. He must have vowed to return. Rosaline and her father lived in constant dread. Many times they thought they saw the Indian peering at them from the shelter of the forest.

One night as father and daughter sat by the door of the open cabin, a shot rang out, and Rosaline's father fell dead at her feet. While she was still in a state of shock, the Indian came and carried her away in captivity. This was the last that was seen or heard of the lovely Rosaline.[3]

Today, some of the residents along the Little Antietam, feel that an old red shed, or perhaps the stone house in which George Adam Geeting lived, might have been the home of Orlando and his tragedy stricken family.[4]

British Drums

Edward Braddock III, born in 1694, followed in the footsteps of his father as he embraced a military career. Like his

7

father, Edward advanced in rank until he became a major general in the famous Coldstream Guards.

September 24, 1754, was probably the biggest day of his life. On that September day, Edward Braddock had an appointment with the king of England and the duke of Cumberland. When he emerged from their presence, he carried with him the title of general and commander of all British forces in North America.[5]

Braddock spent the next several weeks getting ready for his new assignment which would carry him nearly four thousand miles from home. Although he relished the opportunity to achieve military fame, he realized that he was sixty years old, and anything could happen crossing the ocean or in the colonies. Thus he prepared his will before he left.

His task would be to assault and capture the French forts at Niagara, Crown Point, and Fort Duquesne. To do this, roads would have to be cut through the wilderness, mountains would have to be crossed, and rivers forded. At stake was control of North America.

On December 22, 1754, two ships carrying Braddock and his staff left England for Virginia. The weather could not have been worse during the crossing. Perhaps it was a foretaste of things to come. Not until February 19, 1755, did General Braddock get the opportunity to view the New World. The next day Braddock was rowed ashore, and by the twenty-second, he was meeting with colonial officials in Williamsburg.

Plans made in England had called for the concentration of the army at Wills Creek Fort near Cumberland. Existing maps showed little beyond the Conocheague Creek, west of Hagerstown. The only road to Wills Creek was from Winchester, Virginia, and that was eighty-five miles in length, and in terrible shape.

Some of the officers considered sending the artillery and other supplies up the Potomac on boats, but the falls and rapids made that suggestion impossible.

Colonel John St. Clair, Braddock's quartermaster officer, journeyed to Wills Creek to see the situation for himself. He found it far from promising. Actually, all that existed at Wills

Creek was a stockade enclosing a small piece of ground. Colonel St. Clair worried about food for the horses. The area was thickly wooded, with very few homes. It looked as though the army would have to carry its supplies in wagons. Forage for men and animals was too uncertain.

Sailors from the *Norwich,* one of the vessels which had brought Braddock to America, were assigned to help the army cross the many rivers which were without bridges.

In early March, seven British transports arrived at Hampton, Virginia, carrying English troops for the campaign against the French. These were ordered to Alexandria, Virginia. The townspeople had never seen anything quite like the brilliant red uniforms. They had never heard as many drums before either, twenty drums to a regiment. Some of the English soldiers even brought their wives along.

On Friday, April 4, 1755, an advance detail of Braddock's army reached Frederick. On April 17, the main body of troops left Alexandria for Frederick. They marched through wilderness, the road being little better than a trail. A late April snowstorm dumped eighteen inches of the white stuff and made matters worse. However, the snow soon melted.

The soldiers were ferried across the Monocacy, swollen as a result of the snow. The sailors performed their tasks well.

Frederick in 1755 was a town of about two hundred homes, at least two churches, a tavern, of course, and a courthouse under construction.

Poor Braddock. Nothing seemed to go right for him. It was almost as though the entire campaign was jinxed. The general became angry with Governor Sharpe and Marylanders because the wagons promised to carry supplies were slow in arriving. Cattle promised as food were not available either. General Braddock felt the colonies should look upon his army as an agent of deliverance. But it seemed as though the colonies were primarily concerned about their own affairs. Pennsylvania and New Jersey, or at least the general thought so, could not have cared less about the French and Indian War. It was most difficult to obtain funds or promises of other aid from either colony.

But help was on the way. Frederick was to have another

9

distinguished visitor. Much needed aid came to General Braddock from forty-nine-year-old Benjamin Franklin, deputy postmaster general of the North American Colonies. Franklin and his son William dined with Braddock daily. They discussed the campaign. The general desired 150 wagons to carry the army westward. Franklin agreed to round up wagons and supplies for the English in Pennsylvania. When the Franklins left Frederick they made a stop at a printer's shop. Handbills were ordered to distribute to the prosperous farmers in Lancaster, York, and Cumberland counties (in Pennsylvania).

The handbills called for 150 wagons, with four horses to each wagon, and a driver, and 500 saddle or pack horses. The bills stated that Franklin was empowered by General Braddock to pay fifteen shillings per day for each wagon with four good horses, and two shilling per diem for each able horse with a pack saddle.

The horses, wagons, and drivers were to rendezvous with General Braddock at Wills Creek on or before May 20.

Franklin praised the English for coming so far from home, giving up comfort and luxury to defend this land. He pointed out it was now the patriotic duty of the people to support the army. If the items sought were not forthcoming voluntarily, then they would be conscripted by Braddock's cavalry.

Governor Sharpe and Colonel George Washington also arrived in Frederick to meet with General Braddock. In fact, April 1755 was one of the greatest months in Frederick's history.

On Tuesday, April 29, 1755, the Redcoats marched out of Frederick, and crossed the Catoctin Mountains at what is known today as Braddock Heights.

Construction would slow down at the courthouse because the horses being used to haul building materials were now pulling some of Braddock's supply wagons.

The English soldiers made eighteen miles that first day. They had their problems though. Chiggers almost drove them crazy. Most of the soldiers had little red, itchy welts all over them. The march was enlivened by the sight of many deer, rabbits, and other wildlife.

10

By late afternoon the foot soldiers made camp beyond South Mountain, most likely in the Boonsboro-Keedysville area.

The next morning, April 30, the rolling Antietam heard the beat of the British regimental drums as the troops formed to march at six o'clock. They forded the Antietam Creek near the Hitt Bridge or the Upper Bridge of Civil War fame. These soldiers were over one hundred years in advance of others who would wear not red coats, but blue tunics.

Maryland Governor Sharpe, sorry for the difficulties encountered by Braddock, persuaded the general to accept his personal coach as it was better suited to wilderness travel.

Then Braddock also crossed the Antietam riding in a chariot drawn by six white horses, crossing at a ford near the village which eight years hence would be named for Governor Sharpe.

Braddock and many of his men would never see the Antietam again. Each beat of the British drums brought them closer to the Indians and French, hiding in the deep woods of Pennsylvania in ambush. On July 9, 1755, Braddock's men, marching in line almost as though on parade and disdaining the advice of George Washington and others, were caught by complete surprise near Fort Necessity. Braddock was badly wounded, and Washington had several balls go through his coat. The next day, Braddock of the Coldstream Guards died in the American wilderness. He was buried in the middle of the road and the retreating wagons ran over his grave to conceal it from the Indians. His uniform sash is now at Mount Vernon. The British expedition was a disaster. News of the retreat brought great alarm to the few settlers in western Maryland.

Today, there might be a remaining monument to Braddock and his men by the Little Antietam. Near the Mount Hebron Road, which was probably traveled by the British, is Fellfoot. On this historic farm is a large stone barn erected in 1754. Some Washington County historians are of the opinion that the barn was built under the supervision of Colonel St. Clair of Braddock's staff a year in advance of the expedition. The barn would serve as a supply base and house the horses of the

11

army when they came through. This cannot be proven, but it is in the realm of possibility.

George Alfred Townsend, a noted Civil War correspondent, and author of *Katy of Catoctin* as well as *The Entailed Hat*, wrote a poetic tribute to Braddock's men who in 1754 marched to the beat of the drums through the Valley of the Antietam.

SIR JOHN ST. CLAIR

Builder of the First Road Across the Mountain
His name is lost save in a brook of water
    That darkly plunges through a forest glen,
Like that lean army pioneered to slaughter
    Through lonely shades to horrible Duquesne:
    But in that road he hewed across the mountains,
Where Braddock sleeps beneath his wagon wheels.
A living brook goes on from Eastern fountains,
No wars arrest, no killing frost congeals.
His was the skiff that hardily descended
    The wild Potomac to the roaring falls,
His were the floats that the soldiery befriended
    To pass the torrent, under mountain walls.
    His were the bridges over the Opequon
And the Antietam in the morn of time,
    Crossed by a multitude no man can reckon
To sceneries and destinies sublime.
Behind his axes formed the van of movement,
    His picks and shovels were the conquering swords;
And in the rift of light he ope'd, Improvement
    Went single file, through savage-hidden savage hordes.
    Until the pack mules with their bells were merry
Where rolling drums in vain inspired the fight,
    And sheep and shepherds tarried by the ferry
That drowned a host amidst the battle's fright.
High-metted Scot! thine is no glory hollow:
    Shall we forget thee in our westward ho?—
When thy canoe the laden barges follow
    And up thy path the steaming engines blow?
    No! while the sky the Alleghany arches,

12

The good road builders name shall be revealed:
Sir John St. Clair's victorious army marches
Above the army lost on Braddock field.

Washington County as we know it today, was not created
until September 6, 1776, by the Provincial Convention of
Maryland. From 1748 until 1776 it had been a part of Frederick County. Before the Revolutionary War, the governor of
the province made the land grants on behalf of the Lord
Proprietary, and then by the state government. Scharf on
pages 983-986 in Vol. II lists most of these early grants. To
these grants came the early settlers.

Name of Grant	To Whom Granted	Date	Acres
Annadale	Joseph Chapline	Feb. 21, 1764	50
Badham's Refusal	Joseph Chapline	May 12, 1759	50
Clydesdale	Joseph Chapline	Feb. 21, 1764	243
Contentment	Joseph Chapline	Feb. 21, 1764	1,153
Jonah's Last Bit	Moses Chapline	Oct. 12, 1761	67
Little Friendship	Joseph Chapline	July 1, 1760	200
Resurvey of Part of			
Bachelors Delight	Joseph Chapline	Sept. 19, 1763	443½
Tuckett	Joseph Chapline	Sept. 24, 1759	75
Tweed-dale	Joseph Chapline	Feb. 21, 1764	42
Well Done Resurvey	Moses Chapline	Feb. 1, 1764	1,822
Little Thought	Joseph Chapline	Feb. 2, 1763	6,352
Hills and Dales	Joseph Chapline	June 26, 1749	50
Loss and Gain	Joseph Chapline	April 11, 1765	1,168½

II

DRUMS OF THE SETTLERS

Traveling our superhighways today, it is very difficult to realize that in 1750, western Maryland was virtually a wilderness and the western frontier. Although the English, with the leadership of Lord Baltimore and others, had settled and developed the Eastern Shore, western Maryland was still the hunting grounds of the Indians, and just a few log cabins could be found in the dense woods and high grass.

In colonial days most settlements grew up along the coast, making trade and communication with the mother country less difficult.

In Europe and in many parts of colonial America, people were expected to embrace the faith of the king. If not, trouble and persecution could be expected to follow. King Charles I, although not a Catholic, was a good friend of the Calvert family, and granted them a large tract of land. The Calverts were determined that in the new colony, anyone would be welcome regardless of his religious faith.

George Calvert

It only takes a spark to get a fire going. Often one event starts a chain reaction. Many times an individual with a goal or dream can lead people to new horizons. Such a man was George Calvert who lived in England from about 1580 to 1632.

He was a highly educated young man with intelligence and personality to match. He became England's secretary of state, and became very powerful in the government of King James I. The king granted him the island of Avalon and a great manor in Ireland.

In 1624, Calvert decided to leave the Church of England and become a Catholic. This was not a popular thing to do, and he resigned his government post. Calvert's plan or vision was to develop his grant of Avalon. Today we call it Newfoundland. At first things went very well. But then came the winter of 1628 with terrible weather and disease. In addition there was a shortage of food. Calvert, who had been given the title of Lord Baltimore, helped to tend the sick himself.[1]

The winter of 1628 made him realize that he needed a warmer climate to have a successful colony. Still very popular with the King of England and other government authorities, he set out to visit the New World and to look over land in Virginia. The Virginia leaders did not want him there. They thought he was too powerful and would take their land. He refused their effort to make him swear an oath of allegiance to the Church of England. Whereupon the Virginia officials refused him permission to settle in their state.

However, this turned out to be a blessing in disguise. On the way home he noted the beautiful Potomac and wide Chesapeake Bay. The waters were "thick with fish," and the forest full of game. The climate was better, too.

When George Calvert returned to England, he learned that his friend King James I was dead. His son, King Charles I, was now on the throne. Calvert asked King Charles for a charter to settle lands north of the Potomac River. To gain favor, he suggested the colony be called "Maryland" after the Queen of England, Henrietta Marie.

King Charles, in hopes of gaining gold from the New World, signed the charter. However, before he did so, George Calvert died, and his son Cecil inherited the lands, wealth, and title of Lord Baltimore II.

George Calvert and King James I set things in motion for the founding of Maryland, but their sons, Cecil and Charles, carried the plans through to completion.

Two small wooden ships left Cowes, Isle of Wight, England, on November 22, 1633, to sail for the colony called "Maryland." On board the *Ark* and the *Dove* were two hundred carefully selected people. Most of them, including Father White, were Catholics.

15

Food, water, beer, seeds, cuttings, and tools were carefully packed to start the new colony. The time of departure was planned so the settlers would arrive in the New World in the spring of the year when the weather was better, and when they could plant crops.

The journey was rough. There were storms at sea. A terrible storm broke five days out of port. The *Ark* and the *Dove* were separated and almost sunk. But they kept on and in February arrived at Jamestown. The new colonists were treated kindly by the Virginians, and they were able to purchase cows and pigs to take to their new homes.

The weather was balmy when they started up the Chesapeake. The new settlers were delighted at "the wide expanse of the noble bay. They gave thanks to God for the beautiful land which He had given them."

Indian campfires could be seen along the shore. Indian drums and smoke signals sent the message "Canoes, as big as an island, have brought as many men as there are trees in the forest."

The next day, March 25, those stouthearted people who had left England on November 22 set foot on Blakistone Island. They had arrived in Maryland at last.

However, it would take almost another hundred years before the English would reach into the backwoods country and settle along the Antietam.

Why Did the Germans Come?

"The roots of the present are deep in the past."

The cause of German immigration can be traced back to the Protestant Reformation which occurred in 1517. Most of northern Germany became Protestant, while the southern part of the country remained Catholic. The differences of religious thought led to quarrels and conflicts.[2]

Some leaders, anxious to capitalize on the situation by seizing land and making money, fanned the flames. Finally the smouldering fires of hatred burst into flame. In 1618, the Thirty Years' War began. Before it was over, France, Denmark, Sweden, Spain, Italy, and Bohemia had entered the conflict. Most of the fighting, however, took place on German soil.

When peace finally came in 1648, Germany was just about ruined. "Almost a third of the people had been killed or starved to death. Cities were destroyed. Trade and commerce were at a standstill. Fields lay uncultivated. The German people were helpless to protect themselves against tyrants at home or robber kings abroad."[3]

It took Germany over a hundred years to recover. People continued to starve to death. Thus when the opportunity came for the Germans to come to America, they felt they had nothing to lose. The wilderness could not be any worse than the situation at home. So they came for religious freedom, and with the hope of owning a piece of ground where they could farm and live at peace without the threat of war hanging over their heads.

THE GERMAN "MAYFLOWER"

October 6, 1683, was a big day in the port of Philadelphia. On that fall day, the *Conrad* sailed into the harbor. Thirteen German families were on board.[4] They were most happy to see land, having been on the Atlantic for seventy-five days. This was the first organized group of German immigrants to come to American shores. The people could be characterized by the description of the *Conrad*, "sturdy, solid and not too fast."[5]

The Germans came, bringing their Bibles and prayer books with them. Their purpose in coming to America was "the desire to lead a quiet, godly and honest life."[6] Philadelphia was the first home of the Germans in Penn's Woods. Then these hearty people pushed westward to Lancaster and to the Pennsylvania Dutch Country of today. Some branched to the south, to Hanover and down the Monocacy Trail to Frederick and Washington counties. The progress was slow and steady, step by step.

Many of the German immigrants came from the Palatinate. The name at one time referred to the castle of a German emperor. But the geographical area today is known as Bavaria and the Rhineland. The old capitals were Regensburg and

17

Speyer. The land has always been famous for its fertile soil, good crops, and hardworking people.

Therefore, the Germans coming to these shores knew how to work hard and how to eke out a living from the soil. It is good they did, because here they had to start from scratch. Trees had to be cut and cleared so fields could be made ready and planted. Homes and barns had to be built. Everything had to be done by hand.

By 1720 the Germans had reached the Susquehanna River. At first, western Maryland was looked upon as a wilderness necessary to reach the fertile soil of Virginia. In the meantime, the Van Meter brothers had offered a large tract of land in Virginia to Jost Hite. They described the land in such glowing terms that Hite took fifteen German families with him. He obtained 100,000 acres of land. Then he persuaded many Germans in Pennsylvania and New Jersey to go with him to Virginia.

Maryland leaders felt the hearty Germans would be good to settle the backwoods of the colony. They wondered what could be done to induce the Germans to stay in Maryland instead of moving on to Virginia.

In March 1732, Lord Baltimore issued a proclamation aimed to attract Germans. The first part read: "Wee being Desirious to Increase the Number of Honest people within our Province of Maryland and willing to give Suitable Encouragement to such as come and reside therein Do offer the following Terms."[7] Any family arriving within the next three years and promising to settle in Maryland, ". . . on any of the back Lands . . . should receive two hundred acres of their own choosing, completely free for three years; from the fourth year on they should pay a rent of one per cent per acre per year."[8] One can hardly imagine living rent free for three years, and paying a penny per acre thereafter. But these were the terms offered, and they had the desired result. The Germans felt, "Why go to Virginia with a bargain like this?"

Slowly but surely the Germans came, a few at first, but then in an increasing tide. The land looked good. The hills, streams, and woods reminded them of their German

18

homeland. So they unpacked their wagons, cleared the lands, and settled down.

THE GERMANS COME TO MARYLAND

Gradually the Germans made their way to Maryland. It is difficult to determine the exact year of their coming. However, the population of what is now western Maryland was so sparse that Frederick County was not created until 1748. This was twelve years after the beat of Indian War drums was heard at the mouth of the Antietam. At that time Frederick County included part of present day Montgomery and Carroll counties, as well as all of Washington, Allegany, and Garrett.[9]

Fur traders, trappers, and hunters may have explored western Maryland as early as 1715, or perhaps earlier.

> John Van Meter must have crosed the Potomac on his first visit to the Valley of Virginia before the Indian treaties of the 1720's. . . . It is said that he came as an Indian fighter-trader with a company of Delawares on their way south to fight The Catawbas. . . . It was not till June, 1730, that he was given leave by the Governor and Council to take up 10,000 acres lying on the south fork of Shenandoah and 20,000 acres between the Shenandoah and the Cohongoroota, or Potomac, and thence to the Opequon and up the South Branch. At the same time Isaac Van Meter was allowed 10,000 acres, for himself, and other German families, in the region of the Opequon and Shenandoah.[10]

In 1732 the Van Meters moved to the South Branch of the Potomac, and sold their land to Jost Hite. A group of sixteen families, led by Hite, made their way through Pennsylvania to York. From there they had to improve upon Indian trails as they traveled to Harpers Ferry, and on to their final destination around Winchester. The author surmises that they followed the road that leads to Hanover, Taneytown (Maryland 194), Ceresville, Frederick, and perhaps to Crampton's Gap and then across the Potomac.

Old records indicate that Thomas Shepherd lived near Antietam Furnace several years prior to 1734. In that year he bought 222 acres from Jost Hite and established the village of Shepherdstown, the oldest village in West Virginia.

In 1731, Adam Forney bought the acreage upon which the present town of Hanover, Pennsylvania, is located. The Ger-

19

mans who settled in this village named after Hanover, Germany, soon began to move across the border and settled in Maryland. They gradually lost some of their fear of the deep, dark woods. From the time of the early arrivals in Philadelphia, the German movement in Pennsylvania had been in a southwesterly direction. The old Indian trail, known as the Monocacy Road, soon became an important artery of travel from Hanover to Frederick, and on into the Shenandoah Valley.

Some of the Germans made their way to the Valley of the Antietam. Old legends indicate that the valley with South Mountain and Red Hill reminded them of home. Thus before the Revolution, Jacob Hess, George Geeting, and others had settled along the Little Antietam near Keedysville. Sharpsburg, although not founded by a German, had a large German population. The Rohrbacks, Gardenours, Shulers, Neads, and Harmanns were among the first to arrive. Other German families bore the names of Flick, Groffs (now Grove), Schmidt (now Smith), Kretzer, Miller, Piper, Hayberger (now Highberger), and Orndorff.

HOW DID THEY COME?

The exact route of the incoming settlers is open to question. The Germans of course followed the Monocacy Trail to Frederick. A road led from Frederick to Middletown and from there to Crampton's Gap, named after one of the first settlers. Some of the Germans went via this gap to Harpers Ferry and Winchester. Others crossed the mountain at Crampton's Gap and headed north toward what is now Rohrersville. This route explains the German contact with Pleasant Valley. Apparently many of them crossed the mountain and then headed toward the Antietam by way of Rohrersville, Mount Briar, and Red Hill.

An old map at the Washington County Court House supports the author's theory on another route. This route led from Middletown to the Catoctin Creek, and up South Mountain by way of Fox's Gap and the Old Sharpsburg Road; thence down the Dog Street Road to the Antietam.

At Fellfoot some of the settlers turned right onto the

20

Mount Hebron Road and proceeded into the present village of Keedysville. The Little Antietam was forded and the travelers continued on their way, crossing the Big Antietam near the present Hitt Bridge. This route is most likely the path of the early Indians. The writer feels that this artery of travel was used from South Mountain to Williamsport.

Another primary path followed by the Germans and Chapline, was down the Dog Street Road to the present-day Geeting Road, crossing the Antietam at the Orndorff Ford and thence on to the Potomac, crossing at Pack Horse Ford near Shepherdstown.

The Chapline Family

The Chapline coat of arms was granted to the family in 1593. In fact the Chapline name is one of the oldest in England. Various branches of the family lived in Lincoln, Northampton, Hants, and Essex.

According to Hester Dorsey Richardson, writing for the *Baltimore Sun* on July 24, 1904:

> The ancient Manor of Finchingfield, in Essex, was purchased by John Chaplyn in the year 1576, from whom descended Sir Francis Chaplin, Alderman and Lord Mayor of London in 1677. An interesting account of the origin of the name of Chapline connects it with the famous cloak of St. Martin. It will be remembered that while a youth at 15 St. Martin entered the army, and while stationed at Amiens divided his cloak with a freezing beggar at the gate of the city. The night following, we are told, he had a vision of Christ making known to His angels this act of charity to Himself. The half of the cloak which Martin retained to cover himself became the standard of the nation for 600 years. The little oratory in which this famous blue mantle, or chape, was preserved was from it called a chapelle, and the person who was in attendance the chaplain. This, we are told on good authority, was the beginning of the name so familiar to us now.
>
> In the year 1610 Isaac Chapline, ensign in the Royal Navy, came to America in the Starr, as King's Council under Lord De La Warr.
>
> He was granted large tracts of land on the James River in Jordan Parish.
>
> His principal estate he called Chapline's Choice, to which a few years later he brought his wife Mary (said by tradition to have been a Calvert and kinswoman of Lord Baltimore), son John, age 15 years, and several . . . servants.

John Chapline . . . settled in Talbot County where he married and left descendants. His brother William . . . moved to Calvert County . . . where in 1689 his name appears among those who signed the petition to His Majesty, King William, in behalf of the Protestants of that county. His wife was a Miss Travers by whom he had a large family, which spread through Prince George's and Frederick Counties, and through the Western and Southern States.

COLONEL JOSEPH CHAPLINE

Colonel Chapline, the founder of Sharpsburg, was born in Queen Annes Parish, Prince Georges County, Maryland, on September 5, 1707. He died at his estate near Sharpsburg in 1769.[11]

In 1753 he received the first of many land grants along the Antietam. Joseph Chapline had nineteen grants with 13,400 acres. The Antietam Iron Works was included in one of the first grants. This alone contained 6,352 acres. This tract was called "Little I Thought It." Other tracts were called "Love in a Village," "Little Friendship," "Contentment," "Hunting Ground," "Hunting the Hare," "Bachelors Delight," and "Loss and Gain."[12]

On July 9, 1763, Chapline on his grant called "Joe's Lott" laid out the village of Sharpsburg. The settlement was named after the proprietary governor, Horatio Sharpe. It contained 2,127 acres.

Joseph Chapline was a strong-minded, individualistic character. He could become quite temperamental if crossed. Living nearby was Rev. William Williams. The clergyman had served as a Presbyterian missionary to Virginia. However, he got in trouble by performing a marriage which apparently was supposed to be performed by a minister of the established or state church. Therefore, the Williams family moved to Welsh Run. Pastor Williams had three daughters, and Chapline fell in love with Ruhumah. He asked for her hand in marriage. The answer was no. So Joseph and Ruhumah eloped.

Perhaps we should not be too hard on Chapline at this point. The other two daughters of the Reverend Mr. Williams also eloped when denied parental permission. They did quite well for themselves. Jane married William Price, a Hagerstown

22

lawyer, and Sarah became the wife of Colonel Benjamin Chambers, the founder of Chambersburg, Pennsylvania.

When Joseph Chapline arrived in the Valley there were four houses in what is present-day Sharpsburg. One served as a combination blockhouse and Indian trading post. It still stands just northwest of the square on Main Street.

Chapline liked elbow room and hunting. He established his own home at "Mount Pleasant," near the Potomac River. There he lived until his death in 1769. His son Joseph inherited the farm. Incidentally, he was one of nine children born to Joseph, Sr., and Ruhumah Chapline. When the founder of Sharpsburg died, he was buried, as was the custom in those days, in a small enclosure on the family farm. Years later, the remains of this pioneer and his family were moved to Mountain View Cemetery in Sharpsburg.

On March 5, 1768, Chapline deeded to Christopher Cruss, Matthias Need, Nicholas Sam, and William Hawker, vestrymen and church wardens for the Lutheran congregation, Lot No. 149 for a church. The lot was 154 feet wide, and 206 feet deep. If no church was erected in seven years, the lot was to revert to Chapline. Payment was small. "One pepper corn, if demanded, on the 9th day of July."[13]

The log church constructed on Lot 149 served the Lutherans until the Battle of Antietam. It was badly damaged by Union artillery. Gaping holes were made in the walls. The interior was used as a hospital. The damage was beyond repair, and a new church had to be built.

In 1768 the founder of Sharpsburg belonged to the Church of England. However, most of the first settlers were Germans, belonging to either the Lutheran or Reformed tradition. Some years would pass before an Episcopal church was established.

Lot No. 61 was the land Chapline deeded to Abraham Lingenfelter for one shilling.[14] This in turn was deeded to Christian Orndorff, George Kieffer, John Middlekauff, and Conrad Hayberger, trustees "appointed by the Dutch Calvinist congregation in and about Sharpsburg, in Frederick." This occurred on April 2, 1774.

Money for church construction was evidently hard to

23

obtain. The *Maryland Gazette* in its June 8, 1769, edition says, "SIX HUNDRED DOLLARS has been raised by lottery to complete the Reformed Calvinist Church and build a school house."

Actually, Chapline had deeded the lot to Lingenfelter on March 3, 1768, with the intention that the land was to be held for the congregation until the people were able to build.

The year 1765 found Chapline planning with Samuel Beall, Jr., David Ross, and Richard Henderson, the development of the Antietam Iron Works. Antietam Furnace was originally called Frederick Furnace. No doubt this was because the land was at that time in Frederick County. The name Frederick Furnace appears in an early deed.

One of the early visitors to Sharpsburg was Rev. Benjamin Allen. He was a man loved by all. His contribution to the Valley of the Antietam was the first Sunday school. This served not only the purposes of Christian education, but provided a time and place for the early settlers to fellowship and chat. Allen's Sunday school was a big thing in the life of the townspeople. In the winter he held quizzes. Large crowds turned out on Sunday afternoons, or in the evenings when these were held. At one time the Reverend Mr. Allen had 170 scholars. Mr. Allen lived between Sharpsburg and Antietam Furnace.

Jane and Sarah Chapline were very fond of the preacher. They assisted him in Sharpsburg, and also went with him to Antietam where he worked among those employed at the Iron Works.

When the French and Indian War broke out in 1756, Chapline left his Mount Pleasant home, and rode to Fort Frederick. There he commanded a regiment of infantry.

Joseph Chapline was a busy man, founder of a town, owner of large tracts of land, father of nine children, army officer, judge, and member of the Maryland legislature. He was appointed a Frederick County judge in 1748. In 1749 elections were held in Frederick County, and Chapline was elected to the legislature. Thirteen terms he served in this capacity.

The Chapline children were named William Williams,
24

Joseph, Jr., and Deborah (these were twins), James, Ruhumah, Sarah, Jeremiah, Jane, and Theodosia.

Deborah married Captain Alexander Thompson, a Revolutionary War officer. When John P. Smith, a leading citizen of Sharpsburg in a later period of time, helped move the Chapline bodies from Mount Pleasant to Mountain View Cemetery in Sharpsburg, these inscriptions were readable.

Samuel Thompson, 1687–April 29, 1787
One hundred years old
Wife Mary Thompson, 1724–March 6, 1807[15]

These were the parents of Alexander Thompson, Deborah Chapline's in-laws. The Reverend Mr. Thompson served as pastor of the Presbyterian Church at Toms Creek near Emmitsburg.

Several prominent citizens of Sharpsburg, as well as this writer, feel that Joseph Chapline lived originally in a log cabin type dwelling. This may have been on the Clara Line property or in that general vicinity. Then no doubt the stone part of Mount Pleasant and the mansion house proper followed. It is difficult to imagine anyone building a dwelling like the present Mount Pleasant in the midst of the wilderness. No doubt, ten or fifteen years went by before he was able to build the home he desired.

Once again the need to record history, historical fact, not just legend is most obvious.

To visit Joseph Chapline's "Mount Pleasant," high on a windy hill above a great bend in the Potomac, is to step back into history. The beautiful eight-room house, built with bricks shipped from England, is as impressive as Mount Vernon.

The visitor can almost picture George Washington, who may have come here and other notable figures from the early days of our history, as stepping through the front door, and into one of the large drawing rooms.

The fireplaces have cupboards on either side. Around the fireplaces are tiles bearing the Chapline coat of arms. The fire warmed Washington, Gates, and others as they discussed the future and destiny of the colonies.

25

No doubt the rooms heard the strains of the minuet, and other music of the day. Horses galloped across the fields chasing the fox and other game which abounded in the deep forest.

From the upstairs windows, far above the waters of the Potomac, the family could watch the day fade away, and dusk fall on the river.

Joseph Chapline made a lovely choice in the selection of a site for his home. It is well called "Mount Pleasant."

CHAPLINE COAT OF ARMS
COPIED FROM AN OLD PIECE OF SILVERWARE.

The Chapline Coat of Arms.

MOSES CHAPLINE

Joseph Chapline and his brother Moses had good Old Testament names. The qualities of their namesakes were certainly needed on the frontier. Moses, his wife Jeannette Caton Chapline, and ten children lived about two and a half miles from Keedysville, near the Mount Carmel Church.

His wife was a cousin of Charles Carroll of Carrollton, a man who was to be one of the Marylanders signing the Dec-

26

laration of Independence. The Chapline-Caton wedding took place in Jeannette's home near Annapolis in 1740.[16]

Near the same time Moses built a home on Dog Street. Whether he built it before his marriage, or just afterward, is difficult to determine. The large log house had openings to defend against Indian attacks. During Indian uprisings when the fear of attack swept through the valley, the few white inhabitants of the area came to his house for protection. Legend says several Indian attacks were repulsed.

Moses Chapline was an active man. Not only was he a lawyer, but constable of Antietam Hundred in 1749. In the same year he was also the foreman of the first Frederick County Grand Jury. We must remember that what is now Washington County was a part of Frederick County until 1776. In 1749 he gave orders for a road to be made from his residence to the Antietam Creek. The writer presumes he meant the Little Antietam as his plantation or farm bordered this stream. Moses Chapline's tracts of ground were called "Bounded White Oak," "Mount Pleasant" (this seemed to be a favorite name), and "Josiah's Bit."

Moses Caton Chapline sold the family homestead in 1762 to Richard Dean. Dean sold it later to Michael Folkler, who in turn sold it to William Good. Then a Nicholas Shiffler bought it. On January 9, 1901, fire did what the Indians and the years were unable to do, it destroyed the home built by Moses Chapline. Ninety-year-old Betsy Shiffler, who had lived in the house most of her life, died in the blaze.

In November of 1892, Mrs. Dare of Washington, wife of Colonel J. Z. Dare, came to the Moses Chapline home along with her mother, Louisa. Mrs. Dare was a great-great-granddaughter of Moses Chapline. In the family burial plot of her ancestors, on the land they worked and fought for, she placed a monument, bearing the inscription used under the picture on page 28.

1762
Captain Moses Chapline
His Wife Jeannette Caton Chapline
His Son Josiah Chapline
"God Giveth to His Beloved sleep."[17]

28

George and Elizabeth Shiffler have erected a small stone wall around the little farm cemetery.

After Braddock's defeat, Moses Chapline was sent to Ohio to guard the frontier. Among those going with him were Col. Lawrence Washington and Col. Ebenezer Zane. Some of these men remained in the west and were the principal founders of Wheeling, West Virginia. To honor Moses Chapline, they named a main street after him.

The second Moses Chapline married Mary Caldwell. Their son, Moses, married Sallie Lee of the famous Virginia Lee family. One of the children of this union was Mary Lovey. She married Captain Noah Zane, a nephew of the founder of Wheeling and the famous Elizabeth Zane.

James and Joseph Smith

Among the first to come to the banks of the Antietam were James and Joseph Smith. It is thought that they came from Scotland by way of Ireland.[18] On April 17, 1745, James Smith bought 208 acres of land from a tract which had been surveyed for Dr. George Stewart on December 27, 1739. James called the property "Smith's Hills." He found an old log house on the property. This had been erected in 1733 and withstood the ravages of time until 1874. At that time it was blown down by a severe windstorm.[19]

Joseph Smith, apparently the brother of James, appears on the scene two years later, buying 270 acres of "Ellwick's Dwelling." This tract was near "Smith's Hills." The deed was dated February 1, 1747.

The Smiths continued to buy additional land in the Valley of the Antietam. James alone accumulated some four thousand acres prior to October 19, 1779. At that time he sold part of his estate to his son Robert, and his name does not appear afterward in other land transactions. In business dealings, James is referred to as a "wheelwright," "farmer," and "gentleman." He was also active in politics preceding and during the Revolution.

James had ten children. Margaret, born August 10, 1766, married Rev. Martin Hitt in Washington County in 1794. She died in Indiana on February 28, 1839.

29

A sister, Sarah, was engaged to Rev. Daniel Hitt, the traveling companion of Francis Asbury. However, she died of a lung disease in Kentucky in 1803 or 1804.

Ann, who was born in 1774, married Rev. Samuel Hitt in 1800. She died October 21, 1855, at Urbana, Ohio.

Elizabeth and Rebecca also married preachers, Elijah Howard and Francis Standeford.

James Smith must have died between October 19, 1779, and March of 1780.[20] Williams in his history could find no date for the death of Joseph. The scanty material available tends to indicate that the children of James and Joseph moved to Kentucky.

When James Smith sold part of "Smith's Hills" to Christian Orndorff in 1762, he reserved a family burying ground. This was enclosed by a stone fence and was preserved until some time after the Civil War. Now the cemetery has been plowed under.

The Orndorff house.

Robert Smith, a bachelor son of James Smith, inherited his father's land along the Antietam. He was a member of the state legislature during the years 1800-1805.[21] When he died he left his entire estate to Samuel M. Hitt.

John Reynolds, Jr., married Margaret Smith, a daughter of James. In 1779 he sold his land along the Antietam and started for the West but he never reached his destination. In March the party left their camp near Pittsburgh in two boats. About fifty miles below Wheeling the party landed. However, traces of a recent Indian camp were discovered. The Reynolds group got back in the boats and pushed off. The swift current carried them near a point of land from which they received a surprise Indian attack. As Captain Reynolds sought to defend his wife and children, he was shot in the head and fell dead. The Indians captured the boat and took nineteen captives.[22]

Years of suffering and persecution followed. Many times they were forced to run the gauntlet. As the Indians took them deeper and deeper into the wilderness, Mrs. Reynolds saw her little girls fall from hunger and fatigue. She was always fearful when this happened. She knew that if they were unable to get up when the Indians wanted to move on, they would be killed.[23]

Daughter Elizabeth and three-year-old William were taken from the mother. For a long time she feared they were dead. The main party the Indians took to Detroit. Elizabeth and William remained in the custody of a Delaware chieftain by the name of Peter. One day little Elizabeth had the opportunity to speak with a white woman from Kentucky who was also being held prisoner. She begged the woman, if she ever escaped, to send word to her uncles, Joseph Reynolds and Robert Smith, in Washington County.

In Detroit, Mrs. Reynolds never gave up hope of uniting the family and gaining freedom. She was permitted to do sewing, and received regular rations from the British. In time, she was able to persuade the British commander to search for the separated members of her family. The scouts were sent out with large quantities of rum. They promised the Indians they would give them the customary twenty pounds reward given for each prisoner brought in or each scalp taken. This method returned all but Joseph. Soon the mother was able to arrange his escape while his captors were away from the village.

31

The commander of the British troops, realizing what the family had been through, sent them on a ship to Montreal. After their arrival, news of the peace ending the Revolutionary War came to their ears.

Mrs. Reynolds, her children, and nineteen other prisoners were sent to New York City. They had the privilege of meeting George Washington who gave them a pass to go home. A boat took the Reynolds clan to Philadelphia. In that city, the remarkable Mrs. Reynolds hired a wagon and drove home to the banks of the Antietam.

We can well imagine the joy and surprise at the home of the senior Reynolds family. According to his knowledge, the family was still in captivity. However, like the father of the Prodigal Son, we can picture him as looking down the road every day for news of his daughter-in-law and grandchildren. And then at last they arrived and there was great rejoicing.

But what an experience. From the banks of the Antietam to the Ohio River, Indian ambush and death for Captain Reynolds, Jr., a trek through the wilderness and separation of the children, Detroit, Montreal, New York, Philadelphia and home.

Christian Orndorff

Like many other Germans from the Palatinate, Christian Orndorff, his fifteen-year-old son by the same name, and thirteen-year-old daughter Barbara Ann, landed at the port of Philadelphia, probably in 1741.

According to Maryland Archives the name was spelled Ohrendorff, Orendorff, Orendorf, and Orandorff. The spelling used today was used by Christian Orndorff when he signed his will on December 28, 1795.

The father and two children were most likely passengers on the ship *Saint Mark* which sailed from Rotterdam. The name of Christian is included on the membership roll of the German Reformed Church in Philadelphia, covering the period from 1735 to 1755.[24]

The family soon moved to Tulpehocken Creek in Lebanon Valley. Several pieces of land were bought and a mill started. Young Christian II married Elizabeth Ann Hoffman

32

on April 2, 1749. To this union several children were born while they remained in Philadelphia. One of these was Christian III.

Word came to the Orndorffs from their friends that there was lush ground across the Blue Ridge Mountains. Those who had been crossing at Crampton's Gap in Maryland were so impressed with the area that they called it "Pleasant Valley."

Being good businessmen, the Orndorffs made long trips to select sites for additional mills. The lay of the land and possible sources of waterpower were checked. They must have liked what they saw along the Antietam. On November 17, 1762, Christian Orndorff purchased part of "Smith's Hills." Six hundred fifty-nine pounds covered the cost of 514 acres, most of them along the Antietam, and a small tract along the Potomac. Possessions and children made the trip from Pennsylvania to the Antietam in Conestoga wagon.[25]

Across the stream from the house, the Orndorffs built a flour mill and a sawmill. Although most of the early settlers in the valley were Germans, some were English, Scotch, Swiss, and French, the later from the Alsace-Lorraine area. These folks trusted Christian Orndorff and brought their wheat to his mill, and their logs for building to his sawmill. The flour was shipped in large wagons to Baltimore for export. Thus the mill along the Antietam was doing a thriving business.[26]

Family history says that Jacob Hess helped Orndorff with his building program. While working for Christian, Jacob fell in love with the oldest Orndorff girl, Margaret. When Jacob and Peggy got married, the bride's father gave the couple a farm. Soon Jacob was operating his own mill on the banks of the Little Antietam, several miles away.

Christian Orndorff was the father of twelve children. These youngsters romped and played on the spacious front lawn at Mount Pleasant. In the summertime they waded in the cool, refreshing Antietam. When winter came, we can be sure they found some way to slide down the big hills.

Located by the trail leading to the mill, and to Sharpsburg, many distinguished individuals stopped at Christian Orndorff's. These included men like George Washington, and

General Gates of Revolutionary War fame. Often they would stop at Orndorff's "Mount Pleasant," and then continue to Chapline's "Mount Pleasant" down by the Potomac.

The first big white house on the right, after crossing the Antietam, coming from Boonsboro, was built by Christian Orndorff and his family. The big timbers were hewn from the forests nearby. The log house, now covered with weatherboard, has two large chimneys and six fireplaces. The ceiling is seven feet high.

From the yard Christian could see the Antietam, the nearby hills and South Mountain. His view was so nice that he called his estate "Mount Pleasant." The small third story of the house provided shelter to peddlers, travelers, and the many famous guests entertained by the family. The house was built like a colonial mansion, large central hall, and spindle staircase.

The doors are massive, held in place by huge "H" shaped hinges. The stone kitchen where the cooking was done is to the rear of the house. The fireplace is nine feet high, eight feet wide, and three feet deep. Big enough for a lot of cooking.

The windowsills in the house are eighteen inches wide. A fruit cellar preserved the fruits grown in the family orchard. A good spring was the source of the water supply.

As the years passed, Christian and his sons, Christopher and Henry, bought additional land, some from the same James Smith who owned the original tract upon which Mount Pleasant was built.

Christian was one of the first to purchase lots from Joseph Chapline in Sharpsburg. On January 1, 1764, he bought Lot 13, and on October 28, 1765, Lot 47.

Major Orndorff had two lovely daughters, Mary and Rose. Mary was a lovely girl, and had many suitors. When she was fifteen years old, General Gates met her one day, and begged her to marry him the next. He was standing in the hall talking to the major when Mary came down to look in the mirror and see how some new fashions looked on her. Gates was overwhelmed. "Who is that lovely creature?" he exclaimed. When he found it was the major's daughter, he requested that

34

he be placed next to her at tea; this was done, and the old general fell so hard he asked the youthful Mary to become his bride.[27]

She was quite amused at this. She had plenty of young men coming to see her. Supposedly, fifteen young men from Shepherdstown wanted to marry her. She married Jonathan Hager, Jr., the son of the founder of Hagerstown. For a time she lived in a house on the square in the county-seat town. She was widowed quite early in life, and once again suitors came in swarms to her door.

One of these was a distinguished lawyer by the name of Luther Martin. His interest was not met by a warm response. So he resorted to sending her love letters. Some of which were preserved. Martin spoke of Mary as "best and most beloved of women," and "My charming widow." Luther Martin later defended Aaron Burr in court.

Mary was lovely, but Rose seems to have been a psychic. She was frail and delicate, and often went into trances. Rose must have held seances at Mount Pleasant on the banks of the Antietam. People from the surrounding area came to see her. They asked her what she saw in the future for them, and what steps to take in certain matters. They asked her to get in touch with those who had departed this life.

Old papers from that day say that crowds came to consult "Sta. Rosa Vitoza," as she was called. We wonder what the walls of Mount Pleasant could tell us about the consultations Rose held with those who came to her for aid. As her fame increased, the family had little privacy, and some folks, knowing that when in a trance Rose was insensitive to pain, tried to stick pins in her to see if she had feeling.

After Mary's wedding and move to Hagerstown, Major Orndorff packed up the family and left for the "Dark and Bloody Ground" of Kentucky. Before they left the banks of the Antietam with the pleasant view, and the sound of rippling water, Rose made her dad promise to bring her back to Sharpsburg when she died. Father Orndorff was true to his word. Rose now rests from the labors of life in the shadow of South Mountain in the little stone enclosed cemetery on the Mumma farm.

During the Revolutionary War, Christopher Orndorff married Mary Thomas, a neighbor girl. In 1782-83, he built one or two new mills along the Antietam. The old mill had been an extremely busy place during the Revolution, sending forth wagon trains of wheat and flour to the Continental Army.

In 1904, the last of the Orndorff mills was razed. The *Hagerstown Globe* said:

An Old Landmark
Torn Down

The old stone and weatherboard grist mill which for 122 years had stood along the historic Antietam at the bridge between Keedysville and Sharpsburg was recently torn down. The old mill was built in 1782 by Christopher Orndorff.

A stone was found with the date September 2, 1782, and the initials C-O and M-O. (Christopher and Mary Orndorff.) Set in a recess in the old wall was an inscription in German:

June 20, 1783
Christopher Orndorff
Allein auf Gott sets dein vertrauen
Wanen thust eine muhlc bauen,
Auf euschen hilf, verlese dich nicht,
Sonst euschen hilf darf du nicht trauen.

Translated it means:

In God alone put your trust.
When you do build a mill
Do not rely on outside help,
For on outside help, you dare not trust.

These words express the faith of the Orndorffs. They speak well to our day, "In God alone put your trust."

The "Sunken Road" or "Bloody Lane" as it is called today led to the Orndorff plantation and mill. Some say the road was used so heavily by wagons going to the mill that deep ruts resulted in the nickname "Hog Trough Road." Early farmers felt their animals could make it alone to the mill because repeated trips made the route familiar. Farmers

36

jokingly told one another, "Just place a sack of wheat on old muley, and send him on his way. He'll know where to go."

The spot where the observation tower now stands was originally part of the Orndorff estate.

The Mumma Cemetery is one of the prettiest spots in the Valley of the Antietam. This land originally belonged to William Anderson who sold it to John Reynolds, Sr., in 1761. In 1784, William Anderson divided his farm between his sons, Joseph and Francis. Joseph was given the tract known from Civil War days as the Roulette farm. Francis sold his share to the Orndorffs who in turn sold it to Jacob Mumma in a deed dated May 6, 1796. Jacob's son Samuel occupied the farm during the time of the battle. The author wondered why he could not find the graves of Rose and some of the other Orndorffs in the Mumma Cemetery where they are supposed to be buried. The answer came from Mrs. A. Dillion Grove, still living at the age of 101. She is the granddaughter of Samuel Mumma. Her story, supported by other research, is that many of the old stones were destroyed by cannonballs and marching soldiers during the Battle of Antietam.

The National Capitol

The early history of Sharpsburg was closely linked with Shepherdstown. Records prove that in 1790 the leading men of these two towns worked side by side to persuade the federal government to locate the new capitol of the nation on the banks of the Potomac, with each community providing land.

The men said that Sharpsburg would be ideal because it had six good springs and twenty-one wells. Excellent sources of water were also available in Shepherdstown. Eighty-four lots south of Sharpsburg, and 1,400 acres north and south of town were available, some at five pounds and some at four pounds. The owners were listed as David MeMechan, Esq., of Baltimore Town; Basil Beall of Prince Georges County; John Clagett of Washington County; and the heirs of Samuel Dorsey of Anne Arundel County.

A letter sent to the President of the United States on December 1, 1790, read:

The Donations of the Virginia side of the River amount at this period to Twenty Thousand Six Hundred Sixty-Two 2/3 Dollars and on the Maryland side to Four Thousand Eight Hundred and Thirty-Nine Dollars, also Four Hundred and Seventy-Five acres of land Lying Directly in a line between Sharpsburg and the River. Subscriptions are continued open and a probability that they will be considerably augmented.

Henry Bedinger of Shepherdstown and William Good of Sharpsburg signed the letter.

Another letter soon followed. It read:

Sharpsburg Washington County,
4th December 1790

The President of the United States/.
Sir:

Inclosed you have the platts as promised. . . . Some small alterations respecting the donation of the land has taken place. Captain Shepherd has withdrawn his subscription of forty acres of land and has given the whole Tract called Pell Mell containing one hundred and sixty-two acres at $15 per acre, which we thought would be of more advantage than his donation of 40 acres which will appear by referring to the platt. The donation in lands are laid down as directed by your Excellency, as on the platt except an addition of Antietam Creek and the Potomac from Mr. Swearingen's ferry to the mouth of the Antietam Creek, the adjacent lands are laid down as directed and so far as we have been able the prices of land ascertained. . . . We are your Excellency's Most Obedient Servants.

Joseph Chapline
Wm. Good.

"Fellfoot Enlarged"

Two of the most interesting places in the Valley of the Antietam are the Antietam Iron Works and "Fellfoot Enlarged."

"Fellfoot" or "Fellfoot Enlarged" is located on the Dog Street Road. It was surveyed for Thomas Van Swearingen, a Dutch settler in 1734, and patented by Tobias Stansbury twenty years later. In some manner, Conrad Schnebley, a native of Germany obtained the tract of land. His son Caspar was to own 8,000 acres. However, legal involvements with his neighbor John O'Brien cost him heavily, and gradually varying amounts of acreage were sold. Caspar also changed his name to Sneveley. In time it became Snively.

Austin Flook, the present owner of "Felfoot" (in deeds it is spelled with both a single and a double "l"), feels the main house was the old stone dwelling standing west of the Mount Hebron Road, midway between Dog Street and the Mount Hebron Cemetery. There were slave quarters on the estate. The barn is pre-Revolutionary. There is some indication that it was used as a supply depot for Braddock's soldiers. However, the 1754 date chiseled into the wall of the barn, may be wrong. For those deeply interested, check the "4" closely and see if it does not resemble an "8". Jeffrey Wyand is doing some in-depth research on the entire farm which should prove quite interesting when published.

The Snivelys gave the ground for the Geeting Meeting House and the Mount Hebron Cemetery. In fact, Caspar Snively is buried in the cemetery. His marker shows him to be a Revolutionary War soldier, dying on October 16, 1839, age, seventy-seven years, eleven months, and two days.

In 1936 there were thirty-five graves with marked stones at Mount Hebron, and many graves not marked by stones. George Adam Geeting's wife is one of these.

We hope that perhaps this book will inspire earnest students of history to go to the Maryland Hall of Records and other places and make an effort to uncover the secrets of Antietam Iron Works, and "Felfoot."

Antietam Furnace

Antietam Furnace was built by William M. Brown, and operated by Ross, Bell and Henderson of Baltimore. The furnace stood on land originally granted to Joseph Chapline in "Little I Thought It." From Chapline it passed to Daniel Hughes.

During the Revolutionary period many cannonballs and cannon were cast in the Antietam Iron Works. It was a thriving industry from about 1760 until after the Civil War. Now it is in ruins. Here James Rumsey built some of the machinery used in the construction of his steam powered boat.

About 250 yards from the C. and O. Canal, coal, lumber, and ore were received. Iron mills and a nail factory gave employment to the local people. The coke yard was located on an Indian burial ground. A gristmill and sawmill were also included in the operations.

William Brown operated the furnace for quite a few years. Then the business was sold to John McPherson Brinn, who in turn sold it to Samuel Horine and William Clarke of Hagerstown. The next owner was David Ahl. After 1880 operations ceased. Most of the iron ore came from an area one mile north of Harpers Ferry on the Maryland side.

In 1841 the nail factory burned. However, after Mr. Brinn rebuilt it, 200 white men and 60 slaves worked. Three waterwheels, fourteen and seventeen feet high, provided power.

For more information, the reader can check Williams, Vol. 1, p. 247; Scharff, p. 1218; *The Sunday Sun,* December 5, 1948; and *Maryland, a Guide to the Old Line State,* p. 354.

Belinda Springs

Before the Civil War, Belinda Springs, about a mile south of the square in Sharpsburg, was more famous than the town named after Governor Sharpe.

In 1822 John Gardenhour built a hotel near what is known today as Snavely's Ford. He named the hotel after his wife Belinda. The springs contained sulphur water, good for medicinal purposes. Thus like the town of Bath or Berkeley Springs, West Virginia, Belinda Springs soon became famous. Many guests came by stagecoach. Pleasure boats came up the Potomac and thence up the Antietam and docked for wealthy passengers to enjoy the beauty, quietness, and spring water. Actors came from the big cities to produce plays just like summer stock today.

A cave which was said to have been used by Indian warriors was a favorite place to explore. Picnics were held near the entrance.

People from Sharpsburg brought fresh fruits and vegetables down to sell to the city folks. Sulphur water was sent in jugs all over the East coast. Then in 1832 the springs were closed as a cholera epidemic broke out among the C. and O. Canal workers.

Map Showing Donations of Land Offered As Inducement To Locate Captiol Here

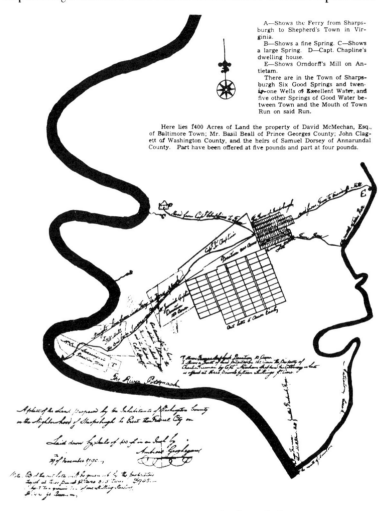

A—Shows the Ferry from Sharps-burgh to Shepherd's Town in Virginia.

B—Shows a fine Spring. C—Shows a large Spring. D—Capt. Chapline's dwelling house.

E—Shows Orndorff's Mill on Antietam.

There are in the Town of Sharps-burgh Six Good Springs and twenty-one Wells of Excellent Water, and five other Springs of Good Water between Town and the Mouth of Town Run on said Run.

Here lies 1400 Acres of Land the property of David McMechan, Esq., of Baltimore Town; Mr. Basil Beall of Prince Georges County; John Clagett of Washington County, and the heirs of Samuel Dorsey of Annarundal County. Part have been offered at five pounds and part at four pounds.

Proposed plat for the nation's capital.

41

Belinda Springs in the 1920s.

The source of Belinda Springs.

Belinda Springs today.

Ferry Hill Plantation

Two of the most interesting books about the Valley of the Antietam are *From Millwheel to Plowshare,* the story of the Christian Orndorff family, and *Ferry Hill Plantation Journal.* Fletcher M. Green, the editor of *I Rode With Stonewall,* found this journal, covering the period from January 4, 1838, to January 15, 1839, in the attic of Ferry Hill Plantation while doing research on Henry Kyd Douglas in 1942. The journal had been written by John Blackford, the owner of Ferry Hill.

Thomas Van Swearingen had been authorized in 1765 to operate a ferry from Maryland to Virginia, now West Virginia. As the years passed, John Blackford, a leading citizen of Boonsboro bought some land from Thomas Shepherd, the founder of Shepherdstown on the Maryland side of the Potomac. This land was adjacent to property already owned by Blackford. In 1816 Blackford expanded his holdings and bought the Van Swearingen Ferry and all that went with it, including the river bottom tracts called "Antietam Bottom," "Ferry Landing," and "Ferry Landing Enlarging." Land holdings belonging to the Bedinger and Hays families were also obtained. These additional seven hundred acres were consolidated with other Blackford property and called "Ferry Hill Plantation."[28]

John Blackford was born on July 18. The year of his birth is unknown, although it was in the 1780s. He was a prosperous man, owning a large plantation and ferry boat operation. He owned stock in the Chesapeake and Ohio Canal, as well as in the Boonsboro Turnpike Company and other businesses.

John Blackford was a community leader, and served as justice of peace, roads supervisor, and a colonel in the militia. In 1830 the people of Boonsboro asked him to serve on a committee endeavoring to persuade the officials of the Baltimore Conference of the Methodist Episcopal Church to build a college in the town.

The Blackfords were members of the Episcopal church in Sharpsburg. They were most generous in their contributions, and also gave some funds to just about all the local churches.

Nine different ministers were entertained at Ferry Hill in the year covered by the journal.

Blackford's third marriage was into the Kanode family. Like many of the other early German settlers, the Kanodes had come from Pennsylvania to the Antietam. Mrs. Blackford had poor health, and during the time of the journal she was confined to her bed as an invalid. The colonel gave her the best medical attention possible. He took her to Belinda Springs near Sharpsburg. He also took her to Shannondale Springs. But the so-called healing waters did not help her.

Mr. and Mrs. Blackford lived in the beautiful two-story red-brick house overlooking the Potomac River. Their lovely home, erected in 1812, they called Ferry Hill. It is still standing, although changed somewhat in appearance. Four other houses stood on the premises. One was "The Cottage," built by Van Swearingen for the ferry boat operator. In the other houses lived a married son, Franklin Blackford, and Charles and Joseph Kanode, the brother and nephew of Mrs. Blackford. Slaves living in "The Cottage" and in properties located in Shepherdstown farmed the land.

Ferry Hill Plantation was a busy place. Crops had to be cultivated and harvested. Wheat was the main money crop. Grain had to be hauled to the mill. Blackford usually took his grain to the Mumma Mill. However, he also used Staub's and Glassford's. Flour and meal were shipped to Baltimore markets. Horses, cattle, sheep, and hogs had to be cared for daily. Blackford seems to have had a large orchard. He manufactured cider, vinegar, and apple butter. Many days were spent in cutting timber, clearing land to plant additional crops, and at the same time gathering wood for fuel. Some of the timber was sold for lumber and shingles.

Blackford was a progressive farmer and took great pride in livestock breeding; pork, sausage, and ham furnished much of the Ferry Hill diet. He also bought a machine to stuff sausage for sale. His wool was sent to mills in Frederick. Twenty-five slaves carried out this huge task. Ned and Jupe seem to have been in charge of the others. Wintertime found them cutting ice from the Potomac and making fences.

Life was never dull at Ferry Hill. Visitors came daily. Some stayed for a day, others for three days, and some for a month. The men did a lot of hunting. Blackford took delight in killing foxes which made life miserable for his sheep and chickens. In the summer there were boat rides on the river and canal, and fishing parties along the Antietam. In the winter all joined in sleighing and skating parties.

During 1838 bad health plagued Ferry Hill. Dr. Richard Parran came almost every day, sometimes twice a day to see Mrs. Blackford. Dr. Otho J. Smith, Blackford's son-in-law, also came on professional and social calls. He lived in Boonsboro. Mrs. Israel Fry, a midwife, came often to attend the slave women in childbirth. Colonel John Miller's wife from Sharpsburg came to sit with the ill Mrs. Blackford.

Some interesting notes appear in the journal. For instance the weather warmed up on February 6, 1838, and:

> . . . a young man named Mintstagh drowned was sceating near the left lock broke through the Ice. . . . Murf has gone to Mummas Mill with a load of wheat. Franklin gone ahead to have the grey mare shod and see the wheat measured at the mill. Will cleaning out the Ice House. Ashberry Elgan and Eaty getting out Ice to fill Franklin Ice House. The Shepherds Town people are getting out Ice commenced yesterday. . . . Murf brought home a load wood from the clearing and took the wagon Body full of the old straw and stuff From the Ice House to the Barnyard. Ned and Jupe in the Boat. Still a very small business at the Ferry Receipts are very small.

This is typical of Blackford's journal. The spelling, grammar, etc., was not changed by Editor Green or this writer. You see the original. Copies of the journal may be obtained from the University of North Carolina Press, Chapel Hill, North Carolina.

The work on the river continued on the eighth, Blackford writes:

> 8th Thursday. Weather morning soft and thawing. Rained smartly in the early part of last night. resumed hauling Ice. J. Kanode came after Breckfast with his wagon and joined in the hauling. have hauled 13 loads and 12 yesterday is 25 in the House say about 23 good loads as hauled this day were not full . . . Will is pounding the Ice.

June 1838 was a busy and eventful month for the colonel. On Friday, June 1, Blackford writes:

Weather warm. sat out at 7 Oclock for Hagers Town. where I arrived a quarter before 11 oclock. dined at Bells Tavern. . . . Bot a pair Boots from H.Fanner. price $5.75. there came on a heavy shower of Rain which prevented me from comeing home. met with several acquantance went into Kalhoofers store where we drank prety freely of Champain wine.

June 2 found him with hangover:

Rose with head ache and bad feelings from haveing taken too much Champain last night. pd. my bill $1.50 sat out ¼ before 8 oclock. Came by Wolfs where there is a dunkard large meeting. spent two hours there eat some Bread and Butter with them. then came on home.

Note that rarely did Blackford use a capital letter to start a sentence. He is obviously referring to a large Dunkard camp or three-day meeting at Wolf's.

Saturday night was very unpleasant for Mrs. Blackford. She "had a cholic and sick stomach." During Sunday afternoon, "Col. Miller wife & daughter came." Ned-Murf were in the boat doing a good business "on acct. of Tunker meeting."

He used the words Dunkard and Tunker interchangeably.

Monday, June 4, found the Blackfords up at 2:00 A.M. He, along with his daughter, Helena, and Colonel Miller, Mrs. Miller and daughter boarded a boat on the Potomac and proceeded to Harpers Ferry. Then on to Washington. The purpose of the visit was to settle some important business matters with the Chesapeake and Ohio Canal Company.

Although Blackford was hostile to Martin Van Buren and the Democratic Party, nevertheless, he had a visit with the president at the White House. However, in his June 7 entry he says little about it. "We then proceeded to the presidents house. Miss Elgen in company where we reviewed the fine rooms and spent a short time with the president to whom I introduced myself, Col. Miller and Miss Elgen and the girls. then reviewed the grounds to the rear of the house."

This is all he had to say about his visit to the executive mansion. Next the group went shopping, dining in Georgetown before taking the B. and O. to Baltimore.

The next day Blackford attended the Maryland Whig Convention, meeting for the purpose of nominating a

46

candidate for the office of governor. John L. Steele won the nomination.

> On the 10th of June the Blackford party took the train . . . and arrived in Frederick at one O clock where we took seats in the Coach. Mr. Daniel Schnebly with us which was 6 inside very crowded and disagreeable ride to Boonsg. where we arrived at Five Oclock. Col. Miller with his family came on home in his carriage which was in waiting for them. Helene and myself lodged with Doct Smith very warm weather.

This of course was a stagecoach trip from Frederick to Boonsboro, taking on that hot June day, four hours.

Sorrow came to Ferry Hill in early October 1838. Blackford writes:

> 7th Sunday. this has been a melancholy day for me and my family. my dear wife Expired in the afternoon about half after 4 Oclock. She appeared to be dieing from 12 Oclock at night. The Doctor Parran called over early, recommended an injection. as Doct. Smith came early in the day. Col. Miller and his two daughters . . . Doctor Parran witnessed her last moments. . . .

Monday, James Shepherd came to Ferry Hill to make the funeral arrangements. In the evening he brought the coffin over. Will and Murf butchered a shoat to feed the friends who would return after the funeral.

On Tuesday, Mrs. Blackford was laid to rest in Shepherdstown with the Reverend Robert Douglas presiding. The saddened husband describes the day.

> 9th Tuesday, weather cloudy and cool. at 10 Oclock the friends began to geather and 11 sat out with the corps. a large procession of carriages which took up some time in crossing. [Remember there was no bridge at the time, only the ferry.] Mr. Douglas and Mr. Hoffmire both attended the interment and then returned to the Prisbaterian meeting house where Mr. Douglas delivered a discours on the occation from the 11th Chapr. 35th Verce of the Gospel of St. John. We then returned home where many of the friends called and partook of some refreshment. . . .

Mr. Hoffmire was a Lutheran minister.

Before the end of 1839, John Blackford would also be dead. In his will, dated November 1, 1839, he divided Ferry Hill Plantation among his three sons. Franklin inherited the ferry boat operations. Henry received "Ferry Hill Place," while William Blackford obtained the "Lower Farm" and the lands formerly belonging to the Shepherds and Bedingers. Jeanette Blackford Smith was given $12,000 in cash and her mother's gold watch. Helena, the unmarried daughter was also given $12,000 and the family portraits. Public sale of Blackford's personal estate was held on December 10, 1839, with $30,917.22 being realized.

In 1846 Henry Blackford sold Ferry Hill Place to his brother Franklin for $17,180. Two years later, Franklin sold it to the Reverend Robert Douglas. When Pastor Douglas moved to Ferry Hill in 1848, he brought his son, Henry Kyd, along. The son was later to write in a book called *I Rode With Stonewall:*

> Born in Shepherdstown, Virginia, I lived in my youth on both sides of the Potomac River. On the Southern side, historic places like Harpers Ferry and Charlestown, where John Brown was hung, were familiar to me as my own garden in Washington County, Maryland. My early acquaintance with the Antietam, Blackford's Ford, and the fields around Sharpsburg was of much service to me at the time of the battles there. For some years before the war I had lived at "Ferry Hill Place," in Maryland and on a hill over against Shepherdstown, where from the gallery of its old house I could look for miles out into old Virginia.[29]

Young Douglas graduated from Franklin and Marshall College in 1859. The following year he earned his law degree at Lexington, and was admitted to the Jefferson County Bar. When the Civil War broke out, he enlisted as a private soldier in the Shepherdstown Company. This unit was assigned to the Stonewall Brigade. Gaining promotions rapidly, he soon won a position on the staff of Thomas Jonathan Jackson. In fact, he was the youngest member of the famous Confederate general's staff. During the war Douglas was wounded six times.

September 1862 found him acting as Jackson's guide through the Maryland countryside. On Sunday, September 14, the Confederate command surrounded Harpers Ferry and waited in readiness to attack at dawn. Douglas had things he wanted to do during the evening:

> As soon as dark came and all was quiet, I notified Pendleton that I

48

would be absent until midnight and rode out of camp. I was on my freshest horse and made my way rapidly for Shepherdstown, about eleven miles. There I crossed the Potomac at Blackford's or Boteler's Ford below the Dam, went up the towpath for a mile, crossed the Chesapeake and Ohio Canal and was soon at "Ferry Hill Place," my home, not quiet three miles from Sharpsburg. Hiding my horse behind the house I spent several hours with my father, and mother, sister and then returned the same way to headquarters. I dismounted, entered my tent a little before 3:00 a.m. and, the night being far spent, I threw myself on the bed without undressing.[30]

When Douglas returned to the Sharpsburg area on Tuesday morning, he found Lee and Jackson surveying the fields of Antietam on ground now occupied by the National Cemetery.

Jackson had been invited to breakfast in Sharpsburg with Longstreet and Stuart. However, he felt he was too busy to engage in such pleasant moments. Mr. Grove's daughter, Julia, prepared the same menu and sent it to Jackson with a member of Longstreet's staff. This pleased the general and he asked who had been so kind.

The reply was, "I dunno, General, but it was the fair one."

Jackson stopped and thought a moment, and said, "Well, since she sent me my breakfast to the field, I will call her Miss Fairfield. He then took a pencil and wrote a note to Julia Grove, saying:

Miss Fairfield,
   I have received the nice breakfast, for which I am indebted to your kindness. Please accept my grateful appreciation of your hospitality.
Very Sincerely Yours,
T. J. Jackson[31]

Douglas described Antietam as "fearful day—one that I am not likely to forget."

After the Confederate retreat from the fields of Antietam during the night of September 18, Ferry Hill and the Douglas family came in for some rough treatment.

When the next day the Army of the Potomac swarmed through Sharpsburg and over three miles to the bank of the river. Long before that, . . . the barn was a black mass of ruins, and its bare stone walls still standing, told the story of its early destruction. Now

49

in a night, as it were, a beautiful farm was laid to waste, its fences disappeared up to the doors of the mansion house, artillery parks filled the wheatfield; corn and fodder and hay soon became the contrabands of war. In front of the house, which from its high eminence looked over into Virginia, were rifle pits; and several rifled cannon, with their angry muzzles pointing across the Potomac, decorated the lawn. My father, mother, and sister were prisoners in their own house, with the freedom from which prisoners usualy enjoy.[32]

Things may have been worse because Henry and another brother were in the Confederate military service. The house was invaded and searched at the whim of the Union soldiers. Mrs. Douglas and her daughter never knew what moment some soldier would stick his head in their room. All the bureaus, wardrobes, and closets were searched. Bayonets and swords pulled garments from their places.

One stormy night in October one of the shutters toward Virginia blew open—they were by orders kept shut at night—and my mother going at midnight to a sick room, passed it with a candle. The sentinel on the river gave the alarm, and the next morning my father was arrested for giving signals to the enemy. He was at once taken from his house, leaving his family absolutely unprotected, and marched on foot to the headquarters of General Fitz-John Porter on his own farm. He requested an interview with the General, but that was declined and he was turned over to the Provost Guard. . . . My father was hurried on that same day to Berlin below Harpers Ferry where he was kept for three days, sleeping at night in the open air without any covering but his cloak, until one of his guard gave him a blanket to lie upon. He was taken before General Burnside . . . and the oath of allegiance was offered him as the price of his release. He declined it and was sent to Fort McHenry without further parley.[33]

There Rev. Mr. Douglas remained for six weeks. At first he was quartered in a stable, then in better facilities. No charges having been preferred he was released. However, young Henry Douglas felt the emotional strain and physical stress of the imprisonment broke his father's constitution. The Reverend Mr. Douglas was never well after his six weeks in captivity. He lived to see the end of the war and then died.

On the way to Gettysburg, Douglas encamped with many other Confederate soldiers near Shepherdstown. This was the 17th of June, 1863:

I visited my home across the Potomac and saw the desolation of war. My beautiful home was barren waste and a common, and the blackened walls of the burnt barn stood up against the sky as a monument of useless and barbarous destruction. I felt it would be hard for me, going into Pennsylvania, to put aside all ideas of retaliation.[34]

On June 18, Johnson's Confederate command crossed the Potomac and camped for the night at Ferry Hill Place. General Johnson made his headquarters in the Douglas home.

Ferry Hill Place served as a small hospital during the 1862 invasion. After reporting to Jackson on the morning of the sixteenth, Douglas felt very ill and exhausted. His commanding officer suggested he go home until dawn of the next morning. Following "Stonewall's" orders, Douglas rode back to Ferry Hill. There he found Brigadier General W. H. F. Lee, the son of Robert E. Lee, the commander of the Army of Northern Virginia. The commander's son had been painfully injured in a fall from his horse near the edge of Boonsboro. The mother and sister of Henry Douglas were treating young Lee and several wounded Confederate officers. One of whom, seeing Douglas entering the parlor unhurt, and feeling that perhaps he was deserting his post, demanded that Henry rejoin his command immediately. But afterwards the man who had spoken so bluntly, "looked as if he would have a hemorrhage when my sister came in and I put my arm around her. He and I served on the same staff for a while . . . but I never let him forget the time he ordered me out of my father's house."[35]

During the Battle of Antietam Alexander R. Lawton, one of Jackson's division commanders, was badly wounded near the Dunkard Church. He was taken to Ferry Hill Place to be treated. After the war he served as minister to Austria. The West Point graduate and president of the American Bar Association never forgot the kind treatment he received at Ferry Hill. From Austria and other places he sent his greetings to those "who still live in the big, red house on the hill."

People who come to the Valley of the Antietam are still impressed by the natural beauty and the friendliness of the people. Fogler McKinsey relates his feelings in the poem "Keedysville."

51

Winding streets and up and down
Here's a lovely Maryland Town.
Here's a pocket far from strife
Where they live a peaceful life.

Creek and mill and old time Inn
Even a train that makes a din.
Old sycamores and willows where
The mill race whispers to the air.

Quiet gardens, homes that sleep
Where its vines and blossoms creep.
Churches tender with the peace
That is rich with God's increase.

Orchards, vineyards, wheat and corn
Beams bright with red of morn.
Melons lovely in the patch
And dreams of love neath every thatch.

Here the old is still abiding
Here the new comes slow to bloom.
Simple families, frank confiding
With no part for hate or gloom.

Sweet and pleasant, still old fashioned
Not by fame or power impassioned.
Just a town in Maryland's heart
Where the soul may do its part.

III

SIFTING OUT THE HEARTS OF MEN

Among the early settlers coming to the Valley of the Antietam was a young man by the name of George Adam Geeting. Like many others, the name was spelled many different ways, including these: Gudhing, Gueding, Guething, Gueting, Guiting, Getting, and Gitting.[1]

For awhile it was thought that he landed in Baltimore, coming from Germany in a ship. However, in all probability, he landed in Philadelphia with other German immigrants.

It seems that he knew the Snively family. Their name also had different spellings: Snavely, Schuebley, and Schnabeli. This family had large landholdings along the Little Antietam Creek. To this area came George Adam Geeting. After awhile he took up residence in the stone house on the corner of the Dog Street and Eakle's Mill Road. It is still standing. He may have obtained his acreage from the Snively family.

In 1759, eighteen-year-old George Geeting arrived in Frederick County,[2] Washington County was yet to be created. Centerville, present-day Keedysville, contained just a few homes. Jacob Hess's mill was the focal point of community activity.

George had worked as a miner in Germany. He was a man of great industry. In the summertime he worked his own farm and helped his neighbors. Spare moments were spent digging wells and working in nearby quarries. A schoolhouse had been built on the Snively farm, so the winters found George Adam Geeting teaching the neighborhood boys and girls. It was built of logs and had a dirt floor.

In 1760, Philip William Otterbein, a German Reformed

preacher from Frederick, crossed the mountain on horseback and came to the schoolhouse to conduct preaching services. Geeting and Otterbein soon became good friends.[3] Tradition has it that Geeting became one of Otterbein's first converts.

Otterbein came to America in 1752. Early in that year, he had heard Michael Schlatter make an appeal for missionaries to the colonies, and he was one of six who answered the call.

Schlatter himself had come to the colonies in 1746 as a missionary to the German Reformed immigrants in Pennsylvania. He had been sent by the synods of North and South Holland. His mission was to organize the German speaking settlers into Reformed congregations.

Today the Atlantic is crossed by our modern jets in six hours or less. Schlatter left Amsterdam, Holland, on June 1, 1746, and arrived in Boston on August 1.

Although only twenty-eight at the time, he greatly impressed his superiors. During the next five years Schlatter was seldom out of the saddle as he traveled in Pennsylvania and Maryland, bringing the Gospel to the Germans. "The crowded history of his activities in those years is told in his Journal, published in 1752."[4] As soon as the roads were fit to travel in the spring of 1747, Schlatter was ready to begin his "Great Journey" into the wilderness beyond the Susquehanna and into western Maryland.

On April 29, 1747, Schlatter wrote in his journal, ". . . left Philadelphia amid earnest prayers that the presence of God might go with me."

On May 8, he arrived in "the newly laid off town" of Frederick. On the journey he stopped in Walkersville (The Glades), Middletown, Saint Paul's on the western pike beyond Hagerstown, and other infant congregations in Maryland, Shepherdstown, and the Shenandoah Valley. Schlatter was appalled at the lack of educated ministers and schoolteachers. He, therefore, decided to return in person to Holland in an effort to get church leaders to see the situation, hopefully to find funds and men to meet the spiritual and educational needs of the Germans in America. This time he sailed on February 5, and arrived in Amsterdam on May 3.

Six young men heard and answered the call to come to the

colonies. They were John Jacob Wissler, John Waldschmidt, Theodore Frankenfeld, William Stoy, John Casper Rubel, and Philip William Otterbein.

Otterbein was born on June 3, 1726, in Dillenberg, Germany. He was one of ten children. Five of the Otterbein lads were to become ministers, and one sister married a minister.[5]

Frau Otterbein seems to have sensed that her son Philip was destined to become a missionary. Widowed when Philip was but twelve years of age, she was very close to all her children. When the Macedonian call came to her son, she:

> ... took the hand of her beloved Philip in her own ... and blessed him in ... affectionate and prophetic words ... "Go, the Lord bless thee and keep thee. The Lord cause His face to shine upon thee, and with much grace direct thy steps. On earth, I may not see thy face again—but go."[6]

Little did those present realize that young Philip William Otterbein would in time become the founder of the first new denomination to be born in America, The Church of the United Brethren in Christ.

Otterbein's first pastorate was in Lancaster, which in 1752 was still largely "the frontier." It was the largest Pennsylvania town west of Philadelphia with five hundred homes and a population of 2,000.[7]

Next came a pastorate near Reading. Then in 1760 he moved on to Frederick. He organized the midweek prayer meetings, which "were probably the first such meetings to be held in America."[8] While serving in Frederick, Otterbein rode horseback to serve and supervise the efforts of nine existing German Reformed congregations. He made several trips via horseback to Winchester, Virginia, and made trips to Walkersville, Middletown, Pipe Creek, and Shepherdstown. While on one such journey, he stopped along the Little Antietam and met George Adam Geeting.

Geeting had been raised in the German Reformed Church. However, he seemed to feel that something was missing, and the services too cold and formal.[9] Thus Otterbein's preaching on the new birth and a personal relationship with Christ warmed his heart.

In many communities lacking ministers, people prevailed

upon the schoolmaster to read a printed sermon between visits of ordained ministers. This was done at the schoolhouse along the Little Antietam. Soon George Adam Geeting, the schoolmaster was conducting church services, and reading a sermon on Sunday morning.

The news of Geeting's efforts reached the ears of Otterbein who soon formed a daring plan.[10] On one of his visits, he took Jacob Hess aside and suggested that during the next service, one of those present should wait until George Adam Geeting started the morning prayer. Then he should reach over on the reading desk and remove the book of printed sermons.

Sunday morning came and the advice was carried out perfectly. While Geeting was praying, Jacob Hess, Sr., reached over and took the book of sermons. We can imagine the preacher's surprise in finding his sermon gone. However, after hesitating a few moments, Geeting gained control of the situation, and delivered a powerful sermon. It was the last time he depended on a book, or someone else's sermons.

But what kind of a man was George Adam Geeting, the teacher-preacher who lived along the Little Antietam?

Dr. Drury, one of the earliest United Brethren historians describes George Adam Geeting as:

> A man of good physical constitution and capable of great endurance. He . . . possessed . . . a good farm, and everything about him was indicative of good condition. The good horses that he kept were long spoken of. He was . . . neat in dress, though he never wore the customary clerical suit. He was possessed of superior gifts. His sympathies were ready and abundant. His understanding of occasions, and adaptation, were much beyond the usual. He had a voice combining sweetness and power. His method of continued attention to books made him capable of great and increasing usefulness. In his preaching he was earnest, yet deliberate. His addresses to the conscience and feelings were always impressive and sometimes strikingly moving. . . . He was . . . a product of the revival movement.[11]
>
> As the years passed, Otterbein was to find in this German convert what he found in no other person with whom his long life and great labors brought him in contact. Geeting was to him a real Timothy.[12]

No field of labor was more enjoyable to Mr. Otterbein than that which awaited him at Antietam, and in no counsels or associations did he more confide or find truer pleasure than in those he enjoyed at George Adam Geeting's.[13]

Brother Geeting's home was Otterbein's retreat, his headquarters when out of Baltimore.[14]

By the mid 1770s Geeting was riding with Christian Newcomer, the Saint Paul of the United Brethren fellowship, into Maryland, Pennsylvania, and Virginia, "sifting out the hearts of men before the judgment seat." Some of the places visited by Geeting in an effort to win converts were: Reading, Lebanon, Lancaster, Manheim, and Harrisburg in Pennsylvania; and Warm Springs, Sulphur Springs, and Martinsburg in what was then Virginia.

Unfortunately, Geeting did not keep a journal like his more famous contemporaries, Newcomer and Ashbury. Newcomer mentions over twenty occasions when he and Geeting were traveling companions on the Lord's circuit. But we are sure there were many others, and undoubtedly Geeting made many preaching trips alone.

Newcomer who lived along Beaver Creek in a lovely stone house said of Geeting: "He preached powerfully. . . . He insisted on the necessity of repentance and conversion, on the knowledge of the pardon of sin, and in consequence thereof, a change of heart and renovation of spirit."[15]

In 1765, Otterbein went to York to become a pastor in that young city. During this pastorate, he attended a "Big Meeting" or revival service at Isaac Long's barn near Lancaster. The preacher was Martin Boehm a Mennonite from Switzerland. Otterbein was so impressed with the message that after the sermon, he embraced Boehm and said in German, "We are brethren." This meeting which probably occurred on Pentecost Sunday in 1767 was the beginning of another beautiful friendship.[16]

Another man was about ready to come upon the scene. This was Christian Newcomer, born in Lancaster County of Mennonite parents in 1749. He felt the call to preach, but like Jonah sought to escape his mission. He did so by selling his farm in Pennsylvania, and fleeing to Beaver Creek just east of Hagerstown where he settled in the spring of 1775. His lovely stone home is still standing. The barn which sheltered his horses was burned recently.

The call of God was inescapable, and finally Newcomer heeded the call to preach. He along with Otterbein, Boehm, and Geeting were the forerunners of a new breed of preachers, calling for a conversion experience among their German listeners. Newcomer was to cross the Allegheny Mountains thirty-eight times on horseback, and even rode to Canada to preach. His saddlebags which carried his Bible and gear are now in the Lovely Lane Museum in Baltimore.

The home of George Adam Geeting, pioneer, preacher, teacher, and farmer.

When Otterbein, Boehm, and others began to preach the necessity of a "New Birth," and a personal experience in religion, severe opposition arose against them. Some were actually excommunicated from their churches. Martin Boehm and George Adam Geeting were treated thus by their communions. These ousted brethren soon gravitated together and became the "United Preachers." Slowly but surely this group was developing a growing sense of fellowship and a deep

A sketch of the old Geeting Meeting House.

conviction of mission. They all became circuit riders, bringing the "Good News," to the German speaking peoples in much the same way that Asbury did to the English speaking peoples. Time and again, these "United Ministers," united in mission and purpose, with the same message of rebirth, would meet to consider how they might conduct their ministry in a more effective manner. Some of these meetings were held at Pipe Creek and still others in Otterbein's parsonage in Baltimore. Their followers became known as "The New Light People."

> Just as Martin Luther, and the Wesleys, and others who are credited with founding religious denominations never intended to do anything except correct wrong conditions in their respective communions, so it was with Otterbein. It was never his plan to start a new church; what he wanted to do was to spiritualize the one with which he and his forefathers had been connected for many generations. Gradually it became apparent that the purposes and ideals for which he strove could not be realized except the new denomination be launched, and he acquiesced.[17]

In 1774 Otterbein became pastor of a German Reformed Church in Baltimore. In the same year George Adam Geeting and the Germans along the Antietam Creek erected a church with Geeting serving as pastor. There has been a debate through the years as to which was the first church or the mother church of the denomination. Lately, most of the credit has gone to the church in Baltimore because it is still standing, now being called "Old Otterbein." Then, too, Otterbein is buried near the church which he served for nearly forty years. However, this church was already in existence when Otterbein went to Baltimore, and was part of the German Reformed faith. On the other hand, the Geeting Meeting House was the first one to be built expressly for the worship of those who were to become members of the Church of the United Brethren in Christ. However, the Geeting Meeting House which stood within the walls of the present Mount Hebron Cemetery where Geeting is buried, gave way to a much needed stone church. This was the Mount Hebron Church which was erected just across the road from the old meeting house in 1845. Both churches were the scenes of many great revivals. All of the church fathers wrote of the "Great Whitsunday Meetings." The Geeting Meeting House and its immediate area "Became the Happy Hunting Grounds" of the United Brethren Church.[18] This gave way to the present Keedysville church erected in 1870. Today all that one is able to see where the meeting house and Mount Hebron once stood is the myrtle-clad cemetery. Thus due to the fact that the Geeting Meeting House was the first building erected primarily for the purpose of religious worship among the followers of Otterbein, it is worthy of being called "The Mother Church."[19]

Whitsuntide or Pentecost Sunday, 1783, was a big moment in the life of George Adam Geeting. On that day, Otterbein and Rev. William Heindel shared in a service on the banks of the Little Antietam.[20] During the hour of worship, Geeting knelt at their feet to receive the laying-on-of-hands, in the rite of ordination. This did not have synod sanction, so Geeting was formally ordained in 1788.

The little log schoolhouse had by this time given way to a large place of worship.[21] The building, erected on the Snively farm, soon became known as the Geeting Meeting

60

House. The exact date of construction is not known. However, this building was the "oldest church built distinctly for and by the followers of Philip William Otterbein in a revival movement. The year 1774 is thought to be the building date. Records existing from June 12, 1775, refer to a congregation of 300 at Geeting's Meeting House."[22]

The church building stood where the Mount Hebron Cemetery is located today. The people in the valley by the stream helped build their house of worship. Some of the early members were those bearing the names of Snively, Baker, Wyand, Hess, Thomas, Welty, Deaner, Zimmerman, and others. Many of them now rest from their labors on land near the spot where the church stood.

The logs came from the big trees nearby. The huge shutters were hung with leather straps. The roof was made with black oak shingles. Two windows were on each side, and two paneled doors in front. The elevated pulpit was between the two doors. Men entered one door, and women the other. A partition ran through the middle, standing about shoulder high. This separated the men from the women.[23] The quaint little chapel in Eyler's Valley near Thurmont is built on this principle with the two doors and the partition in the middle.

Christian Newcomer, writing in his journal, describing the experiences of May 14, 15, and 16, 1796, says: "We held a three day meeting at the Antietam, not far from Brother Geeting's." Whitsuntide 1800 brought a big crowd to the Antietam. Writing about June 1 of that year Newcomer states:

> This morning we had our Love feast. On account of a heavy rain we could not as usual have public preaching under the trees, and as the meeting house could not hold half the people collected, preparations were quickly made to accommodate them in the barn of old Jacob Hess. . . . Otterbein and Brother Geeting distributed the bread and wine.

The big meetings "of the Great Awakening and Revival" movement were very important in the religious and social life of the people. A farmer turned over his entire place for such a meeting. The owner felt honored to have his place selected. It gave him prestige. He would usually slaughter hogs, sheep

61

or beef to feed those coming for services in his woods or barn. Women came together and had a wonderful time baking great quantities of bread, cakes, and pies. Folks exchanged news, visited friends and relatives. Carriages, wagons, and horses brought the crowds, folks coming alone or as family groups. Young lovers always sought permission to ride horseback, the lady behind the lad. Usually there was preaching, singing, and testimony, morning, afternoon, and evening, well into the night in fact.

Between services, the folks cooked, rested, visited, and talked. In those days, men like Wesley and George Whitfield, talked to huge crowds at such meetings. Sometimes people got the "jerks."

In those days the preaching of revival services aimed to make the individual see his need of God, the condition of his soul, and then turn to God in confession and repentance. Many folks wept. Some became so sad over the condition of their life that they fell upon the ground, weeping and shaking all over. At the same time the person would be asking God to be spared and forgiven. The cry heard many times at the "Big Meeting" was "God, be merciful to me a sinner."

Newcomer's account of September 4, 1809, says:

> This evening we had a meeting at Shuey's. I spoke in the English, and Brother Geeting in the German language; we had a soul reviving time, one person fell to the ground and shook in every limb in a remarkable manner. This singular motion they called the jerks. When the person recovered, she praised God with a loud voice.

An individual living at the time said that this action and experience was really the power of God entering a person and causing "a Godly sorrow unto repentance."

Life on the frontier, in New England, and the Middle colonies was far from settled and secure in the period from 1740 to 1800. There were many disturbing factors: Indian wars, Indian raids, political unrest, the French and Indian War, the Revolutionary War, and the birth of a new nation, which had a profound effect upon those living at the time.

The time was ripe for a great spiritual revival which began in Massachusetts in the 1740s. With the preaching of Jonathan Edwards, a new doctrine of conversion emerged stressing the fact of human responsibility and the necessity of choice in turning to God, and also that one should stand in fear if his life was not right with God. "Sinners in the Hands of an Angry God," delivered by the Reverend Mr. Edwards, is a classic example of the preaching in the early years of the period known as "The Great Awakening."

When Edwards preached in Enfield, Connecticut, in 1741 he said, "there was so much a breathing of distress, and weeping, that the preacher was obliged to speak to the people and desire silence, that he might be heard."[24]

Otterbein, Newcomer, Geeting, and Boehm lived in this era, and preached for personal decisions. Geeting "would follow the sinner in his devious ways; showing the severity of God's holy law in a manner which made stout hearts to quail and tremble, and then with feelings and language peculiar to himself, present to the stricken-hearted a loving Saviour."[25]

Many times Geeting as well as other preachers of the day moved their congregations to tears as they sought with God's help to "sift out the hearts of men." Geeting, according to church historians, seemed to have a secret power. Dr. Spayth writes:

> All that ever heard him, saw it—felt it—he alone seemed to be unconscious of it; but love and a childish good nature, like the rays of an evening sun, resting quietly on his round face, was all that could be seen of the great mind, in the midst of sinners crying for mercy or saints shouting for joy. Many were awakened under the preaching of Brother Guething in Pennsylvania, Maryland, and Virginia.[26]

Geeting was a product of the Great Awakening, the revival spirit which swept America in the face of uncertain times, and characteristic of those who called themselves "The United Ministers."

Among churches started by Geeting is Saint Paul's Otterbein United Methodist in Hagerstown. About 1790 Geeting gathered folks together in homes in that city for the purpose of preaching and teaching. In 1807 land was purchased to build a church.

Geeting also rode to Chewsville, between Smithsburg and

Hagerstown, and in 1805 helped to form a congregation which met in a large barn, now the property of Paul Shilling.

A New Church Is Formed

In 1789, the first recorded conference of the United Brethren was held at Otterbein's home in Baltimore. Seven ministers were present. They were Otterbein, Boehm, Geeting, Newcomer, and three others. During their time together they wrote a confession of faith, and the rules of discipline by which they would be governed. In 1815, the first general conference of the denomination adopted the discipline drawn up in 1789.

Washington County with Geeting at the Little Antietam, and Newcomer riding the circuit from Beaver Creek, was the cradle in which the new organization grew to larger dimensions.

Eleven years later, on September 25, 1800, Otterbein and his followers met at the home of Peter Kemp, just west of Frederick and the present Interstate 70. There in the farmhouse "the decision to become a denomination, to assume a denominational name, to name bishops, and to launch out with an aggressive denominational program was made. George Adam Geeting as secretary, dutifully recorded these decisions which gave birth to the first American born denomination."[27]

Fourteen devout men, after much prayer and deliberation, brought forth a new Christian communion with the express aim and desire, "that the church of God may be built up, and sinners converted, so that God in Christ may be honored." These words were written in the minutes of that historic gathering.[28]

Many names had been used to informally designate these men and their converts. Some of them were "The New Mennonites," "Otterbein's People," "The New Light People," and the "German Methodists." However, the name selected by the ministers came from the words spoken by Otterbein when he met Boehm, "Wir Sind Bruder," or "We Are Brethren." Thus the fellowship conceived at the Little Antietam

64

came to birth in Frederick as the Church of the United Brethren in Christ.

SECRETARY AND BISHOP?

George Adam Geeting served as secretary of the annual conference sessions from 1800 to 1812. Family tradition states that he became the third bishop of the new church. However, there are no official records to support this. Otterbein and Boehm served in that capacity until 1813 when Newcomer was elected. If an earlier election was held in the years between 1800 and 1813, Geeting certainly would have been the logical man for the office of bishop.[29]

Whether or nor he was elected is a question very difficult to answer. However, he seems to have acted as bishop in the absence of Otterbein. On numerous occasions he presided over annual meetings and did the work of a bishop. Dr. Spayth says Geeting definitely presided over the 1812 conference.[30] Dr. Thompson, another noted church historian, says, "We find no record of the election of Mr. Geeting to the office of Bishop, but as he did the work associated with the office, he was practically a bishop and we have so classified him."[31]

Williams in his *History of Washington County* calls Geeting the "third Bishop of the United Brethren Church."[32]

The name of Geeting is one of the brightest in the pages of United Brethren history. Two sons, George Adam Geeting, Jr., and Simon, followed in the footsteps of their minister father. For years many people continued to come to the site of the Geeting Meeting House for a special service on Pentecost Sunday. Later, Ephraim Geeting, a great-grandson, married Rachel Russell, the daughter of Bishop John Russell who lived on the Locust Spring farm.

In 1812, George Geeting, Sr., and his wife went to Baltimore to spend a week with Otterbein and other friends. During this time he became ill and started home. The second night he stopped at the home of a friend by the name of Snyder in Ridgeville. During the night his condition grew worse. On the morning of June 28, he knelt by the bed for fifteen minutes in prayer. He was helped back to bed where he folded his hands on his chest. In a few moments his spirit had gone home to be with his Lord.[33]

Sketch of Mount Hebron Church.

The body was brought to the Little Antietam and buried in the Mount Hebron Cemetery. Under a huge tree, a slate stone bears this inscription:

George A. Geeting, Sen.
Born in Nassau, Siegenland, Neiderschelde, Germany
Feb. 6, 1741
& ended his Master's labors & his life
June 28, 1812
Aged 71 years, 4 mo. & 22 days

So ended the earthly life of a humble farmer, teacher, preacher, circuit rider, and man of God.

Among the many contributions coming from the building and those who gathered along the Little Antietam were these:
1. Here George Adam Geeting was brought into the church and joined the followers of Otterbein.
2. Geeting became Otterbein's closest friend, and was his host on many occasions.
3. Here George Adam Geeting was ordained, the first United Brethren ordination.
4. Here the first House of Worship built for the followers of Otterbein was erected.

66

Mount Hebron Cemetery.

The grave of George Adam Geeting.

67

5. Here during nine of the years between 1789 and 1799, the United Brethren ministers met at Pentecost.
6. From here George Adam Geeting went on to become the secretary of the new denomination, and perhaps the third Bishop of the Church.
7. From the hand of Geeting came the work necessary for the first denominational hymnbook which was published in German in 1807.
8. Here great meetings were held until the 1870s.
9. In the Mount Hebron Cemetery Geeting, along with his wife and son, as well as many of the first settlers in the Valley of the Antietam rest from their labors.[34]

In his will, dated September 18, 1811, Geeting said:

> I, George Adam Geeting in perfect health and of perfect mind and memory, thanks be to God, calling into mind the mortality of my body and knowing that it is appointed for all men once to die do make and ordain this my last will ... Principally and first of all I give and recommend my sole into the hand of Almighty God who gave it, and my body I recommend to the earth. First I give and bequeath to Elizabeth my dear beloved wife the two rooms and kitchen and cellar and garden which we now occupy and firewood, stable, and cow which we have now in possession and summer pasture and food in the winter.

Christian Newcomer and Geeting

Christian Newcomer, the Francis Asbury of the United Brethren Church, was born in Lancaster, Pennsylvania, on February 1, 1749. His parents were Mennonites. His father Wolfgang had come to this country from Switzerland. Eight children were born to Wolfgang and Elizabeth Weller Newcomer. In the evenings before going to bed, both parents usually knelt for prayer.[35]

When Christian was very young, "the spirit of God knocked at the door of my heart." He was a very sensitive soul, and seemed to give great thought to sin and the condition of his soul. Once while out in the fields, Newcomer pulled a peach from a tree and started to eat it. However, the seed became lodged in his throat, almost choking him to death. Christian Newcomer never forgot that experience. He wrote:

68

O! the terror and anguish of the soul that struck me; death and eternity staring me in the face, and my God not reconciled; no comfort, no consolation in the soul, it is utterly impossible to describe the anguish which seized me at this instant—suddenly to be removed into another existence, to appear before the awful tribunal of the great Jehovah, and unprepared. O! kind reader, imagine if you can my situation; everything around me began to grow dim, my sight failed, a sudden tremor ran through every nerve, I struggled to catch my breath, but in vain: like a dart, an idea shot across my mind . . . that I should instantly run my back against the trunk of an apple tree, which stood about 25 or 30 yards from me, in order to remove the stone and save my life. . . . Down I came from my horse in an instant, and ran with all my remaining strength towards the tree, though barely able to discern it. At last I reached the spot, bounced my shoulders against the trunk, and out came the peach-stone. O! great Jehovah how did I rejoice;—pierced by gratitude I sunk down on my knees giving thanks to Almighty God for the preservation of my life.[36]

He felt the call to the ministry. Yet he hesitated to make the final step. When his father died, Christian was entrusted with the care of the family. On March 31, 1770, he married Elizabeth Baer.[37] Soon afterward he became very ill and again despaired of his life. He was in a state of inner turmoil.

He seemed to be fighting a war within. Finally like Jonah, he sought safety in flight. Selling his Pennsylvania farm, Newcomer moved to Maryland about 1775. He took up residence in a log house near Beaver Creek in Frederick, now Washington County, Maryland. He found his neighbors to be good, kind-hearted people, yet without a new birth experience. Still Newcomer disobeyed the call to preach. The turmoil kept building and eventually he went through a "dark night of the soul experience."

While suffering mental anguish, Newcomer came down with a bad fever, and almost died. For a week he lingered between death and life. At night when the rest of the family was in bed, he knelt beside his bed pleading for God to be merciful to him. One night he found God's peace. Being almost overcome with joy, he walked out into the yard toward the spring and gave his life completely to the Lord. He was determined to grow toward perfect love and faith.

Returning to Lancaster for a visit, he gave his testimony at the Mennonite meeting, telling them how he had sought to escape God's call, and what he had experienced. It must have been a very moving experience.

He had already become acquainted with Philip William Otterbein and George Adam Geeting:

> ... two preachers of the German Reformed Church, and had frequently heard them preach in the neighborhood of my place of residence. These individuals endowed by God, preached powerfully. ... They insisted on the necessity of genuine repentance and conversion, on the knowledge of a pardon of sin, and in consequence thereof, a change of heart and renovation of spirit. Many secure and unconcerned sinners were, by their instrumentality, awakened from the sleep of sin and death—many converted from darkness to light—from the power of Sin and Satan unto God. They soon collected many adherents to, and followers of the doctrines which they preached, from the multitude that congregated to hear them. Those persons who held to, and embraced these doctrines, were by then, formed into societies, and were called Otterbein's people. . . .[38]

The labors of Otterbein and Geeting spread very rapidly among the Germans in Pennsylvania and Maryland. "From every quarter resounded the call, 'Come over and help us.' "[39]

Newcomer gave himself to the work of preaching and soon became a circuit rider. His journal which he kept from October 27, 1795, to 1830, tells the story of days and nights in the saddle, riding from his Beaver Creek home to Virginia, Pennsylvania, Ohio, Kentucky, and Indiana, crossing the Allegheny Mountains thirty-eight times in behalf of his Lord. He even rode to Canada with the Gospel message.[40]

Christian Newcomer was the "Saint Paul" of the United Brethren Church. He was the guiding light of the church in the years from 1813 to 1830. The movement started by Otterbein and Geeting would grow to reach 750,000, and then in 1968 unite with the Methodist church.

The old log house on his Beaver Creek property became a meetinghouse. A new stone house was erected around 1780. Newcomer's purpose in life is best described in his own words: "Let the days of my life here in this world, be as many as is pleasing in His sight; they shall all be dedicated to Him; I will trust to His mercy and compassion."[41]

These few words concerning Newcomer could easily be

expanded to a book, as could most of the other chapters. We wish more details were available. However, Newcomer was a frequent visitor at the Geeting Meeting House, and George Adam Geeting rode with Newcomer on many preaching trips. We turn now to *Newcomer's Journal* for comments about the meetinghouse and preaching missions.

> April 26, 1796. This day I came in company with Br. George Adam Geeting to what is called Berner's Church, but we were not permitted to speak therein; so Brother Geeting spoke in the graveyard adjoining the church to a numerous congregation, with remarkable power.
>
> September 29, 1797. This day I visited . . . in Woodstock and rode to John Funkhouser's where I again met with Br. Geeting.
>
> October 4, 1797. I set off in company with Br. Geeting on a journey to Pennsylvania. In the evening Br. Geeting preached in Chambersburg.
>
> October 5. We traveled through Shippensburg and Carlisle, and at night held a meeting at John Rupp's.
>
> February 3, 1799. This day Brs. Geeting and Troxell came to my house and prayed with my sick son. The next morning he appeared better.
>
> March 17, 1799. Br. Geeting preached at Fr. Hoffman's in the German, and I spoke in English. [Near Littlestown, Pa.]

August 1799 found Geeting preaching in Rockingham County, Virginia.

> October 2, 1799. Today Brs. Geeting and Abraham Troxell had a meeting at my house. The Lord was present.
>
> November 7, 1799. This day I left in company with Br. Geeting for Pennsylvania. . . . 11th—We rode to Harrisburg. Br. Geeting preached in the German Church. . . . 13th—Br. Geeting preached in the German Reformed Church in Johnstown. . . . 14th—This forenoon Br. Geeting preached in Lebanon.
>
> April 28, 1801. This morning Br. Geeting preached in Liberty in the German language. [Near Frederick.]

Mid August 1801 found Newcomer and Geeting in Cumberland County, Pennsylvania, conducting a big meeting. Five days later Geeting spoke in Chambersburg. The twentieth of September found Geeting in Sulphur Springs, Virginia.

Newcomer's Journal records the following visits to the Geeting Meeting House:

71

May, 1796. On the 14th, 15th, and 16th—we held a three days' meeting at the Antietam, not far from Br. Geeting's.

June 3, 1797. Today a Sacramental meeting commenced near the Antietam. The Lord was present from the beginning. We held a prayer meeting in the evening at Br. Samuel Baker's. . . . Sunday 4th—This forenoon William Otterbein preached from Ephesians 2:1-6. O! how conclusively did he reason. . . . How he tried to convince all of the necessity of vital, experimental religion and a thorough change of heart! The congregation was unusually large, and all seemed to pay profound attention. . . . Otterbein and Geeting administered the Lord's Supper. . . . 5th—We had a glorious time. A great number of young people and hoary-headed sinners were convicted and some happily converted to God!

May 31, 1800. Today I set out for the Quarterly, or Great Meeting as it is generally called, at the Antietam. Father Otterbein was there and preached first from Psalm 11:22-25. At night I spoke from Acts 14:22.

Sunday, June, 1800. This morning we had our Love Feast. On account of heavy rain, we could not have public preaching under the trees; and as the Meeting-house could hold half the people, preparations were quickly made to accommodate them in the barn of Old Jacob Hess. Otterbein spoke first; I spoke after him; then Otterbein and Geeting distributed the bread and wine. The hearts of many were tendered. It was a time long to be remembered.

May 23, 1801. Today a Sacramental meeting commenced at the Antietam; Father Otterbein was present and spoke first; at night we had a blessed time. Sunday, 24th—Father Otterbein preached this forenoon to large congregation with such power and grace that almost every soul was pierced to the heart. I spoke after him, but for a short time, when the people broke forth in lamentations for mercy. May the Lord deepen the impressions made. 25th—Today we had the outpouring of the Holy Spirit, a Pentecost as in the days of old.

June 4, 1802. This day I rode to the Antietam, to Br. Geeting's who had lost his companion while I was away from home. I met father Otterbein . . . tarried at night with Jacob Hess. 5th—Today our meeting commenced, father Otterbein preached the first sermon from Mark 10:29-31. After preaching, we held a small conference with the preachers present.

Sunday, 6th—A vast multitude of people assembled; Otterbein spoke first. . . . Br. Geeting followed him; the Lord's Supper was administered: bless the Lord it was a precious time.

May 19, 1804. A Sacramental meeting commenced at Antietam. . . . Sunday, 20th—This forenoon Otterbein preached again with great energy from Psalm 72. Many drew to the Lord's table with streaming eyes; my poor soul was fed with heavenly manna.

72

Sunday May 21, 1809. We held a Sacramental meeting at the Antietam; the Lord was present and blessed the word spoken.

Preaching Tours

October 3, 1802, Geeting and Martin Boehm administered the Sacrament of the Lord's Supper at a three-day meeting held at Palmer's.

> October 20,1802. This day a Quarterly meeting commenced at Hoffman's in Rockingham county, Virginia. The meeting was held in a barn. I spoke first; Brother Geeting spoke with compassion, and I arose and went among the people, exhorting them to accept the overtures of mercy. Many sought the Lord. The meeting was protracted till late at night.
>
> May 4, 1803. I set off for Lancaster, Pennsylvania; in Middletown I met Br. Geeting. We rode together to Frederick-town, where Br. Geeting preached in the German Reformed Church.
>
> February 7, 1804. I left home for Baltimore, stayed for the night with Jacob Hess. 8th—I stayed at Br. Geeting's. It rained during the whole day. 9th—This morning Br. Geeting and myself set out together, we came to Middle-town where Br. Geeting preached, and at night we came to Br. Kemp's.

Geeting, Kemp, and Newcomer proceeded to Baltimore where Geeting preached in Old Otterbein Church. The group also met the Methodist bishop, Whatcoat.

On April 6, 1806, Geeting preached in Roth's Church near York. On May 21 the annual ministers' meeting began at the home of Lawrence Everhart of Revolutionary War fame near Middletown. This was the first annual session at which neither Otterbein nor Boehm were present. From the minutes it would seem that Geeting presided over the sessions.

April 17, 1807, found Geeting in Baltimore, preaching at Otterbein's church and administering the Sacrament.

May 5, 1808, Newcomer met Geeting at Peter Kemp's in Frederick. Together they rode twenty-eight miles the next day to Littlestown. On the ninth, Geeting preached in York, and on the nineteenth returned home by way of Gettysburg.

June 5, 1808, found Geeting preaching at home along the banks of the Little Antietam. A huge crowd was present. Many tears were shed as a result of his message.

On the thirteenth, Geeting and Newcomer met in Hagerstown and set out for McConnellsburg, Bedford, and West-

73

moreland County in Pennsylvania. On the nineteenth, Geeting spoke in Mount Pleasant, Pennsylvania, on the text "I am the way, the truth, and the life." On the twenty-first of June, Geeting preached in the courthouse in Greensburg, speaking in German, and followed by Newcomer who spoke in English. Before the two returned home, they preached in Somerset and Berlin.

May 15, 1809, saw Geeting preaching at the courthouse in York. Many times the circuit riders would preach from courthouse steps, catching the people on their way to and from the place of legal business. The early church fathers always liked to establish churches in county-seat towns.

September 1809, Geeting preached in Harrisonburg and Winchester, Virginia.

On June 12, 1810, Newcomer set out on a preaching mission in Ohio. Before he did, he stopped at Jacob King's in Hagerstown where he and Geeting prayed for his safety and success. Then it was on to Mercersburg and the West.

February 27, 1811, was a sad day. "This morning the remains of Br. Peter Kemp were interred; a great many people attended the funeral. Br. Geeting preached from Psalm 8:5. I followed him in the English language."

On March 13, 1811, Newcomer found his wife getting weaker and weaker. April 1 he rode to Hagerstown to get some new medicine for her. By the twenty-first, his dear companion was very sick and feeble. On April 22, Newcomer writes:

> This evening at 6 o'clock my dear companion departed this life, and resigned her immortal spirit into the arms of Jesus her Saviour. Peace be unto thy ashes; for many years thou hast been a staff and comfort unto me; soon we shall be reunited where parting shall be no more. 24th—This day the remains of my dear companion were deposited in the grave; Br. Geeting delivered the funeral discourse from Matt. 6:19-21. . . . Her age was 59 years and 22 days. 29th—This day Br. Geeting and Andrew Zeller came to see me, and stayed with us for the night.

May 13, 1812, the annual conference commenced at Schnebly's or the Geeting Meeting House and continued for two days. George Adam Geeting was elected to preside.

On July 23, 1812, Newcomer, traveling near Baltimore,

Kentucky, learned of the death of his dear friend, and oft-times traveling companion, Brother Geeting.

> 23rd—We came to Peter Hays's, an old acquaintance, and stayed for the night. Here I saw a newspaper printed in Hagerstown, Maryland, wherein it stated that the Rev. George Geeting had died at Mr. Snyder's, on his return from Baltimore. So then, one after another of my beloved brethren are called from the stage of action, to try the realities of another world; I am spared, who knows how long? O Lord, grant that I may be fully prepared and ready at any time to obey the summons.

From *Newcomer's Journal* we can see that Geeting rode with him many times and preached in Middletown, Peter Kemp's, Frederick, Liberty, Baltimore, and Hagerstown. In Pennsylvania, Geeting preached in Carlisle, Shippensburg, Lebanon, Chambersburg, Harrisburg, York, Littlestown, Greensburg, and other places in the western part of the state. In the Shenandoah Valley, Geeting preached in Winchester, Harrisonburg, and other places in Rockingham County. He preached Peter Kemp's funeral sermon, as well as a message of hope at the burial of Mrs. Newcomer.

Bishop John Russell

Pipe Creek in Carroll County has given two outstanding individuals to the Valley of the Antietam. Augustus Biggs,

Bishop John Russell.

Sharpsburg's doctor and leading citizen during the mid-1800s came from the Pipe Creek area as did John Russell.

Philip Otterbein was a frequent visitor to Pipe Creek and held many religious services there. Among his converts was the grandfather of John Russell. In fact, Otterbein preached Grandfather Russell's funeral sermon.

Young John had the benefit of a godly home and a wonderful Christian mother. But he realized the faith of his parents was not enough.

75

Crystal Spring, Bishop Russell's home.

He must have his own personal experience. Later in life, John Russell wrote:

> I would pray as well as I knew how; I would sometimes use prayer books, until at length, under an apple tree, my troubled spirit was comforted; gladness so filled my soul that I ran to my mother, telling her what I had obtained. All three of us, father, mother and myself, prayed rejoicingly. I experienced such a power I thought I must tell everybody how I felt.[42]

During the "Big Meetings" which followed, young Russell shared in the services. He told of his experience under the apple tree, read the Scripture for the preacher, and sometimes gave a short sermon.

John's father had hopes of his son becoming a blacksmith. Eighteen months the boy worked as an apprentice. But this occupation was not for him. His interest was in preaching and in leading people to know Jesus Christ. His success in the local area convinced Mr. and Mrs. Russell that God had something more in store for their son. They realized that his calling was to preaching rather than mending wagons and shoeing horses.

John Russell was born on March 18, 1799. Nineteen years

later in Lancaster County, Pennsylvania, he received his license to preach from Bishop Christian Newcomer. Immediately afterward, the teen-age preacher set out on horseback to preach in Virginia. The next year, 1819, found Russell riding and preaching in Franklin, Cumberland, Perry, and Fulton counties in Pennsylvania. He also preached in Washington County during that year.[43]

For all this travel and work Russell was paid the grand sum of eighty dollars. His horse broke down under the strain of travel and work. Rather than give up, young John traveled on foot, walking sometimes all night to keep an engagement scheduled for the next day. When he reached a stream, he had to find a place where he could wade across.

> His exposures were great, his travels extensive and laborious, and his remuneration small. Yet . . . it was not all hardship and disappointment. . . . There were warmhearted brethren and sisters, who greeted him with smiles, followed him with their blessings, and who gave him the best they had. He was entertained by their firesides, fed at their tables, and sheltered within their homes.[44]

In late 1819, Russell traveled to Ohio with Bishop Newcomer and another preacher. Soon he was preaching on the frontier, sharing the plight of the frontier families.

There were no roads, only old Indian trails through the forest and high grass. Young Russell had a hatchet made. As he traveled, he blazed the trees to keep from getting lost.

While still in Pennsylvania, Russell had waded across the Juniata River while overheated. This led to a serious eye disorder which, after his arrival in Ohio, kept him from traveling for a time.

Bad eyes could not keep John Russell down. He preached nearby, and built a schoolhouse. He organized a Sunday school for the boys and girls of the area.

In the meantime, he had been doing a lot of thinking. The United Brethren Church was growing. Something was needed to keep the membership in touch with the events of the day. Those across the mountains in the east did not know what was happening on the frontier, and those in Ohio were unaware of what was going on in the older churches. News was carried primarily by traveling preachers. A better method was

77

needed. A church paper could carry the news from all parts of the church. It could tell about people and places. Inspirational and educational articles could be included, as well as denominational promotions. It was a risk, a venture of faith. No one knew whether such an undertaking could possibly succeed financially. But John Russell believed in it. In fact, he sold his property and invested heavily in the printing venture. In years to come, money from his pocket would often bail the printing establishment out of financial difficulty.[45]

The general conference of 1833 chose John Russell, Jonathan and George Dresbach as trustees of the new venture. "They were authorized to publish at Circleville, Ohio, 'a paper devoted to religious, moral, and literary intelligence.' " The first issue of *The Religious Telescope* came off the press on December 31, 1834. Eleven hundred ninety-seven individuals were subscribers.

After getting the printing venture on a solid basis, Russell moved back to Maryland in 1838. He became pastor of Otterbein's congregation in Baltimore.

Life in Baltimore would be a pleasant change for the Russell family. On the frontier the family had worked together to make ends meet financially. The Reverend Mr. Russell had been paid sixty dollars a year. His wife pulled flax, spun, and wove the cloth into garments for her husband. She spun and wove for the neighbors to make additional income. Russell made his own shoes and repaired clocks for the neighbors.

In 1841 the General Conference of the United Brethren Church established an office in Baltimore to print a paper for the German element of the denomination. The Reverend Mr. Russell was appointed the general agent for the publishing house. It was his task to obtain subscriptions for all church papers, and to promote missions. A year earlier, on his own, Russell had started to publish *Die Geschaeftige Martha* (*The Busy Martha*). Now this was continued under denominational supervision.

Sadly, no details of his work in this capacity have been recorded. They are blank, although they must have been very busy years.

In 1845, Russell was elected a bishop in the Church of the

United Brethren in Christ. He was also named president of the Missionary Society. He strongly opposed slavery and secret societies, writing against both in the church periodicals.

In the meantime, he had obtained a 300-acre farm near Keedysville. He proposed that the denominational seminary be located on his farm, as well as the publishing interests of the church. He desired facilities to handle the quadrennial meetings of general conference. Russell felt the young preachers should study half the day, and work in the fields raising their own food, thus cutting costs, the other half of the day. At one time, at least five young theologians were following this program on the Bishop's farm at the base of Red Hill.[46]

> He was a man of heroic mold, both physically and mentally, and his soundness of heart and purpose matched his otherwise great qualities. His application to his studies and his work made him proficient in thinking and speaking. His hard common sense made him successful in his management of his own affairs and the affairs of the Church entrusted to him. . . . He had the rare gift of working through others.[47]

"Along with his strong preaching and administrative ability, Bishop Russell was unique, resourceful, and witty."

In September 1862 the bishop was living in his fourteen-room farmhouse near Keedysville. Part of the house he had added for his young students. His fields were filled on the nights of September 15 and 16 with the tents and campfires of the Union Ninth Corps. After the battle, his Crystal Spring or Locust Spring farm became a hospital for the more severely wounded cases of that corps. The hospital remained in existence until the early days of 1863. During this time, the bishop went from room to room, and from tent to tent, giving spiritual aid, and assisting in the care of the wounded.

Bishop Russell was a benevolent man. He gave ten thousand dollars, no small sum in those days, for a chair of Bible in the seminary. One of his last acts was to give money in his wife's name for the new church erected in the village of Keedysville in 1870. This building replaced the Mount Hebron Church. After the bell was in place, his daughter called him to come out in the yard to hear its tones. This was the last time he was out of doors. "His death was the first one to be announced by the bell he had purchased." Following his wishes, he was buried at Mount Hebron, but later the body was moved to Keedysville.

The Hitt Family

The Hitts coming from Germany settled in Virginia. But then Martin, Daniel, and Samuel Hitt were drawn to the Antietam by three sisters, Margaret, Ann, and Sarah Smith.[48]

All three Hitt brothers became Methodist ministers or circuit riders. Daniel Hitt was known as "the friend of the Bishop." He was a close friend of Francis Asbury, the father of Methodism in the colonies. Asbury who was known as "The prophet of the Long Trail" often stopped at the Hitt home on his way to and from the Shenandoah Valley. God alone knows how often he forded the Antietam just above the Hitt home traveling to "sift out the hearts of men."

Daniel Hitt was tall and very polite. He had blue eyes and was very neat in dress. Like Asbury, he loved the outdoors and children. Much of the time he was in the saddle, riding to Baltimore, Pittsburgh, and the Shenandoah Valley with the Gospel.

In 1807 Daniel Hitt was chosen by Asbury to ride with him on a grand tour of Methodist churches. The journey covered five thousand miles, from the Carolinas to Maine.

As they traveled, these two men of God compiled a new hymnbook to be used by the Methodists in America. Following the journey, Hitt was sent from the banks of the Antietam, to the growing city of New York to serve as assistant editor of the Methodist Book Concern.

Daniel was free to travel at will. He had been in love with Sarah Smith. However, after the Smith family moved to Kentucky, Sarah died. Daniel devoted the rest of his life to traveling, preaching, and writing.

His last sermon was preached in Greencastle, Pennsylvania. His text was from Jeremiah 13: "My soul shall weep in secret places. Mine eyes shall weep sore and run down with tears." Daniel, like many other preachers of that era, walked around a lot, and often came and stood right before a listener, as though talking to him personally.

On this particular night in Greencastle, a little girl sitting up front, ran back the aisle to her mother, and threw her arms around her neck saying, "Brother Hitt is going to die."

Soon after the sermon Daniel Hitt came down with typhoid fever. His nephew Samuel Hitt came for him and took him back to the house along the Antietam. There he died.

Martin Hitt married Margaret Smith, and Samuel married Ann. Both families moved west. Martin's son Samuel inherited the property along the Antietam. In 1832 the Maryland legislature passed a bill calling for the erection of a stone bridge on the Keedysville-Hagerstown Road. Although John Weaver built the bridge, Samuel Hitt seems to have been of great assistance. The Hitts having been in the area for a long time, and operating the old Hitt mill, saw the new Upper Bridge over the Antietam, named after them.

Asbury Visits the Valley

The Geeting Meeting House apparently had another distinguished visitor in the person of Francis Asbury, "The Prophet of the Long Road," "The Lord's Horseman," and the "Father of American Methodism."

Asbury who rode from Maine to Georgia proclaiming the Gospel, and a man who rode almost 250,000 miles on horseback has an interesting note in his journal for Wednesday, May 31, 1786: "Came to Antietam settlement, and spoke in a Dutch church."[49] Asbury had ridden through eighteen days of rain and had covered 200 miles via horseback during the ten days prior to reaching Antietam settlement.

From all existing records it would seem that the visit was made to the structure erected by the United Brethren on the Mount Hebron Road. The Methodists at the time spoke of the Germans as Dutch, and Asbury was more at home in a revival or evangelistic type ministry than in the formalism of the established German Reformed Church. May 31 would have also been about the time of the great Whitsuntide or Pentecost meetings held along the Little Antietam Creek.

Asbury came to the Valley of the Antietam in May of 1784. At that time he was amazed to see huge chunks of ice floating down the Potomac, carrying huge boulders in the current, and cutting into the banks the same as though hundreds of men would have been at work smoothing the banks.

During the 1784 visit, an Irish woman from Sharpsburg asked Asbury to come and pray with her. She had treated the Methodists poorly. Now in his presence she wished to pray for forgiveness.

Near Pentecost in 1784, 1785, and 1786 Asbury came to the valley. On May 24, 1785, he says, "I crossed the mountains to Sharpsburg, and preached to some honest Germans."

We cannot leave the early preachers of the valley without mentioning the Boveys. They like many of the others came originally from Germany. Gottlieb Bobe was the first to arrive in Philadelphia on August 28, 1750.

A Jacob Bovey came to Hagerstown in the 1790s. Christian Newcomer records visiting the home on June 8, 1813. Jacob, Jr., married Christina Geeting, the daughter of George Adam. Four children were born to this union.

Quite a few of the Boveys became ministers in the United Brethren Church. Among them were Adam, Henry, Michael, John Adam, and Wesley Evers. Many of the Bovey girls likewise married ministers. The diaries of the Reverend Henry A. Bovey are to be found in the archives of the United Methodist Church. They make interesting reading about a tremendous family, and life in another day.

Rebecca Bovey's husband died in 1859, on the eve of the Civil War. The Virginia Conference of the United Brethren Church provided funds to send the widow back to the Bovey homestead. The lovely farm was located along the Antietam Creek, between the Pry farm and the Middle Bridge.

Thus along the Antietam Creek the Reverend Mr. Allen brought Christian education to the pioneer children. And George Adam Geeting, Francis Asbury, Philip Otterbein, Daniel Hitt, Christian Newcomer, Bishop McKendree, the Boveys, and John Russell read their Bibles, meditated and prayed. Then they rode forth to "sift the hearts of men."

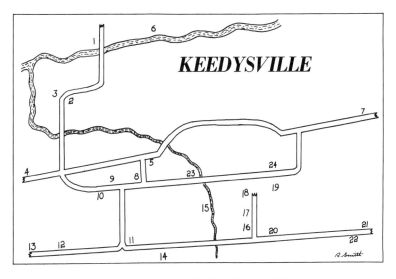

MAP OF THE KEEDYSVILLE AREA

1. The Upper or Hitt Bridge.
2. The Jacob Cost Home.
3. The Pry Mill.
4. Philip Pry's Headquarters, Army of the Potomac.
5. Fairview Cemetery, burial place of the Geetings, Russells, and Costs.
6. The Antietam Creek.
7. Maryland Route 34, Boonsboro to Shepherdstown.
8. Salem United Methodist Church.
9. The Old Stone Schoolhouse, a Union hospital in 1862.
10. The United Church of Christ, a large operating room in 1862.
11. The Home of George Adam Geeting.
12. The Crystal Spring home of Bishop Russell.
13. Geeting Road.
14. The Keedy Homestead.
15. The Little Antietam Creek.
16. Perhaps the first dwelling on Felfoot.
17. Site of the Geeting Meeting House.
18. The Mount Hebron Cemetery.
19. Site of the Mount Hebron Church.
20. Felfoot.
21. The home of Moses Chapline.
22. The Dog Street Road.
23. The Jacob Hess Home, one of the first in Keedysville.
24. Taylor Park.

IV

GRAPES OF WRATH

Grapes contain seeds. Several grapes taste very good. Yet if one eats too many grapes, or accidentally swallows some seeds, pain and discomfort will follow.

In the evenings during the 1840s and 1850s clusters of men sat in the village stores and talked. The men of Sharpsburg talked before and after their lodge meetings. They talked of many things, but one issue on their minds was that of the seeds of discontent sweeping across the country.

During these years there was a variety of reform movements calling for the abolition of slavery. William Lloyd Garrison and later Horace Greeley were most outspoken in their demand for immediate freedom of the slaves. Garrison published a newspaper called *The Liberator.* He said that slavery was a covenant with death, an agreement with hell.

The moderate thinkers recognized slavery as an economic and social problem. They saw many problems connected with freedom, and realized there were no easy answers. Yet slavery must be abolished. Albert Finney, the great evangelist of his day, and Harriet Beecher Stowe were in this group.

As pressure began to mount, the South became more and more defensive. Northern papers were outlawed in many leading cities of the South. Runaway slaves, more and more, were made public examples. When caught, they were taken to a busy spot in the city and publicly whipped to discourage others from following their example.

There were extremists at each end of the line. Never a majority, yet these folks were a dynamic minority. Speeches and writings of Garrison, Greeley, and Southern congressmen had a profound psychological effect on the nation. The matter of slavery was not allowed to rest. It was kept constantly before the people.

Agricultural developments such as the invention of the McCormick reaper, and the great industrial growth of the Northeast played a role in the seeds of discontent. The South did not feel a part of the nation. It seemed as though there were two different societies, two economic systems, and two ways of life.

In the South, of course, cotton was king. There was little farming diversity, especially in the deep South. Slaves were needed to harvest king cotton. After a while there was a depletion of the soil. The land suffered from the lack of fertilizers and crop rotation.

Complicating matters was the difference between the planters and the plain people. The plain folks on small farms were like the average Midwestern farmer, struggling along to make ends meet. On the other hand, the large plantation owners dominated politics, the state government, and to a large extent even the federal government.

For recreation, both the planters and the plain or average people spent much time riding horseback and in shooting matches. These were to give the South an edge in the early days of the war.

One writer has pictured the seeds of discontent in the South like a totem pole. On top was the plantation owner with his wealth and acres of land. Next came the small farmer, or poor white farmer, just making ends meet, and at the bottom, the slaves. The poor white farmers feared the freedom of the slaves, feeling that then they would be on the bottom of the totem pole. But regardless, the North looked, and did not like what it saw. Slavery was wrong, and the press and leaders in the North said so.

On the corner opposite the Lutheran Church in Sharpsburg stands the old slave block. Here children, women, and men were sold to the highest bidder, regardless of the feelings of the person being sold, and regardless of the hardship brought to the family unit, or friendship being broken by the sale.

As time passed, the seeds of discontent were bringing more

and more pain. It is not the purpose of this book to go into great detail about all the things that happened during those years. The reader can do research on the Wilmot Proviso, the Missouri Compromise, the Dred Scott decision, the Kansas-Nebraska Act, Bleeding Kansas, the Lincoln-Douglas debates, and the formation of the Republican Party.

The men of Sharpsburg learned of these things, and discussed them, never dreaming that their town, their farmland, and the picturesque Antietam Creek would help to settle the issue once and for all.

John Brown

Then one day the seeds of discontent came closer. On June 5, 1858, a young man by the name of Johnny Cook, carpetbag in hand, came to Harpers Ferry.[1] He was a good-looking lad from Connecticut, coming South to strike it rich. Though partially trained in law, he would do anything to make an honest dollar.

Someone remembered that Widow Kennedy had a room and he was directed there. Paying two dollars a week for room and board, Cook took a job teaching in the country school. In his spare time he drank with the men of Harpers Ferry and sought to become well acquainted with all the terrain features.

Cook fell in love with Widow Kennedy's daughter and married Mary Virginia. Apparently a child was born to this union sometime before October 1859. He soon quit his job as teacher, and became a salesman of books, specializing in Bibles and in the life of George Washington.[2]

Cook loved his wife. But his greatest love and loyalty was to an old gentleman he had met in Kansas. A man who sat by the campfire at night, with open Bible in hand, expounding the evils of slavery. That man was John Brown, and soon John Brown would be coming to Harpers Ferry.

As a book salesman, Cook rented a horse and buggy, riding throughout the countryside attempting to sell his books. While he traveled, his eyes made mental notes of the lanes and roads, barns, and caves in the lower end of Washington

86

County, and the area around Charles Town and Shepherds-town.

On July 4, 1859, John Unseld rode from the farm he owned near Dargan. He was retired now, and others did his work for him. He was going to Harpers Ferry for a big holi-day drink. Soon he met a bearded man by the name of Isaac Smith, who introduced his two sons and a man by the name of Anderson.

Unseld, like most people of the area, knew everybody else. He soon recognized that these men were strangers. He asked them if they were going to stay. Isaac Smith replied that it all depended on the cost of land.

Unseld, trying to be helpful said:

"Up the road toward Sharpsburg is old Doc Kennedy's place. He died a short time ago, and his widow'd like to sell or rent. It's not very big, thirty acres or so, but it'd do until you get settled here. The big house with two stories is on your right, and then there's a little cabin on the left."[3]

Unseld had no idea he had been talking not to Isaac Smith, but to John Brown. The four newcomers walked from Sandy Hook to the farm, and decided it was adequate for their plans. The kitchen was in the basement, living and bedrooms on the second floor, and an attic to hide things they wanted to keep out of sight.

During the summer of 1859, Brown soon gathered twenty-one men to the Kennedy farm. He paid thirty-five dollars to insure the rent through March 1860. He sent to North Elba, New York, requesting his sixteen-year-old daugh-ter Annie to come and keep house for the men. Oliver Brown's seventeen-year-old wife Martha was to come along.

Folks in Sharpsburg and neighbors soon became curious about the wagons containing long boxes seen heading to the Kennedy farm. Isaac Smith said, "Oh, that's just our pros-pecting machinery." But in reality, the boxes contained Sharp's rifles, and pikes to arm the slaves and overthrow the government.

Annie Brown said that:

After breakfast Father usually read a chapter in the Bible and made a plain, short, sensible prayer, standing while praying. . . . After the meals I cleared off the tables and washed the dishes and swept the floors of the room and porch, constantly on the lookout for Mrs. Huffmaster, our nearest neighbor. She was worse than a plague of fleas. Of our supplies of food, a few things were occasionally bought at Harpers Ferry when the men went to the post office after "The Baltimore Sun," which Father subscribed for. . . . The rest of our food supplies were purchased at the towns from Chambersburg down, a few things at a time or place so as not to arouse suspicion. . . . I was there to keep the outside world from discovering that John Brown and his men were in their neighborhood.[4]

There was still a reward out for the capture of John Brown, stemming from his bloody work in Kansas. Hence the beard, and the reason for Annie's watchfulness.

Cook had done his spying well. But John Brown was disappointed. The Northern backers of his enterprise grew cooler and cooler. Negroes expected to come from Canada to help, never arrived. The men penned up in the Kennedy farmhouse were getting restless.

Brown had to do something. So he went to Chambersburg to meet with Frederick Douglas, the great Negro writer and orator. Meeting in secret, Brown described his bold plan. He and his men would hit the U.S. Arsenal in the dead of the night, arouse the Negroes in the area, and withdraw to the hills. Then using guerrilla tactics, they would strike repeated blows in the South until the yoke of oppression was broken. The Negro would rise up like a great "Army of God."

Douglas was sad. He said, "It will never work. You're speaking of an attack on the federal government. The country will unite against us, instead of joining us."

But Brown could not see it that way. He felt he was an instrument of God sent to raise up the slaves against their masters. He replied, "No, Frederick. No! They'll rise. Thousands of them will join us."

Douglas was not convinced. In his opinion, Harpers Ferry was a trap, and John Brown would not get out alive. Time would prove Douglas correct.

Meanwhile wagons loaded with the long boxes, marked for I. Smith continued to go through Sharpsburg on their way to the Kennedy farm. The stage was set for Brown's fanatical undertaking, an event which would fan the discontent of "the grapes of wrath."

On a chilly, misty October 16 evening, Brown said to his small army, "Come on boys. Get your arms. We're going to the Ferry." The hour had come. There was no turning back. John Brown was ready to launch his raid.

Between eleven and twelve o'clock, "Osawatomie" Brown and his men left the Kennedy farm, proceeded down the Dargan Road, crossed the Potomac on the Baltimore and Ohio Railroad Bridge, and made their way to the U.S. Arsenal. The rest is history.

President Buchanan sent a detachment of marines under the command of Colonel Robert E. Lee to put an end to the uprising. Once again the reader can turn to the many books written on the subject of John Brown's raid, and obtain specific details.

After capturing Brown and what was left of his detail, a Lieutenant Simpson of the Baltimore "Independent Grays" was detached to an old log schoolhouse on Maryland Heights near Harpers Ferry. Sixteen large boxes of arms and ammunition were found. New Sharp's rifles were scattered over the floor. Apparently the weapons had been brought from the farm to serve as a base of supply. The boxes had been shipped from Cincinnati by American Express to Chambersburg.

John Cook was not among the group captured at Harpers Ferry. He had been seen on Maryland Heights. Captain James Ewell Brown Stuart was sent to get him. He had been left behind by Brown in command of the Kennedy farm and the supplies for the uprising. Stuart, later to become famous as a dashing Confederate cavalry leader, found mass confusion at the Kennedy farm. A fire was still burning. Large amounts of food and other provisions were scattered over the place. Those left behind had fled in a hurry. Most damaging of all was a trunk full of papers, letters, and other documents, detailing Brown's plans.

On October 26, Cook, John Brown's advance man, was captured near Quincy in Franklin County, Pennsylvania.[5]

The men taking him captive were both former natives of Washington County, Daniel Logan and Clagett Fitzhugh.

Cook had become apprehensive watching over the Kennedy house. Thus he left the place and rode to Harpers Ferry, only to find his beloved leader trapped in the enginehouse. With that he took off, hiding by day and traveling by night. On the day of his capture he had been without food for nearly three days. Approaching Fitzhugh for bacon and food supplies for himself and imaginary hunting companions proved his undoing.

Brown, Cook, and the other survivors were convicted of treason, insurrection, and murder. The sentence was death by hanging, carried out on Friday, December 2, for John Brown, and for Johnny Cook on December 16, 1859.[6]

On the day of Brown's execution mass meetings and memorial services were held throughout the North. Church bells tolled, and ministers delivered eulogies which brought forth tears. Many politicians and newspapers wrote that he was a martyr to the cause of freedom and justice.

To the South, Brown's deed was one of treason. The man who had murdered in Kansas was guilty of attempting to murder not only Southern people, but the Southern way of life and Southern pride.

The 1860 Election

John Brown's raid and the subsequent investigation came as an "unfortunate prelude to the Presidential campaign of 1860." The Democratic Party was already sharply divided on the slavery issue, and the rights of the individual states. Now new bitterness arising over Brown's raid, threatened to wreck the party. "Alarmed by Douglas's 'Freeport Doctrine', and fearing more antislavery raids, the South insisted upon positive congressional action in support of slavery." Senator Jefferson Davis of Mississippi became a leading spokesman for the people of the South. He said the election of a Republican president would mean the end of the Union. The South said Congress must uphold and support slavery, even if a territorial government failed to do so.

April 23, 1860, found the Democratic National Convention meeting in Charleston, South Carolina. From the beginning there were bitter words between Southern and Western delegates. The West demanded Douglas and the opportunity to decide the question of slavery within the confines of each new state. To the Southern delegates such a stand was unthinkable, and in their thinking, Douglas was as bad as a Republican.

The committee on the resolutions had a task as difficult or possibly even worse than the 1968 Democratic Convention meeting in Chicago. The committee was faced with the task of making a choice between Douglas's idea of popular sovereignty and Davis's congressional protection for slavery. They chose the Davis plan embraced by most of those from the South. Douglas insisted, however, on presenting a minority report. The Southern platform announced that no territorial government had the power to abolish slavery or to deny the right of people to own slaves. Furthermore, Congress was bound to furnish adequate protection to slave owners in the new territories. Douglas on the other hand pledged to uphold the Dred Scott decision handed down by Chief Justice Roger Brooke Taney.

After a heated debate, the convention adopted the Douglas platform. Davis and the delegates from the South withdrew from the convention. Under the heated conditions additional work was impossible. The convention was adjourned, to meet at Baltimore in June. Davis and the others who had walked out arranged to meet in Richmond.

In the meantime, a group of older politicians, fearing what was coming, and seeing the handwriting on the wall, met at Baltimore on May 7. They formed a new "Constitutional Union Party," calling for the support of the Constitution, the Union of States, and the enforcement of laws. Their candidates were John Bell and Edward Everett.

All eyes were now on Chicago. Assembling in "the windy city" on May 16, the new Republican Party met to nominate their candidates for the White House. The leading contender was William H. Seward, former governor of New York and managed by Thurlow Weed, New York's political boss. Seward came to "The Wigwam" so confident of his victory

91

that he had a cannon set up on the lawn of his Auburn home, ready to fire the moment the telegraph brought news of his victory.

Working feverishly behind the scenes was Judge David Davis, leading a group seeking to gain the nomination for Abraham Lincoln. The strategy of Davis and his assistants was "to unite all anti-Seward forces and prove to them that Lincoln was neither radical . . . nor a conservative . . . was the very candidate behind whom the convention should unite." Going against Lincoln's wishes, and making promises after he had said, "Make no contracts that will bind me," the Davis group obtained more and more convention votes. Usually these were gained for Lincoln, only by promising a high position to a favorite son.

The night before the first ballot, Judge Davis met one of his workers in the hotel lobby. The hour was midnight. The judge was just leaving the Pennsylvania delegation. There was a gleam in his eyes. He proudly announced, "We've got them." Medill was happy but curious, "How did you get them?"

"By paying their price," Judge Davis replied. The price was the selection of favorite son, Simon Cameron for secretary of the treasury.

On the first ballot, Lincoln received 50½ votes, twenty-six of them coming from Indiana. Seward received 173½. On the second ballot a great cheer rocked "The Wigwam" when the chairman of the Pennsylvania delegation proudly announced, "Pennsylvania casts 56 votes for Abraham Lincoln." By now Seward was squirming. When the votes were tabulated he still led, but by a slim majority, 184½ to Lincoln's 181. On the third ballot, Ohio's votes gave the Republican nomination to Abraham Lincoln of Springfield, Illinois.

The Republican platform called for the continuance of the Union and for upholding the rights of the states. It denounced the John Brown raid "as among the gravest of crimes." It repudiated the Southern doctrine that Congress must protect slavery in the territories, and said there must be no further extension of slavery.

In June the Democrats reconvened in Baltimore. Many

contested delegates from the South were present. Indeed, three full days were spent going over credentials. When Douglas groups from Alabama and Louisiana were admitted, other anti-Douglas delegates from the South walked out. "The grapes of wrath" were growing.

On the first ballot Stephen A. Douglas received 173½ votes. A resolution was introduced to have him declared the candidate, as he had two-thirds of the votes. However, he had but the votes of those present, not the votes of all the delegates. After the second ballot though, the motion was accepted.

Those who walked out, having previously met in Richmond, met again in Charleston. They adopted the majority platform voted down by the full convention in April, and demanded protection of slavery in all territories. John C. Breckinridge of Kentucky was nominated for the presidency.

Now the Democratic Party had two candidates. Douglas was the choice of the North as he advocated popular sovereignty. Breckinridge was the choice of the proslavery element. Every vote cast for him was a vote for Southern independence.

In October 1860, fifty-three-year-old William Henry Gist sat at the governor's desk in South Carolina's executive mansion. His life revolved around his plantation, politics, and the Methodist Church. For years he had been determined that the South should become free and independent. On October 5, he wrote to the governors of the Cotton States, predicting that Abraham Lincoln would be the next president of the United States. This would be a tragedy. He would hate for South Carolina to take the lead in seceding from the Union, but it would if forced to do so. Governor Gist said, "If you decide to call a convention upon the election of a majority of electors favorable to Lincoln, I desire to know the day you propose for the meeting, that we may call our convention to meet the same day, if possible."[7]

Gist was correct in his prediction. On November 6, the voters of America went to the polls. The results were interesting. Stephen A. Douglas, the Democratic candidate of the North received 1,376,957 votes and 12 electoral votes. Bell

93

and Everett, the Constitutional Union candidates received 588,879 popular votes, but 39 electoral votes. Breckinridge and Lane, the choice of the Southern Democrats gained 849,781 popular votes, 72 electoral votes. Abraham Lincoln received 1,866,452 popular votes with 180 in the electoral column. In Maryland, Lincoln got but 2,294 votes, Douglas, 5,966, Breckinridge 42,482, and Bell 41,760. The Republican Party would occupy the White House.

The vote showed that the people were opposed to secession. Eighty percent of the total vote went to Lincoln, Douglas, and Bell, party candidates who desired to uphold the Union. The sentiment of the people called for the continuance of the Union. If the Southern states had not seceded, there would have been an anti-administration majority of eight in the Senate and twenty-one in the House.

But peace was not to be. Gist called a special session after the "Black Republicans" won. Representatives came from other states. Governor M. S. Perry of Florida wrote, "If there is sufficient manliness in the South to strike for our rights, honor and safety, in God's name let it be done before the inauguration of Lincoln."

On December 18 leaders of South Carolina met at Charleston. A carnival-like spirit pervaded the air. The streets were decorated with flags and bunting. Quickly those assembled passed by unanimous vote an ordinance of secession:

> We the People of the State of South Carolina, in Convention assembled, do declare and ordain, and it is hereby declared and ordained.
>
> That the Ordinance adopted by us in Convention, on the twenty-third day of May, in the year of our Lord one thousand seven hundred and eighty-eight, whereby the Constitution of the United States of America was ratified, and also all acts of the General Assembly of this State, ratifying amendments of the said Constitution, are hereby repealed; and that union now subsisting between South Carolina and other States, under the name of "The United States of America," is hereby dissolved.

That evening in the presence of a great crowd, every member of the convention signed the ordinance. When the last signature was completed, the audience broke into a storm of applause and cheers. Outside and inside the hall, the city went wild with excitement. Bells were rung. Cannon fired salutes. People shouted and hugged each other. The people of South Carolina had spoken and acted.

The seeds of discontent over two ways of life, work, and economic systems had now broken open. South Carolina led the way.

But the cards were stacked against the South. The 1860 census showed 31,000,000 Americans. Of these, 22,000,000 lived in the North or in states remaining loyal to the Union. The South could claim only one city of 100,000 population or more, the city of New Orleans. The North had nearly 20,000 miles of railroads compared to about 10,000 in the South.

The people of the North were shocked by South Carolina's act. They thought the move would be short-lived. But in January of 1861, Mississippi, Florida, Alabama, Georgia, and Louisiana, and Texas on February 1, followed in the steps of South Carolina.

On February 4, delegates from these states met in Montgomery, Alabama, to form a provisional government for the Confederate States of America. On the ninth, Jefferson Davis was chosen president. A divided nation faced Abraham Lincoln as he prepared to leave his Springfield home.

Lincoln expressed his feelings and hopes in one of the most eloquent speeches in history. Standing on the rear of the train which would take him to Washington, to fame, and tragedy, he said to his Springfield friends:

> My friends: No one, not in my situation, can appreciate my feeling of sadness at this parting. To this place, and the kindness of these people, I owe everything. Here I have lived a quarter of a century, and have passed from a young to an old man. Here my children have been born, and one is buried. I now leave, not knowing when or whether ever I may return, with a task before me greater than that which rested upon Washington. Without the assistance of that Divine Being who ever attended him, I cannot succeed. With that assistance, I cannot fail. Trusting in Him who can go with me, and remain with you, and be everywhere for good, let us confidently hope that all will yet be well. To His care commending you, as I hope in your prayers will commend me, I bid you an affectionate farewell.

On a cold windy March 4, 1861, Abraham Lincoln took the oath of office and was inaugurated as the sixteenth president of the United States. Speaking as only he could, Lincoln said, "We are not enemies, but friends. We must not be enemies. Though passion may be strained, it must not break our bonds of affection. . . . In your hands, my dissatisfied fellow-countrymen, not in mine, is the momentous issue of civil war."

The speech offered no plan for resolving the serious crisis and spelled out no compromise. Lincoln did express hope that the South would not look upon the new administration as a threat and would in time come back to the Union.

But as the Southern states seceded, they seized nearly all federal fortifications within state boundaries or off their shores. The day after his inauguration Lincoln received shocking news. Fort Sumter under the command of Major Robert Anderson was low on food and other provisions. Anderson felt only a show of force would cause the South Carolina militia to permit a relief shipment.

Lincoln was in a quandary. What should he do? Give in to South Carolina and evacuate the fort? Or should he send reinforcements and fight it out? To withdraw would mean a loss of prestige for the new administration. On the other hand, sending supplies would probably mean war.

Ward Lamon was sent to talk with the governor of South Carolina. But talk was useless. Lincoln made up his mind to send a shipment of food to Anderson's garrison. He notified South Carolina authorities of the move, saying no men or ammunition would be sent.

Francis Pickens, the new governor of South Carolina, relayed the message to Jefferson Davis. The Confederate cabinet met, and when the meeting concluded, the Confederate secretary of war, ordered General P. G. T. Beauregard, in command of Charleston harbor, to demand the evacuation of the fort, and if met with a negative reply to take it by force. On April 11, Beauregard demanded the surrender of the fort. Anderson refused. At 3:30 A.M. on April 12, he notified Anderson that unless surrender was immediate, he would commence firing in one hour. At 4:30 A.M. April 12, the first shot of the War Between the States was fired. The Civil War was on. Four days later when Lincoln called for 75,000 troops to put down the rebellion, North Carolina, Arkansas, and Tennessee joined the Confederacy. Virginia stuck with the Union as long as possible. But with Fort Sumter and the call of troops she was pushed over the brink. The issue of secession was submitted to a supposedly popular vote on May 23, 1861. It was much like a communist election. Confederate troops guarded the polling places, and in rural areas, Union sympathizers were intimidated.

War Days

In the early days of the conflict, each side seemed like a boxer doing a lot of dancing around, but afraid to throw the first punch. Volunteers and regular army troops flocked into Washington. Once there they waited and waited. The country clamored for an attack on the Rebels. Meanwhile, the Confederates sat across the Potomac in Virginia watching and waiting, threatening the Federal capital.

In mid-July, against the advice of military men, Lincoln, in order to silence public cries for battle, ordered the army to make an attack. Inexperienced men met inexperienced men on July 21, at Bull Run near Manassas. Things were going well for the Union troops until troops fresh from the Shenandoah Valley, led by Thomas J. Jackson, turned the tide. Then the Federals broke and ran. Panic followed. The Washington congressional leaders along with their fancy dressed ladies were swept along with the tide going back to Washington as quickly as possible.

Following this disaster the Union worked on some long-range plans with two objectives. First, to protect the North from invasion, and, two, the capture of Richmond. Western objectives were to gain control of the Mississippi River, and then capture the important railway center at Chattanooga. The Confederacy followed primarily a defensive policy. Jefferson Davis felt the Confederate soldier was called upon to defend his homeland, not to invade the North.

After a fall and winter of inactivity, other than training and drilling, George B. McClellan finally got the Union Army started toward Richmond. The result was the Seven Days Campaign on the peninsula between the York and James rivers in Virginia. By firepower and maneuver, Lee and Jackson were able to defend Richmond from capture.

SEPTEMBER 1862

September 1862 brought excitement and alarm to Washington County and the Valley of the Antietam. After winning the Second Battle of Bull Run, Robert E. Lee launched a campaign into Maryland. By so doing he would draw the Union Army away from Richmond and the soil of Virginia. This would give the Virginia farmers an opportunity to harvest their crops. Victory north of the Potomac would raise the morale of the Confederacy, and lower that of the Union. If successful in Maryland or Pennsylvania, foreign aid might be obtained from France and England, and possibly final independence. If Lee could win in Maryland, Northern politicians might force the administration to sue for peace.

Therefore on September 4 through 7, the Confederate Army of Northern Virginia waded across the Potomac near Leesburg and advanced toward Frederick, the center of a vital road network.

Meanwhile things were chaotic in Washington. Lincoln removed General Pope from command and replaced him with George B. McClellan. "Little Mac" reorganized the army and on the seventh got the Army of the Potomac moving toward Rockville.

Lee had hoped and expected the Union garrison at Harpers Ferry to be relieved once he crossed the river. However, this was not done, and on September 9, from his headquarters just south of Frederick in Best's Grove, Lee wrote Order No. 191, issuing some of the boldest commands ever given by a field commander. He would divide his small army into four parts: "Stonewall" Jackson was ordered to Martinsburg, to dispatch the Federal troops there and destroy B&O Railroad equipment. Then he would proceed to Bolivar Heights. Lafayette McLaws was directed to Maryland Heights just across the river from Harpers Ferry. John Walker was to tear up the C&O Canal and occupy Loudoun Heights in Virginia.

98

Longstreet would proceed to Boonsboro with the rest of the army and await developments there. Once the capture of Harpers Ferry was completed, the various commands were to join D. H. Hill and Longstreet at either Boonsboro or Hagerstown.

The next morning, September 10, the Confederate Army moved west from Frederick to put Lee's bold plan in operation. On the eleventh, Lee heard a rumor that Union troops were coming from Harrisburg toward Hagerstown. To meet this threat, he again divided his army, sending Longstreet to Hagerstown to tend to the matter, while D. H. Hill served as the rear guard in the South Mountain passes.

On Saturday, September 13, the Army of the Potomac close on Lee's heels, entered Frederick where it received a great welcome. Soon after the order to make camp was given, two Union soldiers, Sgt. John M. Bloss and Private B. W. Mitchell of the Twenty-seventh Indiana Volunteers found three cigars with a piece of paper wrapped around them.

McClellan had the opportunity every military commander dreams of finding. The paper covering the cigars contained Lee's plans for conducting his Maryland campaign. Every detail was down in black and white. Someone in the Confederate high command had goofed, and material of the highest classified type was now in the hands of the man who could do the most with it. "Little Mac" had the opportunity of cutting between the two wings of Lee's army and destroying each wing separately, the one at Harpers Ferry, and the other in the Hagerstown-Boonsboro area.

The next day, Sunday, September 14, McClellan sent his First and Ninth corps against the Confederate defenders stationed at Turner's and Fox's Gap. Farther south at Crampton's Gap, General Franklin and the Union Sixth Corps gained a decisive victory over Confederate defenders there. The day had gone against Lee. He had lost the initiative. He had suffered nearly two thousand casualties. His only hope was that Harpers Ferry would fall early tomorrow, thus permitting his scattered forces to rejoin him north of the Potomac. Otherwise he had no alternative but to retreat to Virginia. That Sunday night, Lee sent urgent messages to his

99

commanders at Harpers Ferry, urging them to complete their work as soon as possible, and then rejoin him at Sharpsburg. The fateful decision had been made. Within a week, a little village in Washington County, would become known around the world as the scene of one of history's bloodiest battles, and proclaimed forever as a turning point in the history of the United States of America. By the next evening, Sharpsburg and the Valley of the Antietam would be surrounded by "a hundred circling camps."

Jerry Summers.   "A hundred circling camps."

V

A HUNDRED CIRCLING CAMPS

The little farming village of Sharpsburg stands in a great bend in the Potomac, between that river and Antietam Creek, a picturesque millstream. The Antietam runs north and south, winding through woods, orchards, and fields of grain. The average depth of position between the creek and the river is about three miles. Thus the position selected by Robert E. Lee for the concentration of his army was a peninsula between the Antietam and the Potomac. The ridges about the town offered good defensive positions, but in case Lee was defeated, there was only one good ford offering a line of retreat.[1] This was located about a mile and a half below Shepherdstown, and is known by many names, among them Pack Horse, Boteler's, and Shepherdstown.

D. H. Hill's division, leading the withdrawal from South Mountain, reached the pleasant rolling ridges near the Antietam at dawn on Monday, the fifteenth. Hill's division and the command of Longstreet were placed in line of battle between Antietam Creek and the village of Sharpsburg.[2] It was necessary for Lee to cover both the Hagerstown and Boonsboro roads. George B. Anderson's brigade formed lines on either side of the Boonsboro Pike, near Bloody Lane, supported by the brigades of Ripley, Garland, and Rodes. Artillery was put in position on the hills between the Bloody Lane and Sharpsburg.

About three o'clock in the afternoon of the same day, the long blue columns of the Federals could be seen advancing toward the Antietam. General Longstreet, one of the Confederate commanders, vividly described the advance of the Union forces in these words:

> The number increased, and larger and larger grew the field of blue until it seemed to stretch as far as the eye could see, and from tops of the mountains down to the edges of the stream gathered the great army of McClellan. It was an awe inspiring spectacle as this grand force settled down in sight of the Confederates, then shattered by battle and tiresome marches.[3]

Tidball's Battery A, Second U.S., and Pettit's Battery B, First New York Artillery, were sent forward to the crest of the first ridge west of the Antietam and engaged the Confederate artillery posted at and south of the first angle at the east end of Bloody Lane. These batteries supported the advance division of the Army of the Potomac, that of General I. B. Richardson.[4]

Richardson's division halted and deployed on the east of the Antietam, on the right of the Sharpsburg Road. Generals French and Sedgwick and their two divisions of the Union Second Corps halted on either side of the Boonsboro Pike between McClellan's headquarters and the Middle Bridge over the Antietam. The First Corps under Hooker took position between the Upper Bridge (or Hooker Bridge, as it is now known) over the Antietam, and Keedysville. The Twelfth Corps halted near Keedysville and the Ninth Corps encamped on the Geeting farm at the west base of Elk Ridge.

Lee had withdrawn just in time and now "all eyes were on the Harpers Ferry Road," watching hopefully for Stonewall Jackson.

Before the day ended, J. E. B. Stuart, at Jackson's request, rode to Sharpsburg and gave Lee news and information concerning Jackson's capture of Harpers Ferry.[5]

McClellan and Lee have both been criticized for their actions on the fifteenth. McClellan's troops outnumbered Lee's that day by almost five to two,[6] and he knew that the detachments sent to capture Harpers Ferry could not rejoin Lee for a considerable period of time. The distance from the summit of Turner's Gap to Sharpsburg is only about eight miles, and as Colonel Palfrey expressed it:

102

... it is not easy to see why McClellan might not have attacked in force early in the afternoon of the 15th. He had every reason to believe that delay would strengthen the enemy much more proportionately than it would strengthen him, and he might be sure that delay would be at least as serviceable to the enemy as to him in acquiring knowledge of the ground. . . . If McClellan would have used the priceless hours of the 15th of September . . . as he might have, his name would have stood high in the roll of great commanders.[7]

On the fifteenth, after making a rapid reconnaissance, McClellan decided it was too late to attack the Confederate position, and seems to have done nothing beyond directing the placing of batteries in the center, and indicating the bivouac for the different corps.[8]

So all this day, the 15th of September, Lee stood in front of Sharpsburg with the troops of Longstreet and D. H. Hill alone, while the whole Army of the Potomac was near McClellan.[9]

O. T. Reilly remembered General McClellan passing through Keedysville in the late afternoon of September 15. Mrs. Jeptha Taylor, who lived in the old stone millhouse along the Little Antietam Creek, was ordered by one of McClellan's officers to prepare supper for the general and his staff. This was a big task for Mrs. Taylor. But she did her job so well that the commander of the Union Army gave her a two and half dollar gold piece.

Reilly recalled Union soldiers digging potatoes with their bayonets near the old stone schoolhouse in Keedysville. Every ripe grape was also picked by the hungry soldiers.

September 16, 1862, was a day of intense anxiety and unrest in the valley of the Antietam. The people who had lived in the farmhouses that dotted the golden autumn landscape in this hitherto quiet community had now abandoned their homes and given place to the armed forces. It was day of marshalling and maneuvering of the gathering thousands, preparatory to the mighty conflict that was clearly seen to be inevitable.[10]

Early in the morning the twenty-pound Parrott (Union) batteries of Taft, Langer, Von Kleiser and Weaver, of the First New York Artillery, were placed in position on the ridge between the Antietam and McClellan's headquarters. Two batteries were placed on the ridge south of Porterstown

103

overlooking Antietam Creek, and all engaged the Confederate artillery on the hills near Sharpsburg, where the national and town cemeteries are now located.[11]

After a severe night's march, Jackson's command reached the vicinity of Sharpsburg on the morning of the sixteenth.

> The operations which resulted in the capture of Harpers Ferry had been arduous in the extreme. Men who had taken part in the forced marches of the Valley campaign declared that the march from Frederick to Harpers Ferry surpassed all former experiences. In three and a half days they had covered over sixty miles. . . . The weather had been intensely hot, and the dust was terrible. This night march, coming on the top of their previous exertions, had taxed the strength of many beyond endurance.[12]

Jackson's command crossed the Potomac at Boteler's Ford near Shepherdstown and proceeded on the road to Sharpsburg. Part of the command was halted and stacked arms to the left of the road, about a mile from Sharpsburg.[13]

A little past the hour of noon on the sixteenth of September, 1862, Jackson and Major General John G. Walker reached General Lee's headquarters at Sharpsburg and reported the arrival of their commands.

Tuesday, September 16, was a very hot day in its early hours, with a burning sun and no breeze, but about eleven o'clock the sky became overcast, and an occasional breeze stirred in the Valley of the Antietam.[14]

As Lee was placing his troops, McClellan was not idle. He rode to the left of the Union line to ascertain how well the Ninth Corps was posted and if they were in position to carry Bridge No. 3, or the Rohrback Bridge, as it was called by the local citizens.

> By this time [according to Colonel Palfrey], McClellan's plan for the battle seems to have taken definite shape in his mind. It was extremely simple and ought to have been successful.[15]

McClellan's plan for the impending engagement was to attack the Confederate left in the vicinity of the West Woods with the corps of Hooker and Mansfield, supported by Sumner, and if necessary, by Franklin, and as soon as matters looked favorable there, to move the corps of Burnside against the Confederate extreme right, south of Sharpsburg, and whenever either of these flank movements should be successful, to advance the Union center with all the forces then disposable.[16]

About 2:00 P.M., General Hooker with his corps, consisting of the divisions of Generals Ricketts, Meade, and Doubleday, was ordered to cross the Antietam at Pry's Ford, and at Bridge No. 1, a short distance above, to attack, and if possible turn the Confederate left.[17]

McClellan and Hooker, on horseback together, watched this advance, as it moved westerly until it reached the Joseph Poffenberger farm and lane, then changing front to the left, moved south and encountered the Confederates near the Smoketown Road and the East Woods.

> Hooker's troops were deployed at once. The attack, such as it was, fell upon Hood's brigades, with Meade's division of Federals being principally engaged.[18]

When the fighting ceased at dark, "Hooker bivouacked on the northern slopes of Poffenberger Ridge, Doubleday's division resting with its right upon the Hagerstown pike, Ricketts' division upon the left of Doubleday, and Meade covering the front of both with skirmishers of Seymour's brigade. Between Meade's troops and the ridge were the farm-house and barn of Joseph Poffenberger on the east of the road. . . ."[19] Half a mile in front was the farm of D. R. Miller, the dwelling on the east, and the barn surrounded by haystacks on the west of the road.[20]

Where Were They?

Dusk on Tuesday, September 16, found the two armies encamped on the hillsides, and in the fields of the farmers living in the Valley of the Antietam.

The Confederate Army of Northern Virginia was bivouacked as follows:

The cavalry and horse artillery on the Nicodemus farm. Jackson's corps in and around the West Woods, the Dunkard Church, D. R. Miller's fields, and near Samuel Mumma's. Longstreet's men were encamped primarily on the Piper farm. South of town near the Lower Bridge, Toombs and his

105

small group of defenders were on the heights overlooking the bridge and near the Otto farm.

The Army of the Potomac was located in these positions:

Hooker and the First Corps on Joseph Poffenberger's farm. Mansfield and the Twelfth Corps were near the Cost farm and the Upper Bridge, when ordered up in closer support of Hooker. Marching in a drizzling rain, these men bedded down for the night in George Line's wet cornfield. The Union Second Corps was encamped on the Pry farm, near army headquarters, and in Bishop Russell's fields, just across the road. The Ninth Corps was in position near Henry Rohrback's farm. Some historians feel Burnside had his headquarters in the farmhouse. Part of the Fifth Corps was located near the junction of the Porterstown and Boonsboro roads.

On the evening of the sixteenth, General Mansfield ate supper at the Cost home, and halted the Twelfth Corps near the Upper or Hitt Bridge. However, he received orders to advance in order to be closer to Hooker's men. About 10:00 P.M., the command "Fall in" was given.

Miles Huyette of the 125th Pennsylvania describes the night march:

> We formed and started to join Hooker's corps which had forded the Antietam in the afternoon. We crossed the stream on a stone bridge which is now known as "Hooker's Bridge." The only sound was of scattered picket firing at the front and the mingled noise of men and artillery being rushed into position. After midnight we arrived at the George Line farm. . . . We were massed in "column by company," in a cornfield; the night was close, air heavy . . . some rainfall. . . . The air was perfumed with a mixture of crushed green cornstalks, ragweed, and clover. We made our beds between rows of corn and did not remove our accouterments.[21]

Men of the blue and gray were spending, in many cases, their last few moments on earth, around the fires of "a hundred circling camps" dotting the landscape of the Valley of the Antietam.

The Orndorff Mill.

The Pry Farm—Army Headquarters.

107

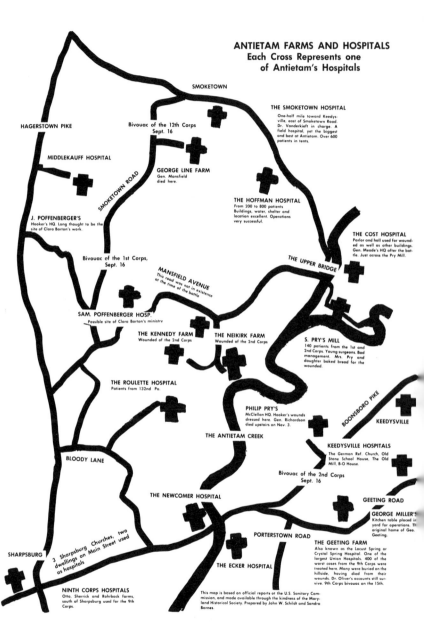

ANTIETAM FARMS AND HOSPITALS
Each Cross Represents one
of Antietam's Hospitals

SMOKETOWN

THE SMOKETOWN HOSPITAL
One-half mile toward Keedys-ville, east of Smoketown Road. Dr. Vanderkieft in charge. A field hospital, yet the biggest and best at Antietam. Over 600 patients in tents.

HAGERSTOWN PIKE

Bivouac of the 12th Corps Sept. 16

MIDDLEKAUFF HOSPITAL

SMOKETOWN ROAD

GEORGE LINE FARM
Gen. Mansfield died here.

THE HOFFMAN HOSPITAL
From 200 to 800 patients Buildings, water, shelter and location excellent. Operations very successful.

J. POFFENBERGER'S
Hooker's HQ. Long thought to be the site of Clara Barton's work.

THE COST HOSPITAL
Parlor and hall used for wound-ed as well as other buildings. Gen. Meade's HQ after the bat-tle. Just across the Pry Mill.

Bivouac of the 1st Corps, Sept. 16

MANSFIELD AVENUE
This road was not in existence at the time of the battle

THE UPPER BRIDGE

SAM. POFFENBERGER HOSP.
Possible site of Clara Barton's ministry

THE KENNEDY FARM
Wounded of the 2nd Corps

THE NEIKIRK FARM
Wounded of the 2nd Corps

S. PRY'S MILL
140 patients from the 1st and 2nd Corps. Young surgeons. Bad management. Mrs. Pry and daughter baked bread for the wounded.

THE ROULETTE HOSPITAL
Patients from 132nd Pa.

PHILIP PRY'S
McClellan HQ. Hooker's wounds dressed here. Gen. Richardson died upstairs on Nov. 3.

BOONSBORO PIKE

KEEDYSVILLE

THE ANTIETAM CREEK

KEEDYSVILLE HOSPITALS
The German Ref. Church, Old Stone School House, The Old Mill, B-O House.

BLOODY LANE

Bivouac of the 2nd Corps Sept. 16

THE NEWCOMER HOSPITAL

GEETING ROAD

GEORGE MILLER'S
Kitchen table placed in yard for operations. The original home of Geo. Geeting.

PORTERSTOWN ROAD

3 Sharpsburg Churches, two dwellings on Main Street used as hospitals

SHARPSBURG

THE ECKER HOSPITAL

THE GEETING FARM
Also known as the Locust Spring or Crystal Spring Hospital. One of the largest Union Hospitals. 400 of the worst cases from the 9th Corps were treated here. Many were buried on the hillside, having died from their wounds. Dr. Oliver's accounts still sur-vive. 9th Corps bivouac on the 15th.

NINTH CORPS HOSPITALS
Otto, Sherrick and Rohrback farms, south of Sharpsburg used for the 9th Corps.

This map is based on official reports at the U.S. Sanitary Com-mission, and made available through the kindness of the Mary-land Historical Society. Prepared by John W. Schildt and Sandra Barnes.

Antietam homes and field hospitals.
108

VI

ROWS OF STEEL

At sunrise, each morn, the calls were played in the following order: drummers, reveille, breakfast, doctors, guard mount, dinner, supper, tattoos and taps.[1]

> As first beams of the rising sun begin to tinge the eastern skies, the clear notes of the bugle, sounding reveille from headquarters are heard, repeated in turn by the regimental buglers. The drums of one regiment commence their rataplan which in turn is taken up by the ear piercing fife and spirit stirring drum of another. . . . At the last tap of the drum every man is supposed to be up and dressed.[2]

Reveille sounded early on September 17 at Antietam. The troops were up and stirring early. The drummer boys excitedly beat their drums calling the men to action, to battle and death. The drummers were young, usually between the ages of twelve and sixteen. On this September day they would beat their drums as their comrades marched into "rows of steel."

Forty Acres of Corn Cut Down by Battle

With the misty dawn of the seventeenth came the great struggle. At daybreak General Hooker sent the divisions of the First Corps under the commands of George G. Meade, Abner Doubleday, and James Ricketts to assault the positions held by "Stonewall" Jackson's forces.

The aim of the attack was the high ground around the Dunkard Church in the West Woods. The right flank of Hooker's advance was on the Hagerstown Pike, and the left along the Smoketown Road.[3]

The cannon on the ridge at Joe Poffenberger's supported

109

Hooker's advance. Then General Gibbon leading brave soldiers from Wisconsin, men who had been nicknamed "The Iron Brigade" for their valor at nearby South Mountain, ordered the Fourth U.S. Artillery to give additional support. The men galloped in to D. R. Miller's barnyard, unlimbered, and fired away from just in front of farmer Miller's haystacks.

Suddenly General Hooker spotted the first rays of the sun shining on some bayonets belonging of course to the Rebs in D. R. Miller's forty-acre cornfield. He gave immediate orders for his cannon to shell the field.

Despite a painful wound in his heel, General Hooker said:

> "Every stalk of corn in the northern and greater part of the field was cut as closely as could have been done with a knife, and the slain lay in rows precisely as they had stood in their ranks a few moments before. It was never my fortune to witness a more bloody, dismal battlefield."[4]

Attack and Counterattack

The First Corps suffered heavily in its attack upon the Confederate position. Moreover, General Lee launched a counterattack sending Hook's Texans into the fray. The fighting was fierce. The First Texas Regiment lost 182 of 226 men present for duty.

Hooker called for help. Up came the Union Twelfth Corps from its bivouac on the Line farm. The two divisions under Greene and Williams swept down the Smoketown Road. General Mansfield, the corps commander, fell mortally wounded.

The field of the battle was covered with smoke. Part of it came from the Samuel Mumma farm. Unfortunately, this farm stood between the two armies. The house, barn, all household furniture, grain, hay, and farming implements went up in smoke. The loss amounted to almost $10,000.

Part of the Union Twelfth Corps pushed on and gained a foothold around the Dunkard Church. By now dead and wounded were in the churchyard where worshippers had talked on Sunday morning. Several holes were in the end of the church, these coming from cannon fire. Someone had taken the pulpit Bible.

It is not my intention to dwell on the actual fighting at

Antietam. An attempt to do this was made in *September Echoes.* However, the stories of the Sixth Wisconsin, the Union artillery, "Fighting Dick" Richardson, and A. P. Hill summarize the terrific combat which many consider the bloodiest day in American history. The Army of the Potomac lost 12,000 men in twelve to fourteen hours of fighting on the seventeenth of September. June 6, 1944, on the beaches of Normandy saw 6,600 Americans fall. Yet this was eighty-two years later with modern weapons, rockets, tanks, machine guns, etc.

Warren Hassler, Jr., author of *McClellan, Shield of the Union,* states this was "the bloodiest single day's battle ever fought on the shores of the New World—a combat which claimed more casualties in one turn of the earth than have ever been suffered before or since by the American people in arms."

Rufus Dawes commanded the Sixth Wisconsin at Antietam. He survived the bloody day to become the father of Charles Dawes, born in 1865. Charles Dawes became a warm personal friend of William B. McKinley, and later vice-president under Calvin Coolidge. He also won a Nobel Peace Prize. But on September 17, Rufus Dawes had no time to think of the future. He had all he could do to save the lives of his men, and his own life. Later in *Service With the Sixth Wisconsin,* Dawes wrote:

> Our lines on the left now came sweeping forward through the corn and the open fields beyond. I ordered my men up to join the advance, and commanded: "Forward—guide left-march!" We swung away from the turn-pike, and I sent the sergeant-major to Captain Kellogg, commanding the companies on the turnpike, with the order: "If it is practicable, move forward the right companies, aligning with the left wing." Captain Kellogg said: "Please give Major Dawes my compliments, and say it is impracticable; the fire is murderous."
>
> As we were getting separated, I directed Sergeant Huntington to tell Captain Kellogg that he could get cover in the corn, and to join us, if possible. Huntington was struck by a bullet, but delivered the order. Kellogg ordered his men up, but so many were shot that he ordered them down again at once. While this took place on the turnpike, our companies were marching forward through the thick corn, on the right of a long line of battle. Closely following was a

111

second line. At the front edge of the cornfield was a low Virginia rail fence. Before the corn were open fields, beyond which was a strip of woods surrounding a little church, the Dunkard Church. As we appeared at the edge of the corn, a long line of men in butternut and gray rose up from the ground. Simultaneously, the hostile battle lines opened a tremendous fire upon each other. Men, I cannot say fell; they were knocked out of the ranks by dozens. But we jumped over the fence, and pushed on, loading, firing, and shouting as we advanced. There was, on the part of the men, great hysterical excitement, eagerness to go forward, and a reckless disregard of life, of everything but victory. Captain Kellogg brought his companies up abreast of us on the turnpike.

The Fourteenth Brooklyn Regiment, red legged Zouaves, came into our line, closing the awful gaps. Now is the pinch. Men and officers of New York and Wisconsin are forced into a common man, in the frantic struggle to shoot fast. Everybody tears cartridges, loads, passes guns, or shoots. Men are falling in their places or running back into the corn. The soldier who is shooting is furious in his energy. The soldier who is shot looks around for help with an imploring agony of death on his face. After a few rods of advance, the line stopped and, by common impulse, fell back to the edge of the corn and lay down on the ground behind the low rail fence.

Another line of our men came up through the corn. We all joined together, jumped over the fence, and again pushed out into the open fields. There is a rattling fusillade and loud cheers. "Forward" is the word. Then men are loading and firing with demoniacal fury and shooting and laughing hysterically, and the whole field before us is covered with rebels fleeing for life, into the woods. Great numbers of them are shot while climbing over the high post and rail fence along the turnpike. We push on over the open fields half way to the little church. The powder is bad, and the guns have become very dirty. It takes hard pounding to get the bullets down, and our firing is slow. A long and steady line of rebel gray, unbroken by the fugitives who fly before us, comes sweeping down through the woods around the church. They raise the yell and fire. It is like a scythe running through our line "Now, save, who can." It is a race for life that each man runs for the cornfield. A sharp cut, as of a switch, stings the calf of my leg as I run. Back to the corn, and back through the corn, the headlong flight continues.

At the bottom of the hill, I took the blue color of the state of Wisconsin, and waving it, called a rally of the Wisconsin men. Two hundred men gathered around the flag of the Badger state. Across the turnpike just in front of the haystack, two guns of Battery "B", 4th U. S. Artillery were in action the pursuing rebels were upon them.

General John Gibbon, our brigade commander, who in regular service was captain of this battery, grimed and black with powder

112

smoke in himself sighting these guns of his old battery, comes running to me, "Here, major, move your men over, we must save these guns." I commanded, "Right face, forward march," and started ahead with the colors in my hand into the open field, the men following. As I entered the field, a report as of a thunderclap in my ear fairly stunned me. This was Gibbon's last shot at the advancing rebels. The cannon was double charged with canister. The rails of the fence flew high in the air.

A line of Union blue charged swiftly forward from our right across the field in front of the battery, and into the corn-field. They drove back the rebels who were firing upon us. It was our own gallant 19th Indiana, and here fell dead their leader, Lieutenant Colonel A. F. Bachman, but the youngest captain in their line, William W. Dudley, stepped forward and led on the charge.

I gathered my men on the turnpike, reorganized them, and reported to General Doubleday, who was himself there. He ordered me to move back to the next woods in the rear, to remain and await instructions. Bullets, shot and shell, fired by the enemy in the cornfield, were still flying thickly around us, striking the trees in this woods, and cutting off the limbs. I placed my men under the best shelter I could find, and here we figured up, as nearly as we could, our dreadful losses in the battle. Three hundred and fourteen officers and men had marched with us into battle. There had been killed and wounded, one hundred and fifty-two. Company "C" under Captain Hooe, thirty-five men, was not in the fight in front of the corn-field. That company was on skirmish duty farther to our right. In this service they lost two men.

Of two hundred and eighty who were at the cornfield and turnpike, one hundred and fifty were killed or wounded. This was the most dreadful slaughter to which our regiment was subjected in the war. We were joined in the woods by Captain Ely, who reported to me, as the senior officer present, with the colors and eighteen men of the Second Wisconsin. They represented what remained for duty of that gallant regiment.

Battery B

Sharpsburg was considered "artillery hell." Early in the morning of the seventeenth, twenty-four cannon of the First Corps banged away at Confederate positions near the Dunkard Church. These were answered by S. D. Lee's five batteries near the church, and Pelham's horse artillery over on the Nicodemus farm. One of the shots from Pelham ended the battle of Antietam for thirteen men from the Sixth Wisconsin.

To the rear of the Sixth Wisconsin was Battery B of the

113

Fourth United States Artillery. The battery was ordered forward from the Poffenberger Ridge to support the black-hatted men from the Badger State.

A Confederate battery on a knoll between the Hagerstown Pike and the East Woods was taking a heavy toll of blue-coated infantry. Battery B was ordered to silence the enemy guns. The commander of the battery, Capt. Joseph P. Campbell ordered his "baby bugler," fifteen-year-old Johnny Cook to sound the proper bugle call. Near the D. R. Miller house, the six guns of the battery opened fire. Soon the Rebel guns fell silent.

Now the problem was heavy fire from the Confederate infantry. General Gibbon ordered two cannon from the battery advance even farther. Captain Campbell sent Lieutenant Stewart and the two guns forward to the vicinity of the D. R. Miller strawstacks, opposite the farmhouse. The guns made ready to fire and spouted flame and smoke in unison. The gray ranks partially broke and sought cover.

But Stewart was in for a hot time. Rebel troops in Farmer Miller's tall corn opened fire on the gunners of Battery B. From a distance of less than fifty yards it was hard to miss.

Within minutes, Stewart's men were all but wiped out. Fourteen men had fallen around the guns. They had to be pulled away so those still unhurt could fire. Some of the men pulled their bleeding comrades back to the haystacks. But in their confusion and pain, several ran back toward the guns and were stricken down not to rise again.

Campbell brought up the other four cannon. The din of battle was terrific. We can imagine the shouting of the men, the pounding of the horses hoofs, the clattering of the wheels, and the screams of the wounded and dying. Captain Campbell dismounted to be joined by Johnny Cook who came running through the smoke of battle, his bugle bouncing at his hip, to be by the side of his commander. Suddenly there was a loud crash of musketry and Campbell started to fall forward. Johnny Cook grabbed him and helped him to his feet. The captain's horse died instantly, pierced by seven bullets. Johnny, with minie balls flying all around, helped his commander to the rear. Soon a soldier took over for the lad.

Battery B

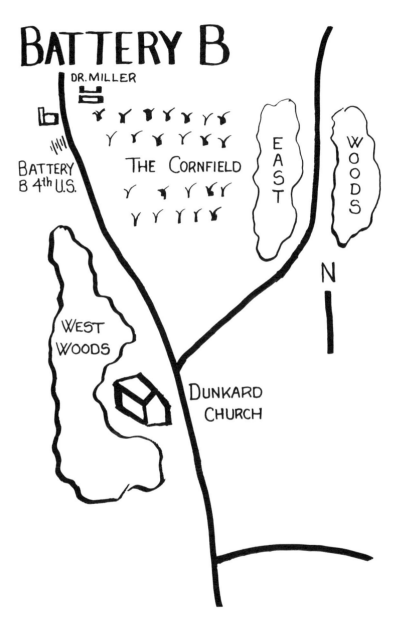

DR. MILLER

Battery
B 4th U.S.

THE CORNFIELD

EAST

WOODS

N

WEST
WOODS

DUNKARD
CHURCH

Campbell ordered Cook to tell Stewart he was now in command of Battery B.

Cook found Stewart and relayed the orders. Now was no time to think of bugle calls. Battery B had suffered heavily. Those surviving had to do two and three jobs. Johnny Cook stepped over the body of a dead artilleryman, and ran to one of the cannon. For the rest of the engagement he loaded and rammed double canister down the barrel.

For his bravery on the D. R. Miller farm, John Cook who at the age of fifteen was called "the baby bugler," won the Congressional Medal of Honor. His citation read: "Volunteered to act as a cannoneer, and as such volunteer served a gun under a terrific fire of the enemy."

All available records indicate that John Cook was one of the youngest men ever to win the nation's highest award for valor. He is buried in Arlington National Cemetery.

Forty of the one hundred men in Battery B fell at Antietam. Most of them on the D. R. Miller farm. One sergeant was hit in the stomach. He was taken to the Miller barn and told his wound was fatal. In agony, he bit his lip, drew his pistol and shot himself in the temple.

Pvt. Horace Ripley of the Seventh Wisconsin had been assigned to Battery B to hold the horses. One was hit in the flank and fell dying. Then came the sound of a heavy thud. Ripley looked and saw a ball had knocked the bit from the mouth of the other horse, and carried away the entire lower jaw. Private Ripley drew his pistol and mercifully put the poor animal out of its misery. At one time he and another soldier were the only men manning one of the guns of Battery B.

A Terrible Ambush

About 9:00 A.M. McClellan stood in Philip Pry's yard, and with his field glasses, watched the three parallel lines of John Sedgwick's division climbing the hills on the other side of the Antietam.[5] General Sumner, commander of the Union Second Corps, was riding with Sedgwick.

Sumner hardly knew what was going on. He saw many casualties and was aware of the fact that the First and

Twelfth corps had been pretty badly shot up. Ambulances were taking many to the rear.

The men of Sedgwick's division were some of the finest in the army. But they were headed for disaster. Lee had just sent reinforcements to the area south of the Dunkard Church. McLaws, Walker, and Early's Confederates were waiting and drawing a steady bead on the men in blue.

Suddenly, without warning, Sedgwick's soldiers were hit on all three sides by a withering fire. The "Philadelphia Brigade" went down almost in a heap. Even the veteran troops had never experienced anything like this. Some regiments gave way completely. Rebel cannon standing wheel to wheel made matters worse. Sedgwick was hit in the arm and bled profusely. Then another bullet slammed into him lifting him out of the saddle and into a hospital for five months.

In twenty to thirty minutes it was all over. Only half of the 5,000 Union soldiers came out of the West Woods alive. In that brief span of time, 2,500 fell to the ground. Many regimental reports say, "We experienced the heaviest, deadliest fire of the war."[6] Oliver Wendell Holmes and many others fell in the West Woods, including H. R. Dunham of whom we shall read later.

Sedgwick was one of the most beloved commanders in the Army of the Potomac. Local tradition says that he was taken to the Deaner house on the Mount Hebron Road to recover from his wounds. He lived to fight another day, but was killed by a sharpshooter near the end of the war in the wilderness of Virginia.

View of the Battlefield.

A lonely grave at Antietam. Courtesy the Library of Congress.

All's quiet along the Antietam, Burnside Bridge.
Photo by A. K. McGraw.

Happy days along the Antietam, September 22, 1862. Courtesy the Library of Congress.

Inhabitants of Sharpsburg taking refuge in the Kretzer
cellar during the Battle of Antietam.

Lee's army in Maryland (Main Street, Sharpsburg—
from a wartime photograph).

121

Hallowed hills and fields. Photo by A. K. McGraw.

VII

FATEFUL LIGHTNING

The Union Corps, the First and the Twelfth were exhausted by 9:30 as was Sedgwick's division of the Second Corps. If only McClellan would have loosed the "fateful lightning" of all three corps on the Confederate position at the same time, or better yet, led the attack in person. But he remained back at Philip Pry's watching the turn of events from a sheltered position. Had "Little Mac" hit Lee at the Dunkard Church and the Sunken Road at the same time, the Confederate commander would have been unable to shift his men from one position to the other.

Now McClellan was ready to launch another piecemeal attack. The divisions of French and Richardson were up at dawn, and consumed a hasty breakfast. Most of the men probably had indigestion from eating on nervous stomachs. From the sound of things across the Antietam, they knew it was going to be a rough day.

The men marched from Philip Pry's and Bishop Russell's farm down to the Pry Ford and Hitt Bridge. Crossing the Antietam they marched through the fields of Henry Neikirk and Farmer Kennedy. Then changing front they proceeded to the Roulette farm and on to bitter conflict in the Sunken Road.

Colquitt's advance line of Confederate skirmishers threw a few shots into the advancing blue lines and then withdrew. A number of Rebels, unable to find shelter and hopeful of avoiding capture, headed for the open cellar door leading under the Roulette farmhouse. Some of the Yanks saw them go in, and slammed the door shut behind them. Union

123

soldiers used the bayonet to drive the Rebels out of Roulette's stable and springhouse.

While passing between the Roulette buildings, a shot from a Confederate shell hit a long row of beehives. The result was disaster for the men of the 132nd Pennsylvania. They were swarmed over by hordes of angry bees. Many a soldier surviving the fighting of the day were covered with nasty red welts from Roulette's disturbed bees.[1]

The Union forces re-formed near the Sunken Road. Their approach is best described by a Confederate defender, General Gordon:

> The men in blue . . . formed in my front, an assaulting column four lines deep. The brave Union commander, superably mounted, placed himself in front, while his band in (the) rear cheered them with martial music. It was a thrilling spectacle. So far as I could see, every soldier wore white garters around his ankles. . . . Their gleaming bayonets flashed like burnished silver in the sunlight. With the precision of step and perfect alignment of a holiday parade, this magnificent array moved to the charge, every step keeping time to the tap of the deep sounding drum. . . . There were four lines of blue to my one line of gray. The only plan was to hold my fire until the advancing Federals were almost upon my lines. No troops with empty guns could withstand the shock. My men were at once directed to lie down upon the grass. Not a shot would be fired until my voice should be heard commanding "Fire!"
>
> The stillness was literally oppressive, as this column of Union infantry moved majestically, toward us. Now the front rank was within a few rods of where I stood. With all my lung power I shouted "Fire!" Our rifles flamed and roared in the Federals' faces like a blinding blaze of lightning.[2]

A Union soldier said, "The Confederates met us with a murderous fire."

In reporting the results of his "fateful lightning," General Gordon stated:

> The effect was appalling. The entire front line, with few exceptions, went down in the consuming blast. Before the rear lines could recover, my exultant men were on their feet, devouring them with successive volleys.[3]

Beyond Henry Piper's cornfield, additional Rebel infantry fired over the heads of their comrades in the Sunken Road and into the ranks of the men in blue.

Federal guns on the hills east of the Antietam were brought to bear on the Rebel cannon in the Piper fields. The gray cannoneers were told to fight to the last. The Union infantry must be stopped. Otherwise the end might come for the Army of Northern Virginia. Confederate gun wheels, limber chests, and caissons were hit and smashed. Rebel artillerymen fell beside their guns. "Never had the Southern batteries taken such a pounding."[4] The rest of the war Antietam would be remembered as "artillery hell."

A Union officer marveled at the bravery of the Confederates in the Sunken Road. In his report he said:

> It is beyond all wonder how such men as the rebel troops can fight on as they do; that filthy, sick, hungry and miserable, they should prove such heroes in fight, is past explanation—one regiment stood up before the fire of two or three of our long range batteries and of two regiments of infantry, and though the air around them was vocal with whistle of bullets and screams of shells, there they stood, and delivered their fire in perfect order; and there they continued to stand.[5]

For over three hours the battle raged without either side giving way.[6] Brave men met brave men and fired shots of "fateful lightning" at each other.

George B. Anderson came to Hill's support. McClellan's big batteries quickly got their range and started a tremendous barrage. The foundations of the homes and barns in the Valley of the Antietam were literally shaken. Residents of Middletown and Hagerstown heard the terrible roar, although ten miles or more away. Black smoke rolled across the hills along the Antietam, blinding and choking the soldiers of the blue and gray.

The Confederate position was very strong. The narrow Sunken Road formed a natural rifle pit. One Union attack after another was beaten back. And believe it or not, some of the Rebels launched counterattacks. One small detail advanced as far as the Roulette barn, considerably to the rear of the main Union line.

Then the Union division of Israel B. Richardson came up. Here was a commander who was always at the front. He personally led his men after the Rebels retreating from South Mountain. On September 17, he led his men across the

"Fighting Dick" Richardson.

The Sunken Road.

Antietam, and now in the Roulette fields he was supervising
the deployment of his troops. The division was a proud one.
The men had faith in themselves and in their gallant commander. The band was drumming the march. The Irish Brigade was in front, the green flag fluttering in the breeze. The
famous "Fighting Sixty-Ninth New York" was ready to give
any and all who stood in front of them a dose of "fateful
lightning."[7]

Richardson halted his men in a protected depression. He
ordered them to remove all unnecessary equipment. Blanket
rolls, and canteens were removed. Finally, only rifles and
cartridge boxes were left. Regimental commanders moved up
and down the line among their troops, giving them last min-
ute instructions and pep talks.

Then it was "Forward" into the fray. Onward went Israel
"Dick" Richardson's division until it was within thirty yards
of the Sunken Road. Men were falling all around. Confederate General G. B. Anderson fell mortally wounded. Robert
Rodes was hit in the thigh. Gordon took three bullets, but
remained on his feet.

In the midst of the smoke, death, and destruction was
Richardson on foot leading his men, his face blackened with
127

powder, sword drawn and pointing at the enemy, he was yelling at the top of his voice.[8] No wonder his men were inspired. No wonder they almost achieved total victory. Such a leader men will follow to the very jaws of death.

By now one Confederate draped over the rail fence had seventeen bullets in his body. Gordon was struck by a fifth ball ". . . squarely in the face . . . barely missing the jugular vein."[9] He:

> . . . fell forward and lay unconscious with my face in my cap, and it would seem that I might have been smothered by the blood running into my cap from this last wound but for the act of some Yankee, who as if to save my life, had at a previous hour during the battle, shot a hole through the cap, which left the blood out.[10]

Richardson's division was now pushing the Confederates from the Sunken Road into the Piper fields within sight of the Sharpsburg Road.[11]

The end was in sight. Victory was almost in the grasp of the Army of the Potomac even though "Little Mac" was still safely back at the Pry farm. Thanks to Richardson and his division, Lee's army was on the verge of being cut in two. Just a little bit more and Union soldiers would be on the hill where the National Cemetery is now located. From that height and strategic spot they would command Sharpsburg, the approaches to Burnside Bridge, and the Confederate rear.[12]

"Affairs were critical."[13]

> This was a fearful situation for the Confederate center. I put my staff officers to the guns while I held their horses. It was easy to see that if the Federals broke through our line . . . the Confederate army would be cut in two and probably destroyed, for we were already badly whipped and holding our ground by sheer force of desperation.[14]

Double charges were fired into the advancing men in blue. In a few moments the Confederate battery lost nineteen men and fifteen horses.[15] In an effort to silence the few guns blocking his way to the Sharpsburg Road, Richardson obtained a battery of horse artillery and started forward to silence the Rebel guns.

Then it happened, a shell fragment from one of the deadly

Confederate cannon hit Richardson in the hip and down he went. This was a tragedy for the Union Army. Not only did it prevent a possible decisive victory on the Antietam hills, but it may have cost the army dearly. Lincoln needed a man of Richardson's stature to lead the troops of the Republic.

With the wounding of Richardson, the fighting died away in the Piper fields and in the Sunken Road. The brave leader was taken to Philip Pry's home where an infection set in, claiming his life on November 3. One of his men wrote, "No one but a soldier could understand our sorrow at seeing him carried off the field."[16]

At the Sunken Road was delivered the most telling blow of which the Federals could boast in the fighting at Antietam.[17]

Thomas L. Livermore, a soldier in blue, said, "The gray dead lay so thick in the road that a man could have walked its length without touching the ground."[18]

After the battle local citizens came to survey the carnage of death, and also to see if they could be of help. An unknown little old lady was greatly moved by what she saw. Seeing young men twisted in death, and hearing the moans of the dying, she got down on her knees in the lane, and asked God to bless the men laying in "this bloody lane."[19]

Winfield Scott Hancock arrived on the battlefield of Antietam about 9:00 A.M. on the day of the battle. Before the end of the day, he at the age of thirty-eight, would no longer be in command of a brigade, but in command of a division.

When "Fighting Dick" Richardson fell near Bloody Lane, General McClellan sent for Hancock and ordered him to assume command of the first division of the Union Second Corps. Hancock in his official report wrote:

> Early in the afternoon of the 17th I was directed by Major-General McClellan in person, who was on the field, to take command of Richardson's division, and to command the center of our forces, General Richardson having been so seriously wounded as to require his removal.

Hancock was a worthy successor to Richardson. Not only would he lead the division to new and greater heights, but in time as commander of the Second Corps, his leadership would make it one of the best in the entire army.

Hancock was the man who selected the Union position at Cemetery Ridge at a place called Gettysburg. His troops withstood Pickett's charge. Hancock falling wounded in the struggle.

Passed over by Radicals after the war, and ignored by Grant for whom he had performed valiantly, Hancock served as a true soldier. After the war, this young man, who assumed command of a fine division at Bloody Lane, granted terms of reconciliation equal to those of Lincoln to the people in Louisiana and Texas. He was in charge of U. S. Grant's funeral, and almost won the election to the highest office in the land in 1880.

Capt. William H. Graham, commander of Battery K, First U.S. Artillery supported Richardson's division during the fighting at Bloody Lane. In fact, "Fighting Dick" told him to have his battery ready for an advance which he expected to be ordered by General Sumner. While Richardson was relaying this message to Graham he fell mortally wounded by a ball of spherical case from a Confederate battery.

Graham had to use other horses to bring his caissons back to a less exposed position. The horses assigned to them had been killed. On September 17, Graham had seventeen horses killed, and six severely wounded. Some of these the young captain expected to die.

Graham's official report ended with these words:

> In closing this report I feel called up to mention the conduct of a citizen, a Mr. ——, who resides near the battlefield. This gentleman drove his carriage to my battery while under a severe artillery fire, and carried off my wounded who were suffering very much for the want of surgical attendance, and distributed ham and biscuit among the men of the battery. He also returned a second time to the battery. One of his horses was wounded while performing this service.

For many years this Good Samaritan has remained unknown. Some thought it might have been one of the Pipers. However, the Piper family had taken shelter near the Potomac River.

According to the *Hagerstown Morning Herald* in an article published on April 27, 1962, the man who aided the wounded of Graham's battery was Martin Eakle of Eakle's Mills near Keedysville. Aaron Snyder had gone up to Red Hill to watch the battle unfold. While he was there, he saw Martin Eakle drive up with a wagon and two horses. He was on his way to the battlefield with water, ham and biscuits. Pat Eakle said Mr. Snyder had told him the story, stating as did Graham that one of Martin's horses was wounded. At times the wagon, horses, and Mr. Eakle were obscured by the smoke hanging over the battlefield.

VIII

TERRIBLE SWIFT SWORD

By noon the sounds of battle were increasing south of Sharpsburg, near the Lower Bridge. During the morning hours, the Georgia regiments posted rifle pits above the bridge and were able to hold the Federals in check.[1]

However near noon, large numbers of Union troops forded the Antietam down by Snavely's Ford, almost within sight of Belinda Springs. They swept up the hill toward Sharpsburg, and hit the Georgia riflemen on the flank.[2]

Earlier in the day, the Eleventh Connecticut, the Second Maryland, and Sixth New Hampshire had tried to storm the bridge. However, they were met with a withering fire and forced to fall back.[3]

With Rodman applying pressure on the flank, finally about 1:00 P.M. a gallant charge by the Fifty-first New York and Fifty-first Pennsylvania carried the bridge.[4]

The stubborn fighting and steep hill seemed to exhaust the Ninth Corps. The Union divisions paused to regroup, and to get a new supply of ammunition. During the lull, William B. McKinley, a young commissary sergeant with the Twenty-third Ohio, galloped up on the heights above Sharpsburg with hot coffee and sandwiches for his comrades.

Finally about 3:00 P.M., or nine hours too late, the Ninth Corps launched its drive toward Sharpsburg and the Harpers Ferry Road.

The small band of Confederates fell back through the Otto farm. Some took shelter in the old mill at the edge of town. It looked like the jig was up. Confederate infantrymen stopped behind stone fences to fire a round or two, and then continued their withdrawal. A stand was made along the fences in what is today Branch Avenue.

The end was almost in sight. McClellan had victory in his grasp. Lee's line of retreat was almost cut off. The Army of Northern Virginia was close to being cut in half. Robert E. Lee's command was close to disaster. No reserves were left to send to the Confederate right.

But "A terrible swift sword" of deliverance was on the way. Early in the morning A. P. Hill, seventeen miles away at Harpers Ferry, received a communique from Lee urging him to make haste to Sharpsburg.[5] Within the hour, Hill was underway, moving to Lee's relief.[6] "For fate or fame,"[7] Hill was to have the final word at Sharpsburg. His was to be the final act.

It was hot and dusty that September afternoon. But there was no time to rest. The fate of the Confederacy was hanging in the balance. Hill was everywhere, urging the laggard forward with the point of his dress sword.[8] Every sound from the hills of Sharpsburg seemed to say, "Come quickly, come quickly."

About 2:30 the head of the Light Division reached Boteler's Ford near Shepherdstown.[9] Hill, dashing and picturesque in his red battle shirt,[10] galloped ahead with his staff to assess the situation.

When Lee met Hill near the field of battle, tradition has it that Lee embraced him in thanksgiving. Hill was directed to come in on the right. He galloped back to his men, urging them once again to make haste.

It was now around 4:00 P.M. The Ninth Corps was pressing on. The Harpers Ferry Road was in sight. But suddenly out of the dust of Sawmill Road, the brigades of Hill charged onto the field. Forward with the Rebel yell and the bayonet toward the Yanks they came. "At the critical moment A. P. Hill was always at his strongest."[11]

As the Union forces advanced, a gap had been created between two of the columns. Into this gap Hill sent his men. The effect was devastating. Some of the Confederates wore blue uniforms which added to the confusion. General Rodman, seeking to stabilize the Union force, ". . . fell desperately wounded by a ball through his breast. The loss of their commander at a critical period caused confusion . . . in the division."[12]

"With his terrible swift sword," Hill met the Union onslaught, stemmed the tide of battle, and forced the Ninth Corps back to the vicinity of the Lower Bridge.

With his characteristic enthusiasm, Hill had marched his 2,400 men seventeen miles in eight hours, forded the Potomac, climbed a steep hill, and was able to say, "We have met the enemy and they are ours." Hill said, "My troops were not a moment too soon." His "terrible swift sword" had brought deliverance to the Army of Northern Virginia.

With characteristic appreciation of his command's performance, Hill lost no time in issuing the following congratulatory address on September 24:

Soldiers of the Light Division:

You have done well and I am pleased with you. You have fought in every battle from Mechanicsville to Shepherdstown, and no man can yet say that the Light Division was ever broken. You held the left at Manassas against over-whelming numbers and saved the army. You saved the day at Sharpsburg and Shepherdstown. You were selected to face a storm of round shot, and grape such as I have never before seen. I am proud to say that your services are appreciated by our general, and that you have a reputation in the army which it should be the object of every officer and private to sustain.[13]

It seems that A. P. Hill was always a thorn in the flesh to General McClellan. Perhaps the following purported romantic involvement will give some light on the matter:

There was a report in the Army of the Potomac . . . that General McClellan and General A. P. Hill were both in love with the beautiful Miss Nellie Marcy, daughter of General Marcy, when they were at West Point, that she smiled on both of these gallant gentlemen . . . but that in the end she married McClellan. It so happened that in all McClellan's campaigns around Richmond [as well as at Sharpsburg and Shepherdstown], Hill was always to the fore, and it seemed that whether struck in the front, flank, or rear, especially early in the morning, it was by A. P. Hill. McClellan's soldiers began to get tired of this sort of thing, and attributed it to spite and vengeance on the part of Hill. Early one gloomy morning, before the sun had appeared, there were shots of artillery and rattle of musketry which told of a spirited attack. Hill was at it again. The long roll was beaten: there was commotion and confusion and the rush to arms, in the midst of which one hardened old veteran unrolled himself from his blanket and in an inimitable tone of weariness and disgust, cried out, "My God, Nellie, why didn't you marry him!"[14]

The Aftermath

Thus the bloody Battle of Antietam came to an end just as the setting sun, a crimson red, sank beyond the western hills.

General Longstreet, one of Lee's corps commanders, wrote:

> For fourteen long hours more than one hundred thousand men, with five hundred pieces of artillery, had engaged in titanic combat. As the pall of battle smoke rose and cleared away, the scene presented was one to make the stoutest heart shudder. There lay upon the ground, scattered for three miles over the valleys and the hills or in improvised hospitals, more than twenty thousand men. Horace Greeley was probably right in pronouncing this the bloodiest day in American history.[15]

"Never had the Army of Northern Virginia fought a battle so doubtful, save at Malvern Hill, and never one so long," declares Douglas Freeman.[16]

"The sun," wrote one soldier, "seemed almost to go backwards, and it appeared as if night would never come." Lee had thrown into action every organized infantry unit north of the Potomac.[17]

In three distinct localities, the battle had waxed fierce. In reality Lee had fought three battles, one on each of the three segments into which the field was divided by natural objects. First, Jackson had met and stood off the Union attacks upon the Dunkard Church and the West Woods. Then the tide of battle raged at the Sunken Road where the centers of both armies spent themselves in sanguinary struggle. Lastly, A. P. Hill arrived just in time to save Lee's army, as the Union Ninth Corps was driving to cut off his line of retreat.

Colonel Palfrey gave this graphic description of the ensuing night:

> The blessed night came, and brought with it sleep and forgetfulness and refreshment to man; but the murmur of the night wind, breathing over the fields of wheat and clover, was mingled with the groans of the countless sufferers of both armies. Who can tell, who

135

can imagine, the horrors of such a night while the unconscious stars shone above, and the unconscious river went rippling by?[18]

Of the less than forty thousand Confederate infantry engaged, more than ten thousand were casualties. Some units had been almost wiped out. The Texas brigade lost 560 out of 854.[19]

> Grievous as the losses had been, and desperately as the outcome had hinged, time after time, on the arrival of Lee's scant reinforcements, what could the morrow hold except disaster more complete? Every division was in line; in all northern Virginia there were no troops except Thomas's brigade at Harper's Ferry that could possibly be called upon. . . . Another series of attacks like those that had been delivered all day would certainly drive the army into the Potomac.[20]

So, at least, thought nearly all the officers who made their way during the evening to a council of war held by Robert E. Lee in the home of Jacob Grove on the square in Sharpsburg. As general after general rode in wearily from the front, he asked quietly of each, "How is it on your part of the line?" Each told the same story; their men were worn out; the enemy's numbers were overwhelming. Lee asked Hood where his fine division was. Hood replied, "Dead upon the field, sir."[21] To a certain extent each commander regretfully had to say the same.

When all had reported, Lee said not a word about retreat, but said that the army could and would defend its position if McClellan attacked on the morrow.[22]

There was little sleep that night in the ambulance corps, according to R. L. Walker, Confederate officer.

> . . . all night long their lanterns could be seen flashing about the battle-field while they were searching for and bringing in the wounded, of friend and foe alike. In company with General Barksdale of Mississippi, whose brigade was on my left, I rode over that part of the battlefield where our troops had been engaged, to see that none of the wounded had been overlooked. While passing along a worn fence, in the darkness, we heard a feeble voice almost under our horses' feet: "Don't let your horses t-r-e-a-d on me-e!" We at once pulled up, and peering over the pommels of our saddles into the darkness we could distinguish the dim outlines of a human form extended across our path. "Who are you?" we inquired. "I belong to the 20th Mas-sa-chu-setts, reg-i-ment," answered the voice; "I can't

136

move—I think my back's broken." We sent for an ambulance and gave orders to care for the poor fellow, who was one of Sedgwick's men. This was but one of the very many instances of human suffering we encountered that night.[23]

Charles Coffin found the area around the Dunkard Church thickly strewn with dead. He wrote:

> I recall a Union soldier lying near the Dunkard Church with his face turned upward, and his pocket Bible open upon his breast. I lifted the volume and read the words . . . [of the 23rd Psalm]. Upon the flyleaf were the words: "We hope and pray that you may be permitted by a kind providence, after the war is over to return."[24]

Almost, But Not Quite

This was the story of the day for General McClellan and the Army of the Potomac. Every attack, though partially successful, seemed to lack the final drive and effort necessary for a complete Union victory on the fields of Antietam.

At Bloody Lane and at the Lower Bridge, disaster was in the making for the Confederates. In both areas, the Army of the Potomac was within yards of victory, just a little more and the Army of Northern Virginia would have been cut in

Hawkins Zouaves Monument near the Harpers Ferry Road.

two. But it was not to be. Victory was in sight, almost within the grasp of McClellan, but not quite. And in that statement we find some of the irony and the tragedy of the bloodiest Wednesday in our history.

IX

DIM AND FLARING LAMPS

At last the sun went down upon the fields, and hills, and the woods near the Antietam. The cannon ceased firing. Muskets were quiet, and weary men wiped sweaty brows. The horses that were still alive sought fresh green pasture.

But the work was not finished. On the field of battle, behind trees, in gullies, lanes, and fencerows, were stretched the forms of the dead, the dying, and the wounded. For the ambulance corps, it would be a long night. By "dim and flaring lamps," soldiers searched for their comrades attempting to bring them aid. For many, especially in the Burnside Bridge area, morning would never come. They died from their wounds before their comrades ever reached them.

Eighteen thousand men were wounded at Antietam, ten thousand men in blue, and eight thousand in gray. Most, but not all, of those engaged in the Miller cornfield, the West Woods, and Bloody Lane, were taken to barns, houses, churches, schools, and open fields to be treated while the daylight hours remained. These men were treated through the night by surgeons and nurses, using "dim and flaring lamps"; the lamps, in many cases, making the difference between life and death.

South of town, men of the Ninth Corps worked feverishly to get their comrades to the Otto, Snavely, Rohrback, and Locust Spring farms where their wounds could be cleaned in the field hospitals, where the wounded could find comfort and nourishment, or perhaps die in peace.

Never had America known such a long and dreadful night, a night when men wearing the blue and gray treated their comrades, or searched for those yet on the field of battle by the light of "dim and flaring lamps."

Hospitals in the early part of the Civil War were pitiful and inadequate. Almost any building was considered as a possible hospital site.

Before the war there was no such thing as a General Hospital. There were no well-trained army nurses, no special diets, and no humane means of transporting the wounded. One has to wonder how many died in the jolting wagons which took the wounded from Antietam to Frederick. Each bump and jolt brought new pain and misery.

Some blamed the government for this condition. There was a lack of beds, blankets, pillows, and socks. The fellows complained that all they got to eat was "hardtack and salt junk."

The bivouacs and camping areas were plagued by insects and every kind of "creeping thing." Men died daily from pneumonia, dysentery, and other camp diseases.

Today, some in the military go on sick call to escape disliked duties. But in the early part of the Civil War, many soldiers fought against going to the hospitals. In a lot of cases they received better care in camp from their comrades than in the hospitals. In some hospitals rotten straw was used for bedding. In camp clean pine boughs were used.[1]

A young soldier from the Fifth Wisconsin, writing from Camp Griffin, near Washington, on November 12, 1861, said:

> We need beds and bedding, hospital clothing and sick-diet, proper medicines, surgical instruments, and good nurses,—and then a decent building or a good hospital tent for the accommodation of our sick. I suppose we shall have them when the government can get around to it, and in the meantime we try to be patient.[2]

In New York City, the Woman's Central Association of Relief was formed. A Dr. Bellows was chairman. He went to Washington with plans for the "U.S. Sanitary Commission." This organization was to be subject to the army, yet would supplement government care, always ready to meet any need.

Lincoln at first looked upon this as "a fifth wheel to the coach." However, the women of America backed Dr. Bellows and the Sanitary Commission was born.[3]

Patriotic women across America formed aid societies. At first, some of them asked that their donations of bedding, clothing, and bandages be used only for men from their hometown or state. However, they soon saw the need to let their gifts be used wherever there was need.

The railroads transported the boxes free of charge. Express companies reduced fares by 50 percent, and the telegraph firms remitted their charges.

The Sanitary Commission sent medical inspectors to inspect camp rations and cooking, hospital ventilation, drainage, cleanliness, quality of materials in use, and hospital administration.

Eighteen of the best doctors in the country prepared concise guidelines on health in camp and the treatment and care of the wounded. These were of great value in the field hospitals.

Another innovation was "kettles on wheels." These were small portable furnaces used to prepare hot soup for the wounded.

After seeing the misery caused by jolting wagons, hospital cars were invented. These were cars with beds suspended by strong rubber.

Soldiers' homes or lodges were established in key cities. These were free hotels for soldiers who were broke. Eight hundred thousand men slept in them during the war.

The Sanitary Commission helped relatives trace pension and back-pay benefits after loved ones became casualties. A "Hospital Directory" was maintained listing the patients in the 233 general hospitals of the army.[4]

The hospital supplies and money used by the Sanitary Commission to carry out its work came from loyal women who organized 10,000 aid societies. Branch offices were established in ten key cities, among them Boston, New York, Philadelphia, Chicago, and Cincinnati.

When materials arrived at a branch office, they were sorted and all items similar in content placed in one box. The box was stamped with the list of contents, and then sent on to Washington or Louisville for the use of the armies in the East and West.

Some of the boxes arriving in branch offices came with letters. One such box arriving in Chicago contained shirts, underwear, towels, socks, and other toilet and sewing articles. The note read:

> Dear Soldiers, The little girls of ——— send this box to you. They hear that 13,000 of you are sick, and have been wounded in battle. They are very sorry, and want to do something for you. They cannot do much, for they are all small; but they have bought with their own money, and made what is here. They hope it will do some good, and that you will all get well and come home. We all pray to God for you night and morning.[5]

The offering of these children was left intact and sent on to a hospital.

In another incoming package a note was found attached to a pillow. It read:

> My Dear Friend, You are not my husband nor son; but you are the husband or son of some woman who undoubtedly loves you as I love mine. I have made these garments for you with a heart that aches for your sufferings, and with a longing to come to you to assist in taking care of you. It is a great comfort to me that God loves and pities you, pining and lonely in a far-off hospital; and if you believe in God, it will also be a comfort to you. Are you near death, and soon to cross the dark river? O then, may God soothe your last hours, and lead you up "the shining shore," where there is no war, no sickness, no death. Call on Him, for He is an ever present helper.[6]

Some of the letters were written by young girls with the hope of finding a pen pal, or better yet a boyfriend. This note was also found in a package arriving in Chicago:

> My Dear Boy, I have knit these socks expressly for you. How do you like them? How do you look, and where do you live when you are home? I am 19 years old, of medium height, of slight build, with blue eyes, fair complexion, light hair, and a good deal of it. Write and tell me all about yourself. . . . Direct to . . .
>
> P.S. If the recipient of these socks has a wife, will he please exchange socks with some poor fellow not so fortunate?[7]

Throughout the war, the women of the North came together in churches, town halls, and private homes to prepare and pack items for shipment to the Sanitary Commission. Some worked until they were weary to the bone. Many a

142

soldier, however, owed his hospital comfort to these women of compassion.

Houses were rifled of all bedding that could be spared. Canned and dried fruits were taken from the cellars. Families tried to save on milk, butter, and eggs so they could sell more of their products, diverting the profit to Sanitary Commission work.

Festivals, cake walks, musical programs, fairs, and just about every legitimate means imaginable were used to make money to purchase needed items.

Children got into the act, too. In our day, the boys and girls have backyard fairs for the March of Dimes and other worthy charities. During the 1860s, the children of America held "Sanitary Fairs for the Soldiers." They sold candy, lemonade, pens, bookmarks, dolls, frogs, etc. They acted out plays and shows, charging admission, of course.

Many notes were answered by the Union soldiers. Some resulted in lasting friendships, others in marriage. In one box was a hospital gown with a large pocket. The pocket contained hickory nuts and gingersnaps, and were sewed shut so the contents could not spill out. A note was pinned on the outside:

> My Dear Fellow: Just take your ease in this dressing gown. Don't mope and have the blues if you are sick. Moping never cured anybody yet. Eat your nuts and cakes, if you are well enough, and snap your fingers at dull care. I wish I could do more for you, and if I were a man I would come and fight with you. Woman though I am, I'd like to help hang Jeff Davis higher than Haman—yes, and all who aid and abet him, too, whether North or South.[8]

Another dear soul wanted to be sure only a wounded soldier received her goodies. On the top of a box of cookies was this message:

> These cookies are expressly for the sick soldiers, and if anybody else eats them, I hope they will choke him![9]

Comfort bags were main items in most boxes. These usually contained a small needle book with twelve good needles, a pin cushion, thread, buttons, and other items needed to keep clothing in good repair. Some contained a jackknife to

Smoketown Hospital.

Crystal Spring farm.

The Crystal Spring.

The Jacob Miller farm.

144

whittle away the hours, a New Testament, and often a plug of tobacco.

The soldiers always hoped to find stamps and stationery in their bags. Army pay was low, and the men were usually broke. The sutlers took advantage of this situation by charging ridiculous prices for stationery.

The Sanitary Commission brought comfort and aid to the wounded at Antietam. The commission supplied 28,763 pieces of dry goods, including shirts, towels, bedticks, and pillows. Thirty barrels of old linen for bandages were used at Antietam. Three thousand one hundred and eighty-eight pounds of farina helped feed the troops, along with 2,620 pounds of condensed milk, and 5,000 pounds of beef stock and canned meats. Three thousand bottles of wine and cordials were used to help calm the wounded.[10]

Several tons of lemons and other fruits provided vitamin C for the wounded at Antietam. Crackers, tea, and sugar were provided in large amounts. Rubber cloths, chloroform, opiates, and surgical instruments were supplied to the doctors working in the fields, barns, and churches along the Antietam. The supplies came from centers in Boston, New York, and Philadelphia to Washington, and thence by wagon to Antietam.

During that terrible Wednesday, September 17, 1862, the Union Army of the Potomac, led by General George B. McClellan, sustained the following losses: 2,410 killed, 9,549 wounded, and 753 missing.

The Confederate Army of Northern Virginia lost: 2,700 killed, 9,024 wounded, and 2,000 missing.

Caring for such a large number of wounded soldiers presented great problems. Medicine, bedding, doctors, attendants, and supplies were needed. Not only were there almost ten thousand Union wounded, but General Lee left nearly eleven hundred of his most seriously wounded on the battlefield. For the most part, these were men who could not be removed when the Army of Northern Virginia withdrew across the Potomac.

What happened to the men wounded on these fields? This

writer had often asked the same question. Hence, some research and this chapter.

The officer in charge of caring for the 10,000 Union wounded and the 1,100 Confederate wounded left behind at Antietam was Jonathan Letterman, medical director, Army of the Potomac.

On September 15, Letterman had examined all possible hospital sites in Boonsboro and Keedysville. Medical directors of the various corps were given orders to establish hospitals on a divisional level. These were to be close to the fields of expected conflict, yet secure from the shot and shell of the enemy. The houses and barns were to be easily accessible, and well supplied with hay, straw, and water.

Barns were preferred to houses. The barns would provide better ventilation, and more freedom for the doctors to move about. As the hospital sites were selected, medical supplies were brought forward to await the expected battle.

Supply Difficulties

Very few hospital tents were available at Antietam. This was due partly to the haste of the movement from Virginia to Maryland. The good fall weather was another reason. Some of the wounded had little shelter until early October.

After the battle, messages were sent to Frederick to hurry fresh supplies to the battlefield. Apparently there was a supply bottleneck at Monocacy Junction. The doctors were fearful of running low on medicine, bandages, stimulants, and other needed items.

Food supplies were also short. Letterman obtained an order to get twelve wagons in Frederick to bring food to the hospitals. He was able to get but two, and these with great difficulty. Had it not been for the local citizens and the Sanitary Commission, many of the wounded at Antietam would have suffered hunger pangs as well as pain from their wounds.

Many of the ambulances had been left at Fortress Monroe in Virginia. Hence, there was a shortage of these at Antietam. The ambulance corps itself had not had the opportunity for much training. Yet the wounded were recovered and brought

146

to the field hospitals in fairly good time. The biggest problem was on the right, near Burnside Bridge. Letterman says that some of these men were not recovered from the fields of battle until 2:00 P.M. on Thursday, September 18.[11]

The outdoors seemed to aid the patients.[12] The pure, fresh country air brought healing. Dr. Letterman in his official reports states:

> The results of the battle only added additional evidence of the absolute necessity of a full supply of pure air, constantly renewed—a supply which cannot be obtained in the most perfectly constructed building. Within a few yards a marked contrast could be seen between the wounded in houses and barns and in the open air. Those in houses progressed less favorably than those in barns, those in barns less favorably than those in the open air, although all were in other respects treated alike.[13]

The big barns and kind people in the Valley of the Antietam greatly helped the wounded. Letterman expressed his gratitude by saying:

> The capacious barns, abundantly provided with hay and straw, the delightful weather . . . and the kindness exhibited by the people, afforded increased facilities to the medical department. . . . It gives me no little pleasure to say that the wounded had every care that could be bestowed upon them—that they were promptly, willingly, and efficiently tended to.[14]

Lanterns of Mercy

Early on Sunday morning, September 14, a wagon with a white canvas top, drawn by eight long-eared mules, pulled up in front of 488½ Seventh Street in Washington, D.C.

Major Rucker of the U.S. Army had sent the wagon with four men to get Clara Barton. Miss Barton supervised the hurried loading of the wagon. To save vital space for medical supplies, she carried just a few personal articles, tied up in a handkerchief.

Then the driver, Cornelius M. Welles, turned the wagon around in the middle of the street, and the strange looking group started on their journey from Washington to the fields of Antietam. The beginning of the journey was made "in full gaze of the whole city in its best attire, and on its way to church."

147

They made good progress for those days. By nightfall they were near Frederick. A campfire was made, supper prepared, and then they hit the sack. The men rolled up in blankets and slept on the ground . . . Clara slept curled up in the wagon.

As she prepared to go to sleep, Miss Barton must have thought of the events of recent days. On the thirteenth, she had been told to go to Harpers Ferry immediately as medical help was needed.

But Harpers Ferry was surrounded by the Confederates, and there was no way to get in. Now she was on the road, following the main body of the Union Army, somewhere in the vicinity of South Mountain.

On Monday morning the Barton crew saw first-hand evidence of the struggle at Turner's Gap on Old Route 40. Dead horses were by the roadside and in many fields.

Clara met many hungry, battle-fatigued, and demoralized Union soldiers. Some stated, "We are always getting beaten and wind up retreating."

It is difficult to tell whether some of these men were stragglers, or perhaps they were suffering nervous and emotional fatigue from the fighting in the mountain pass.

Clara Barton knew an army moves on its stomach, and that combat and expected combat often produces hunger. Therefore, at every available stop, Miss Barton bought all the bread the folks would sell her. She cut the freshly baked loaves into slices and then passed them out to the hungry soldiers she met.

At South Mountain, Clara left her wagon, and made a personal search of the battlefield. She wanted to be sure no young soldier had been missed, and left to suffer.

A young Union officer rode up asking for a few words with her. He said, "Twenty-five wounded Rebs are hiding in a nearby farmhouse." They had been left behind by the retreating Confederates.

A civilian doctor treating the men told the lieutenant that the Rebs were hungry and in need of food. He begged for two cows from the herd the officer was taking to Antietam.

"Milk," said the doctor, "will make the difference between life and death for these men."

The young officer, a Harvard divinity student before the war, wanted to help, yet the cows belonged to the government and he did not want to get in trouble with his superiors.

Miss Barton smiled. "You can do nothing except your duty. But I am neither bonded nor responsible. Ride on lieutenant."

The young officer smiled. He bowed, and spurred his horse. When the cattle and those herding them were out of sight, there was an addition to Clara Barton's wagon, two fat cows trailing behind.

She called to Sergeant Field and said, "We can't be encumbered by these straying beasts. Drive them on to that house, the one with the sheltered windows, and put them inside the fence. Then close the gate because I don't want them to get out."

By noon, Clara's wagon was caught up in a train several miles long. The wagon train was heading for the fields of Antietam.

Miss Barton was upset. She had missed the action at Harpers Ferry and South Mountain. She certainly did not want to miss another opportunity to be of service.

Ammunition wagons had first priority in the wagon train, then the wagons containing food and clothing. Last of all came the hospital supplies.

Her mind was working. She was making a plan. Her crew would pull out of line early in the evening. The mules would be fed, and they would go to bed early.

At 1:00 A.M. she awakened the men and persuaded them to harness the team and get going. They would steal a march on the others. By nightfall she was close to Antietam Creek, near the armies poised for battle.

The night air was stifling, and Clara felt a great sense of doom.

Early on the morning of the seventeenth, Clara Barton was on a hill watching the smoke of the battle with the aid of field glasses. She learned that Hooker had suffered heavy losses and had asked for reinforcements. Following some artillery, she arrived in the rear of Hooker's line sometime after ten o'clock. For two miles she had passed wounded men.

Dismounting from her wagon, Clara headed for a house which was being used as a hospital.

She met a Dr. Dunn, an old friend, who expressed delighted surprise in seeing her.

Dr. Dunn was not very well supplied. He had his instruments and a small amount of chloroform. All the sheets in the house had been torn up, and now they were out of bandages. With nothing to stop the flow of blood, men were bleeding to death. Four tables had been set up on the porch. The doctors were using green corn leaves to dress raw wounds.

Clara had her crew unpack the boxes of bandages, cotton, quilts, and stimulants sent to her by patriotic women from New England and the Midwest.

Several times during the day the hospital came under fire. They did not have to go far looking for wounded. Many severely wounded men walked to them.

Miss Barton had brought twelve bottles of wine. She dipped bread in the wine and gave it to the soldiers to ease their pain.

She came close to losing her life at Antietam. As she stooped to give a wounded soldier a drink, she felt a sudden twitch of the left dress sleeve. With that hand she was holding the cup of water to his lips. The bullet went through her sleeve. Then, "The poor fellow sprang from my hands and fell back quivering in the agonies of death. A bullet had passed between my body and the right arm which supported him, cutting through the sleeve and passing through his chest from shoulder to shoulder."

Although she had never performed an operation, Clara cut a minie ball out of the right cheek of one painfully wounded soldier.

At times the artillery fire was so great and the tables upon which the wounded lay for surgery were jarred so badly that the surgeons had to momentarily stop their work.

Night fell, and with it, despondency on the part of one doctor. He had but two little candles to use during the night. He knew that many would die unless he had the light to give them immediate attention.

150

Clara gently led the tired doctor to the door, and pointed to the barn where "lanterns glistened like stars." She had learned a lesson on the last battlefield. Candlelight is undependable and can easily start a fire in a pile of straw. This time she was prepared. She had brought a large supply of lanterns. Thus the work of bringing aid to the wounded would continue without hindrance during the long night hours—a night of pain and death.

Some of the men had not eaten since the evening before. Miss Barton soon had thirty helpers giving hot gruel to all who were able to eat. She used kettles from the farmhouse. All night Sergeant Field, her devoted helper, and others kept the fires going and served hot food to the hungry.

For three days Clara Barton, truly an angel of the battlefield, worked until she was utterly exhausted, and all her supplies gone. By this time though the Sanitary Commission was on the scene.

Clara's assistants put her to bed on the floor of her now empty wagon. They covered her up, and she slept like a baby, despite the jogging wagon, most of the way back to Washington.

God alone knew how many men on the Union right owed their lives to her thoughtfulness and care.

Dr. James Oliver

James Oliver III was born June 28, 1836, in Athol, Massachusetts. Many of his early recollections are those connected with his hardworking, blacksmith father.

As a young lad, James taught grammar school. Then in 1859 he began to study medicine at Harvard Medical School in Boston. Graduating on July 16, 1862, Oliver went immediately to the state house where he was examined, and promised a position as assistant surgeon, Twenty-first Massachusetts Volunteers. Receiving his commission on August 1, twenty-six-year-old James Oliver set out to find his unit.

Taking the train from Boston to Baltimore, he was thrilled with the views of New York and Philadelphia. In the Maryland city he found a freighter sailing for Fortress Monroe, and enjoyed a sail down the beautiful Chesapeake.

151

Reaching the fortress, he was confronted with the news that the Twenty-first had left Newport News and had gone to join Pope's army in the vicinity of Fredericksburg. Going by way of the Potomac to Aquia Creek, he finally reached the Twenty-first at Falmouth, just across the river from Fredericksburg. Dr. Oliver soon had the opportunity to put his medical skills in practice by caring for the wounded from Second Bull Run. Then it was on to Maryland.

Saturday night, September 13, 1862, Dr. Oliver slept near Middletown, Maryland. In midafternoon the Twenty-first was ordered up the Fox's Gap on Old Sharpsburg Road. On his way, James Oliver met General Reno on a stretcher, dying of wounds, and being treated by Dr. Cutter.

By the time Oliver reached the side of Dr. Hastings, the senior physician of the Twenty-first, the ground was covered with dead. Young James helped amputate a leg by the light of a candle. Sinking to the ground from exhaustion, Oliver awoke the next morning to find himself lying next to a dead Confederate.

As the great battle grew near, Oliver was sent on detached duty to the Fifty-first New York. This gallant unit supported by the Twenty-first Massachusetts, and accompanied by the Fifty-first Pennsylvania, finally carried Burnside Bridge. During the engagement, Oliver was at the Rohrback barn, partially protected by a ridge. However, shells from both armies passed over the barn, and fragments flew in every direction.

Those who fell in the fighting around the bridge were brought to the Rohrback barn, and as quickly as possible moved back to Locust Spring, the site selected for the Ninth Corps Hospital.

After dark, Dr. Oliver accompanied an ambulance to Locust Spring. The vehicle of mercy was filled with men with compound fractures of the legs. James was never able to forget their groans as the bumps and stones in the road added to their misery. One poor lad begged to be taken out of the ambulance, and placed by the roadside where he could die. Oliver spent the night of September 17 working at Locust Spring.

On the twentieth, Dr. Oliver was sent to Pleasant Valley

where he remained until October 11 when he was ordered back to Locust Spring. However, he did ride from Pleasant Valley to the fields of Antietam to see the presidential review in early October.

After the war, Oliver was chairman of the Massachusetts Committee on Education, and twice represented his area in the state legislature.

The young physician kept a journal of his experiences while on duty at the Locust Spring Hospital. The record was copied by Fred W. Cross and through the kindness of Thomas Kendrick, a grandson of Dr. Oliver's, is presented for you to read.[15]

Ordered Elsewhere

Oct. 11

This morning while sitting at my tent, the Col. of my regiment handed me a note which on reading, I found to be a communication from Burnside detailing me to Sharpsburg to assist at the hospital at that place. Tis about 12 miles from here. Regret to leave these pleasant quarters, but know that I shall be happier when I can be of service to my fellow beings. Duty always before pleasure, and acting on that motto I shall soon be on my way.

Locust Spring Hospital

At four o'clock p.m. Well, here I am. Enjoyed the ride over very much. There are many pleasant hours here in spite of the hardships which must come. I sometimes think that friends at home fear our hardships are more than they really are. I ask no sympathy from anyone as long as I have my health.

(Severe Cases)

Oct. 12

The Surgeon has placed me in charge of sixty patients. All the cases are severe ones, they being those who were so sick and badly wounded as not to be able to be removed with our troops after the battle of Sharpsburg. As I examined the patients I came to the conclusion that half of them would die.

Day Is Done

It is terrible to see them growing daily weaker, then when nature gives out to see them die. Ah, they pass to a state of existence where there is no more suffering of a physical nature, where there are no more soldiers' graves, no groans of terrible import. The conflict for them is over. They have performed their duty and gone home. Will the country ever appreciate the sacrifice they have made for it! Home, friends, ambitions, hopes, and aspirations—everything has been freely laid aside to respond to the call for action and battle.

And now many a noble fellow feels that he must die. Their last thoughts will be of home, of dear ones who cannot be with them in their last hours. O God, bless and comfort the soldiers.

A Hospital Service

It is Sunday. We all collected together today, sung several hymns, a man then offered prayer and read to us from the Bible. The spirit of devotion is too often dormant within me; but today my soul bowed in deepest reverence before the throne of the Eternal—and earnest heartfelt prayer ascended to the gates Heaven, and I trust, found acceptance there. After the prayer (which was a real hell-fire one) we sung "Happy Day" and "Old Hundred." Would like to go to a New England Church service today, but as I cannot, must content myself with thinking of it.

Have attended to all my patients as usual. One case worries me. He is suffering from a shell wound. A piece of the shell remains in his leg which I have not as yet succeeded in finding. Surgeons have endeavored to find it but could not do so. Shall chloroform him soon and have it out if possible.

Amputations Performed

Oct. 21

This morning assisted the Chief Surgeon of the 2nd Ward perform some amputations. In the P.M. went to ride. Wish I had more of the system about me. Only write when the Spirit moves.

Dr. Bowditch Comes

Oct. 23

This has been a mighty cool day for our sick soldiers—cool of course for all, but the sick soldiers feel changes in weather more readily than those in health. Dr. Bowditch of Boston came out to see us last night. It is a great pleasure to see familiar faces from the North, particularly when we can look upon a few like his, and know that he is a noble and interested friend to us. He went through every ward with me and showed deep interest in all the cases, is keenly alive to the good of the country and especially for the relief of the sick. He would gladly have everything conducted with credit and is trying to see that the soldiers are better cared for than they have yet been. Someone has a mighty work to do in that line.

This hospital has been established now more than five weeks, and all we have received has been through the Sanitary Societies. May God's blessing rest upon these whose untiring efforts have supplied these stores. Those societies have saved the life of many a soldier. The stores sent by kind hearted ones at the North may be given to their own friends in the hospital.

With Dr. Bowditch

Oct. 24

I've spent most of this day with my friend Dr. Bowditch. He is a professor in Harvard, has charge of the chemical (clinical) department of that College and is considered one of the best, if not the best, physician in the country of diseases of thorax. I have, ever since I first knew him, found him to be my beau-ideal of a man and a physician; he has a heart as well as a head, sympathizes with the poor, and treats them with greatest kindness.

Physicians see so much of suffering, are so constantly hearing the groans of the sick that they often become hardened to it, and are apparently indifferent to the feelings of those they come in contact with, but this man is an exception. He is firm but always kind.

Yesterday we visited the battleground. He wished first to see where our forces were drawn in line of battle; where the reserves were stationed, etc. Then I took him to the left where Burnside's forces had been stationed; of this portion I could give him a more detailed account, as it was the part where I was during the battle. Pointed out to him where we lay, and were shelled by the Rebels; where our advance was moved down to the bridge; where the brave New York Zouaves made their splendid charge; where we had our hospitals. The Dr. shuddered as he thought how our men must have suffered as they lay there in the ditches, and on the ground all night bleeding and suffering dreadfully from their wounds. There are many mounds on the battle-ground showing where our men are buried, and as the Dr. looked at them, tears filled his eyes, and he would say "Poor fellows." Pictured to him as well as I could the terrific grandeur of the scene, when the cannon opened their deafening, thundering roar, and the hissing of the shells as they flew about our heads. Ah! what a sight for human eyes, to see their country men falling thick and fast around them, and to know that a brother's hands may be dealing death to a brother.

On our way back to the Hospital we passed a church which was completely riddled with shot; also passed through hospital at Sharpsburg. Everything there was comfortable.

An Early Snow Storm
Nov. 7

We are having a New England storm; ground is covered with snow, which continues to fall. Wish we were far enough south to escape snow storms, for it makes the sick men shiver in their tents, although they are as comfortable as they can be. I have two nurses for every five patients; each nurse is on duty twelve hours; if they are not neat and kind, we send them back to their Regt., and others take their places. There is no need after the first two or three days of a battle of a soldier's suffering for want of attention; our army is full of lazy surgeons who won't work at any rate; one to do his duty faithfully is obliged to be on his feet from morning till night. Gracious heavens! Cannot a man who is not wounded by cruel shot and shell work willingly for one who is suffering from the effects of those horrid, death dealing missiles?

155

Time Goes Slowly—Howlers Come

Nov. 9

A rough, cold day. Sunday.

Time drags some days for the same routine of duty has to be gone through with each day. At the same time news of the onward march of our forces makes me impatient to be with my Regiment. Am much more comfortable where I am at present, but notwithstanding all the hardships of camp life, I would rather be with them than shut up (as it were) and far away from them.

We have been visited today by a band of singers, alias (Howlers) who promenaded up and down between the tents. What in the name of common sense can lead them to think their singing is good and pleasant for others to listen to is more than I can imagine. Such howling and screaming. Oh heavens! I won't think of it.

Letters From Home

Nov. 21

This evening as I sat here in my little office feeling quite lonely a whole pile of letters was brought me from my Reg. Among them letters from New York. Have had a glorious evening's treat in reading them all. To me it seemed like a social gathering of friends; purely and thoroughly did I enjoy it. The writer of each letter seemed to be with me as I read the sentences they had written, and I recall the expressions of their faces as I used to see them. Shall go to bed tonight feeling very happy. What a blessing the power of expressing our thoughts on paper is, and what a comfort to tired, weary ones far from home and loved ones to receive such messages as those I have been reading. Thanks to my friends who wrote them. May they be as highly favored when they are absent from their homes.

Thanksgiving Evening

Nov. 29

Last Thanksgiving evening I took my pen and wrote the above two words when the other Dr. came in and urged me to go to singing school with him, so I gave up to his entreaties and went; don't know what I go for, for it is perfect misery, still tis lots of fun to hear them.

We had a good and pleasant dinner on Thanksgiving day, but I wanted the pleasant love like faces of home to make it seem natural. My father's kind voice, my mother's cheerful face, and the sure bright eyes of my dear sisters were all wanting—they would have removed all heaviness from my heart, and made it in every sense Thanksgiving fay [sic].

We have a professed cook here, and it is supposed, our meals are served in New York style.

This has been a stormy day. Nothing of importance has transpired. My Southern patients are groaning half the time.

Visiting the Sick Helps

Nov. 30

A beautiful day, clear and cloudless. Have been sick and do not yet feel strong, but am well enough to attend to my patients which is a pleasure as well as a duty. When I feel very tired I go to one of my tents and sit for awhile with a wounded or sick man, have a social chat with them and feel all the better.

Discharges

Dec. 5

We have sent off fifty patients today, and two of the Surgeons have been released and permitted to join their Regts. again. I for once am one of the lucky ones. Some of my patients said they went away reluctantly. I have become much attached to many of them.

A Cold Day

Dec. 6

Has been an outrageous cold day, really seems like Dec. in Mass., the snow lays in drifts. I supposed we had left most of the cold weather with friends North, but as if we needed something to remind us of them they have sent it down here to us. Have just received a long letter from Rosella; she writes she is well and contented.

A Visit to Boonsboro

Dec. 7

Have been this P.M. to visit a patient at Boonsboro. The cold was intense with a high wind. Citizens here say that cold weather seldom reaches them before January. Am reading Victor Hugo's work "Les Miserables."

Another Battle (Fredericksburg) Poor Leadership

Dec. 17

This is a sober night; another great battle and no good results. What have we to show for it? Ten thousand slaughtered human beings! We have men directing our army that are wholly incapable of grasping the magnitude of their positions. We have shown ourselves a weak minded, giddy headed race. . . . As a military people we are a mere cipher, as stupid as a mule. We have not displayed the first act of military strategy since the war began. Shall probably leave this Hospital in a day or two to join my Regt. Shall pass through Washington enroute for camp; wonder if I shall meet any of its fools.

The Locust Spring Cemetery

Dec. 20

Have been raising a monument in a little burying ground for the dead, it is made of wood and painted white; on the front side is the inscription, "Sacred to the Memory of the Union Soldiers who lost their lives in defense of their country at the Battle of Antietam." On

157

the other side is the following—"Erected by the attendants at Locust Spring Hospital." The spot has been surrounded by a substantial stone wall; at the head of each grave there is a small board painted white and as far as could be ascertained, the name of each soldier lying beneath, together with the No. of Regmt. to which he belonged is written upon it. There is a larger cannon weighing 1685 pounds within the enclosure. She did her duty nobly, as did the soldiers, and her resting place may well be near them. A small piece of the muzzle is broken off. There is one thing about this little burial place that causes me to feel very sad; there are eight graves we were obliged to mark "Unknown." In future days, a mother, father, sister may see them and say—recorded the name. . . . Oh, how many hearts are bleeding with anguish for the loss of brave ones fallen in battle; and they must live on for years in sadness caused by this unholy war, by this strife between parts of this once great nation. I never look on these graves but I think of the mothers at home.

Dr. Oliver Evaluates His Experience

Dec. 21

A beautiful day has just past, cool enough for comfort. Snow has fallen twice, but melted as fast as it came. Have been sick for nearly a week, but am now nearly well again, and shall be on my way to my Regmt. very soon. To sum up the past ten weeks that I have spent here, I find they have been weeks of profit and interest to me; have not only learned many things useful in my profession, but much of human nature. I have seen what I never would have believed had it not come under my own observation. I refer to persons who have come here from the North to take care of their own sons; of all the number, I have never seen a single case where they have offered either by word or act to assist in caring for any of the others—even when their sons did not require half their time, and if we would not take part of that which belonged to the other and give it to them, they were offended. Oh, selfishness beyond degree!

Christmas Preparations

Dec. 24

Have been busy today in foraging for a Christmas dinner for the patients (in number now about fifty). Procured fourteen chickens, of which I shall have a "stew." This with onions prepared with salt and butter will constitute the first course. Have 26 qts. of milk, of which to make pudding which will make the second course. Apples, the third. Hope they will enjoy it.

Frederick City, Md.

Dec. 27

Well, here I am in a pleasant inland city of considerable importance, just now on account of the several hospitals located here;

158

there are over 4,000 wounded and sick ones here. Have met several of my old patients since I came to the city; it seemed like meeting old friends; am also well pleased to learn that all of them are getting along nicely.

Thus ends Dr. Oliver's account of his service at the Locust Spring Hospital.

Dr. James Oliver repeatedly told Fred Cross, "If you ever go to Sharpsburg, you must visit my old hospital site at Locust Spring."

In 1919 Mr. Cross was standing on the porch of the Nicodemus Hotel when John Nail said, "You ought not leave this section without going over to Red Hill and getting the wonderful view of the battlefield from the summit."

On Thursday, September 18, George Snavely took Mr. and Mrs. Cross and their two daughters to the summit of Red Hill. Before them stretched the entire battlefield. Mr. Cross found it a place where he "would like to muse and linger."

As he looked out over the Valley of the Antietam, Cross realized that the site of Dr. Oliver's hospital must be very near. In answer to his inquiry, George Snavely replied, "Yes, I know the place very well. It's the Geeting farm. I'll take you there on the way back." Twenty minutes later, the Cross family was at the Locust Spring, "and quaffed the waters of that sacred spring." He said he even sensed the presence of Dr. Oliver.

A little white shed stood on the farm. It is said that this building was used as the hospital morgue.

Writing in 1924, Mr. Cross said:

> The Locust Spring is one of my sacred spots. It always seems as though the spirits of the dear old Doctor and of the brave boys he cared for come to welcome me ... and as I drink from the spring's clear waters I always find myself repeating the words of assurance in the grand old creed,
>
> "I believe in the communion of saints, the forgiveness of sins, the resurrection of the body, and the Life Everlasting."[16]

At least three times in his manuscript, Mr. Cross tells of experiencing the presence of Dr. Oliver at the Locust Spring on Geeting farm.

One of the "almost but not quite" of Antietam involved

159

the famed Ninth New York Volunteers, better known as the Hawkins Zouaves. This combat unit, named after their thirty-year-old colonel, Rush Hawkins, made the greatest dent in the Confederate right, reaching the high ground near the Harpers Ferry Road at the point now marked by the Ninth New York Monument.

The Ninth "almost" broke Lee's lines, chasing some of the Confederate defenders into the streets of Sharpsburg. But in the Ninth Corps' advance, the 89th and 103rd New York were unable to keep pace with the Zouaves. Thus a gap developed between the flanks, and into this gap stormed A. P. Hill.

Had the Ninth been supported and the Brigade in line, the story of Antietam may have been far different. Just like Richardson at Bloody Lane, the Ninth New York had victory in sight, almost in hand, but not quite.

The Ninth was led that September day by Colonel Kimball, and paid a heavy toll in its gallant advance from Burnside Bridge to the Harpers Ferry Road. The color company was just about wiped out. Twenty-two-year-old Captain Adolph Libaire won the Medal of Honor for his courage in rescuing the flag in the fields which are now threatened by a housing development.

As the men of the Ninth fell victim to Confederate fire, they were taken back to the Rohrback farm and examined by Dr. Humphreys, a man loved by the entire unit. If they could possibly be moved, the men were then taken to the Jacob Miller farm and safer quarters. Lt. Matthew Graham of Company A was one of the men examined at Rohrback's, and then moved to Miller's where his leg was amputated.[17]

Soon after the battle, the regiment moved to Antietam Furnace and to the iron works where they camped for several weeks. One day Colonel Kimball assembled the men and they all went to the Locust Spring Hospital to visit their wounded comrades.

In the early part of October tents were erected at . . . Locust Spring and a division hospital established there. The wounded from Miller's house and grounds were transferred to the new location. [Despite] the distance between the regiment and this hospital the

160

men still continued to get passes from camp and take the long tramp to visit their suffering comrades. None of the boys had anything to bring, and had no way of procuring anything that would add to the comfort of the patients. All they had to offer was sympathy and cheering words.

Lieutenant-Colonel Kimball marched the regimental band all the way from camp one Sunday to play for the sick boys. They gave their best selections of marching tunes and other music and devoted several hours to alternately playing and visiting from bed to bed, or to be more correct, from man to man, as there were no beds, all the men lying on the ground or on such makeshift protection from direct contact with mother earth as the soldier nurses could improvise out of the materials within reach.

Lieutenant-Colonel Kimball and several commissioned officers, together with a number of enlisted men accompanied the band on this occasion. Their presence had a good effect on the wounded boys, who kept them busy answering questions about the regiment. The regiment appeared to be uppermost in the thoughts of each of them. They wanted to know how it looked on parade; what number of men were present for duty; what kind of a camp they had; what Burnside and the other generals had said in their reports in relation to the charge of the regiment in the battle and a hundred similar questions. It was always the regiment; its welfare, its *esprit de corps* and its standing and reputation in the corps and in the army.[18]

This must have been about the first Sunday in October 1862. For just about this time, Surgeon Humphreys was ordered to assume the post of division surgeon. The men of the Ninth were glad for his advancement. Yet they hated to see him go. Each man in the Ninth had "the utmost confidence in his skill, . . . and the wounded had perfect faith in his ability to 'pull them through.' " Therefore, the move caused much uneasiness in the ranks of the Ninth New York. However, in time, they came to love his successor, Dr. Squires of the Eighty-ninth New York.

Hospitals

Dr. Theodore Dimon, acting surgeon of the Second Maryland, has also left behind some memories of Antietam. Born in Fairfield, Connecticut, on September 19, 1816, he was the youngest member of the Yale class of 1835. Next came the Medical School of the University of Pennsylvania. Graduating in 1838, Dimon opened practice in Berkshire County, Massachusetts, and then moved to Utica, New York. After a short

161

stay, he became resident physician of the state prison located in Auburn, New York. The California Gold Rush lured the good doctor from the office to a three-year period in the goldfields.

In 1861 Ted Dimon was forty-five years old. But when war broke out he volunteered his services, and became surgeon of the Nineteenth New York. He transferred to the Second Maryland, a unit which he loved very much. Although he was mustered out of the army shortly before Gettysburg, he had much to do with the establishment of the National Cemetery in that Pennsylvania city. Visiting the battlefield shortly after hostilities ceased, Dr. Dimon was appalled at the manner in which the soldiers had been, and were being buried. He took some other officers and approached Governors Curtin and Seymour of Pennsylvania and New York and urged them to create a soldiers' cemetery at Gettysburg.

Dr. Dimon's journal became the possession of George H. Dimon of Branchville, New Jersey, and Mrs. Ernest Flemming of Utica, New York.

When he rode down South Mountain toward Keedysville on September 15, 1862, Dr. Dimon was very hungry. He sent his Negro helper to obtain food. However, the lad had no luck. Then the doctor found a woman baking bread in a brick oven. He "bought a loaf of splendid bread and a pound of glorious butter," and wrapped it in a cabbage leaf and rode away.[19]

The logistics of the Army of the Potomac left much to be desired. The Second Maryland came to Antietam with few blankets, and little or no protection from the rain. It apparently lacked good food, too. On the morning of September 16, Captain Wilson found two stray bullocks. He killed them and shared the meat with the Sixth New Hampshire. The men grabbed every stick and rail fence they could find to roast or cook their meat. This was one time the men had beef for breakfast.

The Second Maryland was a part of the Ninth Corps and was ordered to a position near the Lower Bridge. Near dusk, Dr. Dimon found two large strawstacks, surrounded by fences to keep the cattle away. After a supper of hardtack and whiskey, he made his bed for the night. Col. Bob Potter of the Fifty-first New York shared the warmth and cover of the strawstack.

Cannon fire from the heights above the bridge unnerved the cooks on the morning of the seventeenth. Dr. Dimon and his friends laughed at the men as they in their anxiety kept upsetting and spilling things.

By midmorning the doctor became restless. He rode forward to see what was going on.

The Second Maryland was sheltered in a protective hollow. Colonel Duryea rode off to see General Sturgis. He came back with his shirt collar buttoned, a sign he was ready for action. Sturgis had asked him, "Do you want to win your star?" Naturally the answer was, "Yes."

To win his general's star, all Duryea had to do was take the bridge on the other side of the hill. The price was high.

Two hundred to three hundred yards ahead was the bridge soon to be known as "Burnside Bridge." Dr. Dimon realized there would be huge losses resulting from an attack on the stone span over the Antietam. With his trained eyes he started looking for a first-aid station.

What he found was not ideal, but it would have to do. Dr. Dimon located a barn built of round poles and covered with thatch. He immediately got some idle soldiers to spread straw on the ground, and erect barricades for protection from cannon fire.

With the attack of the Second Maryland and Sixth New Hampshire on the bridge, the barn was soon full of wounded men. A small door placed on two barrels served as a hastily constructed operating table. In the midst of an operation, fragments of a shell came through the thatch roof and fell harmlessly to the straw and blood at Dr. Dimon's feet. The wounded Union captain survived this operation and the trip to the General Hospital in Frederick. But there he died, still fifty miles from home. From 11:00 until 2:00 P.M. the doctor was very busy. Then there was a lull.

The writer feels that Dr. Dimon was located on the H. R. Rohrback farm. However, this may be wrong. At any rate, the physician rode up the lane and found what was left of the

163

Second Maryland. His good friend, Captain Wilson, was dead. He would not eat any more beef. A cannon shot hit him in the forehead and carried away the top of his head. Four hundred men had stormed the bridge; 150 fell dead or wounded.

Dr. Dimon's improvised hospital was within Confederate artillery range. Orders came to move the wounded to the rear. Ambulances were brought up and many of the wounded moved to the Big Spring or Geeting Hospital.

Once the area was cleared, Dr. Dimon rode to Big Spring. He found everything under control there, but was told a large number of wounded were at a place farther on with no doctor. The surgeon of the Second Maryland says this was Millards. He must have meant Miller's. George Miller's home on Red Hill was used as a hospital. However, Dimon must have been at J. F. Miller's.

He speaks of two houses and a barn joining the main house. He also calls his place of work "The Red House Hospital." J. F. Miller lived in a large red-brick house east of Burnside Bridge, and just off the Churchey Road. The smaller house on the opposite side of the road, Dimon used for his own quarters. The family volunteered to cook for the doctor and his patients. Many of the wounded were from the Thirty-fifth Massachusetts, a relatively new unit in the army.

Dr. Dimon obtained a lantern and made his rounds until midnight. Then he crawled gratefully into a "regular bed."

Having great difficulty in getting supplies from Keedysville, the doctor went looking himself on the morning of the eighteenth. He got two kegs of whiskey, and rode to discuss conditions with Dr. Church, the medical director of the right wing of the Army of the Potomac.

Returning to the Miller house, he rode over Burnside Bridge. This again points out the fact that it must have been J. F. Miller's rather than George Miller's on Red Hill. Near the bridge he gave one keg of whiskey to his comrades in the Second Maryland. While visiting with these men, he found a soldier from Ohio who had laid on the field all night. His leg had been broken by a minie ball.

Near the bridge Dr. Dimon met and saluted General Burn-

Another view of Jacob Miller's house.

side. The commander of the Ninth Army Corps looked sadly at the heaps of dead men near the bridge. Fighting was expected to resume and no men could be spared for burial details.

Back at Miller's, Dimon counted 147 wounded in his care. He lost his temper with some of the army cooks and helpers. They had looted the medicine chest and were drinking the whiskey saved for the wounded. The doctor decided to put an end to such practices. The men, caught in the act, were taken out to the orchard and strung up in the apple trees by their thumbs, toes barely touching the ground.

During the next few days, Dr. Dimon removed many fingers and toes from his patients. He had eleven major operations at Miller's, amputating arms and legs. Three men died at J. F. Miller's, two who had been shot through the lungs, and another soldier from the Second Maryland. The poor fellow developed tetanus the day after the removal of his arm.

The Sanitary Commission made a detailed report of the Antietam hospitals. We can almost picture the doctors and nurses working by the light of "dim and flaring lamps" to bring help to those who had fallen. A summary of the main hospitals is presented with the hope the reader will do more research into the matter.[20]

The Smoketown Hospital was located on the road from Hagerstown to Keedysville by way of the Upper Bridge. Near the Smoketown Road intersection, a large hospital was established with Dr. Vanderkieft in charge. Most of the patients were boys from Pennsylvania, members of Hooker's First Corps.

Those in charge had a shortage of towels and bread. The men were pleased with their medical treatment, but daily clamored for fresh bread. A Dr. Harris of the Sanitary Commission sent six barrels of flour which helped.

The Smoketown Hospital was strictly a field hospital in tents. Yet it was a model of its kind. The sanitary inspector felt it was the most successful hospital. Eleven men lost their legs at the thigh in surgery at Smoketown.

Nearby on the north side of the road was a branch of the Smoketown Hospital containing sixty-seven patients from Williams's Division of the Twelfth Corps. This hospital was located in a dry grove of trees.

Proceeding toward Keedysville, on the right-hand side of the road was the Hoffman Hospital. All patients were from Sumner's Second Corps. Dr. Doughtery, corps medical director, was here to supervise and coordinate activities at the adjoining Neikirk and Kennedy hospitals. Dr. Hayward was chief of the hospital. Eight hundred and twenty-five men were here at one time. The only thing lacking was surgical appliances. The location was described as excellent. The wounded were doing well at the time of hospital inspection, and operations were remarkably successful.

One-fourth of a mile southwest of the Hoffman farm was the White House or Dr. King's Hospital. Dr. Donnelly and four assistants treated 1,052 wounded men. This hospital was evacuated as soon as there were tents and room at other field hospitals.

North of and adjoining the Joseph Poffenberger farm was the Middlekauf farm. Three hundred were treated here. Some feel this was the site of Clara Barton's work. However, the Sanitary Commission reports, "This hospital was shelled and evacuated early on Wednesday, and filled on Wednesday evening."

A widow Snyder lived east of the Hoffman farm. Forty members of the 107th Pennsylvania Reserves were treated by Dr. Hutchinson on her premises. The hospital was closed on September 29, 1862.

At Samuel Pry's Mill, 225 from the First and Second corps were treated. Dr. Wilcox was one of the physicians. This hospital received a poor report from the inspector. He said: "Surgeons are young and often under stimulation. Management bad."

At another hospital west of the Antietam and one-fourth mile south of Pry's Mill, 1,396 men were treated. These men were from French's Division of the Second Corps. Dr. Grant, medical director of the division, was in charge. There was no shelter, and little by way of blankets and hospital clothing. The location was poor, too.

The wounded of Richardson's Division were treated on the Kennedy and Neikirk farms, about a mile to the rear of Bloody Lane where most of the men were hit. Some were also in a hospital at Army Headquarters on the Philip Pry farm. Fifteen hundred men were given medical attention on these three farms near the Antietam Creek. The surgeons were overworked. Supplies, as can be expected, were fine at Army Headquarters, but there was a great need at the Kennedy and Neikirk farms.

The Big Spring Hospital with its three branches was located on the "road under the mountain from Keedysville to Porterstown." Here the worst cases of the Ninth Corps were treated. At first Dr. Cutter was in charge. Many of the 670 patients lacked hospital clothing, covering, and bedding. The organization was listed as "faulty and patients unhappy." See Dr. Oliver's accounts.

Samuel Poffenberger's stone house (now on Mansfield Drive), served as a hospital for 215 men of Hooker's Corps. Dr. Chaddock and Young administered treatment, assisted by a captured Confederate physician. This hospital received a fine report, "Faithfully managed, every patient properly and kindly treated. Success good. No ambulances. Dr. Chaddock has been overworked; has had but one assistant except a Confederate Surgeon, who has taken care of his patients very faithfully." As was true in several other cases, the hospital was named after the chief doctor, and sometimes referred to as "Dr. Chaddock's Hospital."

Adjoining Sam Poffenberger's farm was the Michael Miller or "Dr. Taylor's Hospital." It was also called "The Brick House Hospital." Two hundred and twenty-five of Franklin's troops were treated here. It was "Well managed and officers full of resources. Surgery excellent."

Dr. Warner's Hospital was actually the Sherrick and Otto farms south of Sharpsburg on the road to Burnside Bridge. One hundred and four men were treated on these farms, mostly from Harland's Brigade of the Ninth Corps. Many were severe cases.

Other Ninth Corps hospitals were located on the Porterstown Road at the Thomas and Miller farms. They were also known as Dr. Storr's and Dr. Humphreys's hospitals. Five hundred men were treated on these two farms.

In Sharpsburg, Dr. Miller was in charge of the 450 patients located in the three churches and two large dwellings on Main Street.

The Sanitary Commission listed 1,325 Confederate wounded as being in Union care. Most of them were located at David Smith's near the present Antietam train station, Stephen Grove's at Mount Airy, Widow Grove's and in other homes on both sides of the road leading from Sharpsburg to Shepherdstown.

Many buildings in Keedysville were used as hospitals. One hundred and ten men were housed in the Brick Store; 200 men from Gibbon's Brigade, mostly Wisconsin men in a barn; 125 were treated in the Old Mill; 40 in the old Brown House; 50 in the old Stone School House; 160 at C. Keedy's; and several hundred others scattered over the community. Counting those who came and went, 1,000 to 1,400 Union soldiers were treated in Keedysville. The "Hospitals have exhibited want of organization and thorough discipline. Patients have

168

suffered from lack of fresh air, cleanliness, and regularity of treatment."

Immediately after the battle, a great many relatives came to the Valley of the Antietam looking for their loved ones. Many insisted on moving their friends home. However, rest and quietness were greatly needed. Dr. Letterman and other Union doctors had a terrible time trying to convince the well-meaning relatives of this fact. Their minds had one main thought, "Let's get our friends home as quickly as possible."[21]

Dr. Letterman moved the wounded from Antietam as quickly as possible. Always, their well-being was uppermost in his mind. The wounded were not shipped out until he felt they were ready. After all, the trip to Middletown and Frederick was slow and painful. The ambulances stopped in Middletown and the men were given food, drink, and rest. Spare horses and ambulances had to be ready. There could be no breakdowns along the road. The trains had to be ready and waiting in Frederick to take the wounded on to other destinations. The entire business required a great deal of time, patience, and coordination.

Not only did Dr. Letterman have between 8,000 and 10,000 Union soldiers to treat, he also had the Confederate wounded from South Mountain. These were collected and treated in Burkittsville and Middletown.

In October 1957, Miss Catherine Letterman died in Albuquerque, New Mexico. She was the daughter of the man who had taken care of Antietam's wounded by "dim and flaring lamps."

She could be proud of her father. The Army Medical Corps made great strides forward under his leadership. His plans put into effect at Antietam marked a new beginning in the care and treatment of the wounded. During the horrible Civil War, those wounded at Chancellorsville, in the Wilderness, and at Gettysburg were brought from the field under his supervision. Later the German Army adopted his methods.[22]

One of the good things done by McClellan was that of placing Letterman in charge of the wounded. "Little Mac" held Letterman in high esteem. The doctor was his best man.

The government, recognizing Dr. Letterman's contributions, named a general hospital in San Francisco after him.

Yes, when Catherine Letterman died in 1957, she could look back and see the great improvements made in the U.S. Army in the field of treating the wounded. She could take satisfaction in knowing that many of these steps began with her father, a man who worked at Antietam by "dim and flaring lamps."

EVENING DEWS AND DAMPS

Many feel that every person gives off vibrating brain waves. These are just like sending and receiving electrical impulses at the radio stations. We are all sending and receiving vibrations all the time. Some of the vibrations are positive, some are negative.

Some in the psychic field insist that buildings and land also produce positive and negative vibrations. Regardless of the truth of this matter, we often wonder what the forests, fields, homes, and barns of the Keedysville-Sharpsburg area might tell us if they could talk.

When evening comes and shadows fall, and the dew brings dampness to the earth, no doubt these historic spots could tell us of many things, violence and bloodshed, love and valor, journeys of red men and red-coated soldiers, the coming of the Chaplines and early settlers, the preaching of George Adam Geeting, and presidential visits to homes and land made sacred by the bloodshed of thousands of young Americans.

Perhaps the Valley of the Antietam would speak to us of the "Communion of Saints." If we believe that our loved ones are with God, and God is with us, then although we see each other no longer, still we are not far apart. In "The Evening Dews and Damps" the visitor might feel the presence of the great souls who have trodden the fields of Antietam.

Fred Wilder Cross, historian for the state of Massachusetts in the 1920s, was one of whom Antietam spoke in "the evening dews and damps." He always tried to visit the

Geeting farm or the Locust Spring Hospital when he came to the area. Cross said:

> And the spirit of the good Doctor Oliver always seems to stand beside me, and as I drink from the abundant fountain voices come to me with which my own voice joins, and together, the living and those whom the world calls dead, unite in the great words of promise, "I believe in the communion of the saints, the resurrection of the body, and the life everlasting."[1]

Antietam Farms

Philip Pry: Headquarters, Army of the Potomac. Bivouac of part of the Second Corps on September 15 and 16. Field hospital for Second Corps.

Jacob Cost: Scene of last supper for General Mansfield, commanding Union Twelfth Corps. Field hospital with Dr. Wilcox in charge. Headquarters for General Meade, commanding a division in the First Corps.

Hoffman Farm: Large Union hospital. One of the best.

Line Farm: Bivouac of the Twelfth Corps late on the night of the sixteenth. General Mansfield, corps commander, died in the old Line farmhouse.

Joseph Poffenberger Farm: Bivouac of the First Corps on the night of September 16. General Hooker's headquarters. Union artillery placed on ridge.

Middlekauf Farm: Field hospital. Thought by some to be the scene of Clara Barton's work. Yet it was shelled and evacuated on the afternoon of the battle.

The Henry Piper Farm: The key to the Confederate Center. Generals Longstreet and D. H. Hill ate supper in the farmhouse the evening before the battle. Piper family took refuge down along the Potomac River. Seventh Maine charged into the orchard. Longstreet and a group of orderlies and cooks were all that was left to hold the center at one time. Longstreet held the reins of the horses while his staff manned cannon.

The Samuel Mumma Farm: This family gave the ground for the historic Dunkard Church. Occupied by Confederates early in the battle. Later fired so barn and buildings could not be used as hiding places for sharpshooters.

Roulette Farm: Men of the Second Corps trampled through the fields on the way to storm Bloody Lane. Angry bees stung Pennsylvania troops. Barn used to care for men of the 132nd Pennsylvania.

Bishop Russell or Locust Spring: Bivouac of the Ninth Corps on the fifteenth and part of sixteenth. Site of large field hospital for the worst Ninth Corps casualties.

Henry Rohrback Farm: Bivouac of Ninth Corps on night of sixteenth. General Rodman and Colonel Kingsbury of Connecticut died here. Dr. Oliver worked here on September 17.

Otto and Sherrick Farms: Former was scene of Confederate bivouac on the nights of the fifteenth and sixteenth. Later, it along with the Sherrick farm became a hospital for the Ninth Corps.

Stephen Grove Farm: Confederate and Union hospital. General Porter's Headquarters after the battle. Visited by President Lincoln who shook hands with his wounded enemies.

THE PHILIP PRY FARM

Philip Pry moved into his beautiful ten-room brick house in July 1844. From his vantage point, high on a ridge overlooking the Valley of the Antietam, he had an unsurpassed view of the entire area.

His farm was surrounded by history. Several hundred yards away British soldiers, part of Edward Braddock's command, crossed the Antietam at what would become known as the Pry Ford.

Upstream just a little way was the Hitt home, the favorite stopping point of Bishop Francis Asbury as he rode his preaching circuit.

Across the Boonsboro Turnpike toward Red Hill was Bishop Russell's home, and the scene of Indian raids.

The Pry family had worked hard, and lived quietly and peacefully. Then on Sunday, September 14, 1862, that peace was rudely shattered by the booming of the cannon over on South Mountain.

Little did Philip Pry know what was in store for him and

173

his farm. A friend stopped and told him that General George B. McClellan, commander in chief of the Union Army of the Potomac, was eating supper at Mrs. Taylor's in the old Mill House in Keedysville. The general was inquiring about high ground and a place to establish army headquarters.

It wasn't long before a column of blue-clad soldiers were seen heading out of Keedysville, up the hill to the high ridge overlooking the surrounding countryside. A dozen or more of them turned right, and galloped down the Pry lane.

A dashing young officer bounded up on the porch, and said, "General McClellan, the commander in chief of the Army of the Potomac, desires to make his headquarters here."

Mr. Pry thought the young officer said his name was "Custer." It just might have been, because a young cavalry officer from Michigan by the name of George A. Custer was on McClellan's staff.

The Pry farm became a beehive of activity. Flags were unfurled, tents set up, and stakes driven in the front lawn. These would support telescopes to be used by the staff to observe the field of action.

General McClellan was in excellent spirits. He told Mr. Pry that he expected a big engagement and hoped to give, "Bobbie Lee the whipping of his life." He told Mr. Pry not to fear, and promised to give transportation to the rear for Mrs. Pry should the need arise.

On Wednesday, September 17, the bloodiest day of the Civil War occurred. McClellan was up about 4:00 A.M., and from the Pry home, he and his staff watched and plotted the Battle of Antietam.

A Mr. Rohrer was brought from Keedysville to plot smoke from artillery bursts on a large map in the yard.[2] Several times McClellan went up to the attic, stood on a barrel and looked out from a trapdoor between the two chimneys over the field of action. He had an excellent view of the Miller cornfield, the Sunken Road, and the Lower Bridge.

In midmorning General Hooker was brought to the Pry home to have his wounded foot dressed. While being treated, he was approached by a reporter about taking command of the army and leading an all-out assault on the Confederate positions. Hooker refused to do so.

About 2:00 P.M. Brigadier General Israel B. Richardson was brought from the Sunken Road, severely wounded, to receive the best care army headquarters could offer. He was getting ready for a final attack on the Confederate position on the Piper farm when he was hit in the hip by a shell. Many feel that had it not been for his wound, he would have pushed on into the streets of Sharpsburg, thus cutting Lee's army in half. This would have brought a major victory. However, it was not to be. General Richardson remained a patient at the Pry home until November 3, when he died in an upstairs bedroom at the age of forty-seven. A picture of the general still hangs in the room.

Near midnight on the seventeenth, McClellan from Army Headquarters at the Pry farm made the decision not to renew the attack on the eighteenth.

It is hard to imagine the scene at Philip Pry's. Couriers coming and going. Soldiers of the Second Corps bivouacked in the fields for the third night, tents, and horses all over the place.

But even more was in store for the Pry farm. In October, the president of the United States, Abraham Lincoln, came in person to the farm to visit the wounded General Richardson.

Many feel that Lincoln spent the night of October 1, 1862, in a field tent on the Pry farm. The story coming from the Pry family is that Lincoln, being disappointed with McClellan, would not sleep in the house with him. However, the family talks with pride of a note received from the White House bearing Lincoln's signature, and conveying thanks to Mrs. Elizabeth Cost Pry for the fine breakfast given to him earlier in October.[3]

The Battle of Antietam just about ruined Philip Pry. He had to wait until November 27, 1865, for his first payment for military damages to his farm. His fields were heavily damaged during their occupancy by the Union Army during September, October, and early November 1862. Most of his livestock, crops, and fruit were also used by the army and by army horses.

175

According to Mr. Pry, General McClellan had promised him that a board of appraisers would be appointed to appraise the value of the property used. Such a board was appointed, but the army moved before the task could be completed.[4]

Philip Pry listed his damages as:

800 bushels of wheat (unthreshed) at	$ 1.40	$1,120.00
5 barrels of Flour	7.00	35.00
720 bushels of Corn	.75	540.00
24 loads of Hay	10.00	240.00
38 bushels of Corn	.75	28.50
2 beef Cattle	22.00	44.00
10 Sheep	8.00	80.00
7 large Hogs	12.00	84.00
15 Shoats	5.00	75.00
25 Pigs	1.00	25.00
75 bushels of potatoes	1.00	75.00
150 bushels of Apples	.25	112.50
Amounting		$2,459.00

"Alleged to have been furnished to the Army of the Potomac by order of Generals Hooker and Sumner." (See Cl. G. 1759/1873 in the National Archives.)

When a claim was submitted, an agent came to investigate. In the claim of Mr. Pry it was Agent Sallade of the Quartermaster Corps. The individual making a claim had to appear before a justice of the peace and under oath state that his claim was true. His loyalty to the Union during wartime was investigated, and character witnesses sought. Philip Pry's loyalty was attested by Jonathan Thomas, Daniel Bovey, and John Cost, the Keedysville postmaster.

Jacob Cost, C. M. Keedy, Samuel Keedy, Alfred N. Cost, Ezra Lantz, F. Wyand, and David Bell testified that they were farmers and neighbors of the Prys. They reported visiting the Pry farm frequently in the fall of 1862, and personally knowing that Philip lost heavily. They all said that General McClellan occupied the house for nearly two weeks in September. The horses of the commanding general's escort cavalry, the horses of the Twelfth and Thirteenth Pennsylvania Cavalry, and the horses of the ambulance corps consumed 900 bushels of wheat in straw. Pry said, "They stayed until the rick was all eaten up."[5]

Burnside's and Hooker's Corps along with cavalry burned all of the Pry fences. This was another large loss. Twenty acres of ripe corn, all ready to be picked, was eaten by the horses. Another claim issued by Pry said that eighty-five acres of the farm was used as pasture by Union horses. He asked ninety cents an acre rent, as well as fifty dollars rent for use of his house as a hospital.

But this was not all. Pry was connected with a lumber business in Keedysville. Fifteen hundred feet of lumber were taken to build Union hospitals. This amounted to $450 which was paid at a later date.

There is a volume of material in the National Archives relating to damage at the Pry farm. These amounts were paid:

1. Claim 77/23 paid on November 27, 1865; Amount, $2,662.50.

2. Claim 95/1030 paid on August 17, 1872; $339.78.

3. Claim G 2695 amounting to $1,241.25 was also paid. However, there was a claim by the government that this was an overpayment. It seems as though this was the fault of a Mr. Keedy who represented himself as a collection agent. Thus Philip Pry had to repay $1,209.38. He states in his testimony that he had great difficulty in collecting the money to repay the overpayment.

William B. Hill of Baltimore was hired to represent the Prys, then an Attorney Rittenhouse. However, the damage to the farm in 1862, waiting for government payments, an overpayment, legal fees, and attempting to get the farm back in shape proved a terrible burden to Mr. Pry. In 1873 he sold the farm and moved to Tennessee.

William T. Hamilton, writing from the U.S. Senate Chamber on February 25, 1874, said of Philip Pry:

> Before the war he was a prosperous man, owning one of the finest farms in the county lying in the vicinity of the battlefield of Antietam. He is now in serious circumstances. I have known him for thirty years, an upright, honest man and good citizen. His loyalty is unquestioned.

At the time Williams published his *History and Biographical Record of Washington County,* Dawson Kefauver owned the Pry farm. Mr. Williams wrote:

> His beautiful home is the house where General McClellan made his headquarters during the battle of Antietam. . . . The farm contains 125 acres and was purchased at a bargain by Mr. Kefauver, who has since been offered a large price for it because of its historical connections. . . .
>
> There has been much talk of the erection of an appropriate monument to General McClellan on the premises of the house where he had his headquarters and it is only fitting that such a memorial should stand there.[6]

Williams wrote in the early 1900s. In 1971 there is still no memorial at the Pry farm to General McClellan or to the Army of the Potomac. There is nothing denoting Lincoln's visit to the wounded General Richardson. A marker stands at the end of the tree-lined lane saying, "The Pry House— General McClellan's headquarters during the battle of Antietam." But that is all.

The author had hoped that this property could be made into a museum depicting all the history of the Valley of the Antietam. There would also be room for camping along the banks of the stream, for a retreat center, and a rustic chapel of peace overlooking the fields of America's bloodiest day. However, the farm was sold on October 29. Soon a housing development will cover the area where McClellan, Hooker, Richardson, Custer, and Lincoln once walked.

Israel B. Richardson, a native of Vermont, was admitted to the United States Military Academy at West Point on July 1, 1835. According to the staff records, 1835-1842, he was found deficient in mathematics and discharged on 2 February 1836. He was readmitted to the Point on 1 July 1836, and placed in the class of 1841. He graduated thirty-eighth in a class of fifty-two members. Richardson was commissioned a brevet second lieutenant and assigned to the Third Infantry.[7]

During the 1840s Richardson served in Florida, Missouri, and Texas. He took part in the Mexican War, winning a citation for gallant and meritorious conduct in the Battle of Chapultepec. After the war, he served as a captain in the Third Infantry.

178

Richardson resigned from the military on September 30, 1855, and took up farming near Pontiac, Michigan. There he remained until war broke out in the spring of 1861. In May of that year he was appointed colonel in command of the Second Michigan Volunteers, and assigned to the defenses of Washington. Promotion was fast. By July he was in command of a brigade, and a year later Richardson wore the two stars of a major general.

He took part in the Battle of First Manassas, and served on the peninsula between the York and James rivers from March to August 1862. On September 14 he led his division up the slopes of South Mountain. On Wednesday the seventeenth he was in front of his division, leading them through the Roulette fields to assault Bloody Lane. Near the Sunken Road, approaching victory, he fell. When he died at the Pry farm on November 3, his body was taken to Pontiac for burial.

THE NICODEMUS FARM

North and west of the Dunkard Church was the Nicodemus farm. On the hills of this farm, Major John Pelham, "Lee's Boy Artillerist," only twenty-four at the time of Antietam, stationed the cannon of the horse artillery on September 16.

In the evening, Pelham was cooking a ration of beef, when Heros Von Borcke, a giant Prussian soldier on "Jeb" Stuart's staff, rode up. Von Borcke loved to eat and was always good at finding food. He opened his knapsack, which was overflowing with goodies given to him by local ladies. The two were eating a delicious meal when a drizzling rain started. This time it was Pelham's turn to share. He invited his German friend to share the comfort of a nearby haystack.

At 3:00 A.M. the roll of drums was heard across the fields of Joe Poffenberger. General Hooker was arousing the men of the First Corps, getting ready for the assault on "Stonewall" Jackson.

When the darkness lifted, the First Corps of the Army of the Potomac was seen advancing toward Sharpsburg. The attack might have been successful had it not been for Pelham

179

and the horse artillery which blasted gaps in the Union advance. Sixteen men in blue went down with one shot.[8]

Colonel Hunt, commander of McClellan's artillery, seeing the havoc being wrought by Pelham ordered a heavy fire to be brought upon the horse artillery. What followed was part of "artillery hell." Many of Pelham's draft horses used to pull the cannon were hit and had to be shot in the head to end their suffering.

However, most of the cannon were withdrawn. Jackson, being greatly impressed with Pelham sent him fifteen additional cannon.

By this time, Hooker had advanced half a mile, and Jackson was in danger. But "the boy artillerist" was not to be denied. Once again he came to the rescue and immediately ordered his nineteen cannon to fire double canister. Throughout the day, when the need was the greatest, Pelham was there with the horse artillery to help repel Union advances. By noon his men and horses were just about worn out from galloping, limbering and unlimbering on the Nicodemus farm and in neighboring fields.[9]

Norwood Penrose Hallowell tells an interesting personal experience at the Nicodemus farm that day. He wrote a little booklet called *Remarks Written for My Children at the Request of Their Mother*. He tells the following story:

> Your Uncle Edward . . . was one of the few men I knew who really seemed to enjoy a fight. He appeared to go into action with grim delight, and to go out of it with something like regret. . . . I shall never forget him on Antietam day, as he dashed by with General N. J. T. Dana's staff, . . . with the light of battle on his countenance. Throughout the same Antietam night he wandered over the field, turning up the faces of dead men as he searched for the brother whom he thought was dead. Holding my shattered left arm, I had walked right through the rebel ranks, whose men were in such confusion and too busy with their onward work to notice or to care for my presence. A shot in the back, whether by chance or design, dropped a Union soldier who preceded me by a few yards. Before long I gained the little farmhouse marked on the maps as the Nicodemus House. The yard was full of wounded men, and the floor of the parlor, where I lay down, was well covered with them. Among others, Captain O. W. Holmes, Jr., walked in, the back of his neck clipped by a bullet. The baggage train had not been up for many a

day, so that I had replenished my wardrobe by appropriations of chance clothing from various sources. It so happened on that day that I wore the light blue trousers and dark blue blouse of a private soldier. When the rebels, a little later, were busy in the yard, paroling some and taking others to the rear, paying marked attention, of course, to officers, I was glad to have taken the precaution to remove my shoulder straps and to conceal them with my sword under a blanket.

The first Confederate to make his appearance put his head through the window and said: "Yankee?" "Yes." "Wounded?" "Yes." "Would you like some water?" A wounded man always wants some water. He off with his canteen, threw it into the room, and then resumed his place in the skirmish line and his work of shooting retreating Yankees. In about fifteen minutes that good-hearted fellow came back to the window all out of breath, saying: "Hurry up there! Hand me my canteen! I am on the double-quick myself now!" Someone twirled the canteen to him, and away he went.

An Irishman in the yard, whose side had been scooped out by a shell, was asked by a rebel whether he could walk. He replied humorously: "Would I be here if I could? I'll just leave it to yourself." And then he died. For a while the farmhouse appeared to be midway between the opposing forces. Shells broke the window panes, and ploughed up the wounded in the yard, but not a shot went through the house.

During some fifteen or twenty minutes only we were within the rebel lines. Late that afternoon ambulances carried us off to Keedysville. Not us alone. I directed someone to bring along many jars of preserves which burdened the tables and the shelves of the little house. My recollection is uncertain as to the time which elapsed before my arm received attention. Sometimes I think it was twenty-four hours. At other times I make it thirty-two hours.

At all events, when they did get at me it was much swollen, and they and I scooped out the maggots from my side and arm which had been generated by the wound. The long delay was all right. Every one was immensely busy, too busy with more urgent cases, until a cavalryman from Philadelphia had looked at me as he passed, and, looking again, had asked my name. "Hallowell," I replied. "Are you from Philadelphia?" "My father is Morris L. Hallowell of that city," I said. "What!" he exclaimed. "Why, I know him!" It was not long before he had several surgeons at me. Among them was Surgeon Thomas Antisell, the Medical Director of the 12th Army Corps. He said there was a chance to save the arm, and asked me whether he should try. I may have told him to take the chance, but I think I told him I did not care. At all events, after etherization I found the arm there, where it now is, a beautiful exhibit of the surgical operation known as exsection. The surgeon handed me three quarters of an inch of bone to keep as a souvenir. I told him to throw it away. When coming out of my stupor I heard someone say, "He will hardly pull through." I did not then care a rap whether I should pull through, and I think they might have buried me alive without protest. It may have been the next day or later when a woman of masculine but not ungainly presence burst into my room, exclaiming, "Who has some brandy?" My flask was at her service. She disappeared, to return in time to sit by my side and to say that her wounded husband, in the adjoining room, was sinking fast when my brandy revived him. The husband was General Francis C. Barlow.

While lying on my cot I was startled to see my brother Ned come wandering in. He looked at me a second, saying, "They told me thee was dead." He then attempted to get up to the top of the house or, it may be, to an attic by a rude set of steps, as I remember them, or perhaps a ladder. He had maintained his search for his brother, albeit his oncoming typhoid fever had unhinged his mind. My loud calls brought attendants, who persuaded him down and cared for him. The next surprise was my blessed father. How in the name of all that is rational his beaming face was then and there permitted to shine upon me I know not. Was he tired out? Not a bit tired. Father never tired when he had something to his fancy to put through. Into a hack Ned and Lieutenant-Colonel Palfrey and I were hustled. Had anyone ever before seen a hack in Keedysville? Ned carried on pretty hard, pulling at the curtains, and starting at uniformed men who he thought were after him for desertion. We were driven to Hagerstown. There father put us into an empty freight car. At this juncture the thought came into his mind that the floor of a freight car would not be a suitable place for him. Through an open door of a house near by he espied a rocking chair. No one was in the room to consent. The train might start at any moment. Promptly he appropriated the chair, and made off with it. His triumph was cut short by a pursuing woman. Her he pacified by a token of good will big enough to put a rocking chair into every room of her house. As the train started, a little contraband boy begged to be taken along. Father yanked him into a dark corner of the car, and off we started on an all-night journey to Philadelphia. Lieutenant-Colonel Palfrey, under pressure of great suffering, begged hard to be put off at the several stations where the train stopped. Altogether it was a great night for father as he sat contented, comfortable, and satisfied in that rocking chair, with three officers and one little contraband under his masterful control. At Philadelphia the contraband disappeared. The others were taken to our home, the House called Beautiful, as Doctor O. W. Holmes has written. Wounded officers of the 20th had been there before. Our home was a hospital, so to speak, whose matron was your Grandmother Hallowell, and whose nurses were your three sister aunts, Anna, Emily, and Susan. Among the officers cared for was Captain George A. Schmitt, then late professor of German at

182

Harvard College. Captain Schmitt had received five wounds, of no great import, at the Bluff. He would lie on his cot in the parlor, patient and sufficiently polite, but somewhat uncommunicative. Evidently something was not just right. He kept the sisters guessing for some days, when at last Anna had an inspiration. She filled a pipe with tobacco, which she handed to him with lighted taper. Schmitt's broad German face beamed with smiles, and thereafter he overflowed with conversation.

In 1868 your mother and I made our wedding trip to Antietam and other places. Of course we hunted up the Nicodemus house, where we found a worthy couple of that name. They proved to be Union people who had fled upon the approach of the battle. . . . I startled the old lady by asking after a little clock which had stood in a certain place on that day. . . .[10]

At the time of the battle, Alexander Davis, or "Uncle Alex" was working as one of the Nicodemus hired hands. In fact, he spent most of his life with the family. When Mr. Nicodemus died, Davis accompanied his widow to Sharpsburg and became the handyman at the Nicodemus Hotel.

Few men knew more about the battlefield than "Uncle Alex." On several occasions he related to Fred Cross how he buried fifteen soldiers from Massachusetts in a little hollow just south of the Nicodemus house. He distinctly remembered burying a Jimmie Hayes. A close check of the records by Mr. Cross revealed that the Nineteenth Massachusetts had fought near the Nicodemus house, and had lost fifteen by death. Among them was James G. Hayes of Company G.[11]

"Uncle Alex" buried other men from Massachusetts near the barn, and of all places, the spring house. One soldier was buried near the front door of the farmhouse. He also filled up an old unused well with shells, guns, cartridge boxes, canteens, and other items from the battle.

THE MUMMA FARM

Jacob Mumma was born in Cumberland County, Pennsylvania. He, like so many who came to the Antietam Creek, was of German ancestry. Moving to Washington County, he purchased the Christian Orndorff farm along with the mill on May 16, 1796. He worked hard and prospered. Soon he bought two adjoining properties. Jacob Mumma died about 1840.

John Mumma was born at Mount Pleasant in 1787. Years later he would purchase the homeplace and the mill from his father. John died about 1836. His brother Samuel was the Mumma owning the historic property in the 1860s.

On September 15, 1862, the Confederates urged the Mumma family to leave before the bullets and shells started to fly the next morning. One gallant young Rebel even offered to assist Lizzie and Allie Mumma over the fence. But the girls were angry over the invasion, and even more distressed over having to leave their nice farmhouse. They spurned the soldier and his offer of help. During the evening the Mummas took refuge at the nearby Hoffman farm. The next day they joined many other Dunkards who sought to escape from the battle by taking shelter at the Manor Church of the Brethren.

On the seventeenth the Mumma farm went up in smoke. Samuel lost just about everything he owned. A rumor spread that the Confederates had salted the spring. This was untrue. Earlier in the week father and son had gone to Hagerstown for salt. It was stored above the spring, and some fell into the water when the heat weakened the bags.

The Mumma farm was between the Union and Confederate lines. An article in the *Hagerstown Herald* tells the plight of the farm:

> Destruction of property. . . . Among the heaviest sufferers in Washington County is Samuel Mumma, Esq., whose house and barn were burned, together with all their contents. They were between the two great armies. We learn that Mr. Mumma lost all of his household furniture, including the wardrobe of his family, and all his grain, hay and farming implements.

Mrs. Virginia Mumma Hildebrand, a granddaughter of Samuel Mumma, Jr., kindly shares a copy of a letter, her grandfather received in 1906 while he served as Sharpsburg's postmaster.

New Bern, N.C.
March 19, 1906

Postmaster
Sharpsburg, Maryland

Dear Sir:

Please be so kind as to give me the correct name of the man who owned or lived in the brick house that was burned at the Battle of Antietam or Battle of Sharpsburg, being called by both names.

I belonged to the 3rd North Carolina Infantry, Colonel William L. Derassette, Ripley's Brigade, D. H. Hill's Division.

This house stood immediately in our front as the battle was being commenced and at times—was in the enemy's lines. General Ripley, to prevent its occupation by sharpshooters, and protect his officers from being picked off, ordered it to be burned. A volunteer call was made as to who would go and do it. Five or six privates from Company A volunteered and I took charge of them, being at that time Sergeant Major of the Regiment. After firing the house we all got back to our lines, myself being the only one hurt. Ripley ordered me to carry orders down to his line to 44th and 48th Georgia Regiments to come up and take a rail fence in their front. He was shot soon after I left him. I carried the orders down to the Georgia troops and being weak from the loss of blood, went off the field by an old church and on to our hospital. Then a woman young and beautiful and black-haired, helped to bandage my arm. Have often wondered if she was any of the family and where they went when caught between the lines of battle.

I wish to write up the particulars of the event truthfully and there are some particulars about the family I would like to have.

On the next campaign, Gettysburg, by the command to which I belonged, we assisted to capture General Milroy at Winchester, Virginia, and I had to lay up for repairs and did not get any further.

My brother, now deceased, said that he saw the old gentleman, or thought he talked with the owner of the house burned, and said that he hoped the next time they fought, they would get out of his cornfields, as he gathered no corn or crops that year.

Hoping to hear from you with a line of particulars, as to where the family went that morning, Wednesday, September 17, 1862, I am,

> Yours respectfully and truly,
> James F. Clark, Late Sergeant Major
> 3rd North Carolina Regiment.

Mrs. Hildebrand said: "Although my grandfather was a Union sympathizer and his family had lost everything at the hands of Sergeant Clark, he was not one to bear a grudge. In

185

fact he was rather pleased to hear the particulars of the burning." His reply was as follows:

Sharpsburg, Md.
March 22, 1906

Mr. James F. Clark
New Bern, N. C.

Dear Sir:

In reply to your letter of March 19th asking for some information concerning the burning of the brick house on September 17, 1862, I will say that the house referred to was owned by my father, Samuel Mumma, Sr.

The house, a large brick colonial one, near the Dunker Church, was burned at the Battle of Antietam.

My father was told that the family had better get away, so we left on Monday afternoon, September 15th, took nothing with us as they were cannonading then, and we were afraid there would be a battle at once. Some clothing was gotten together and the silverware packed in a basket ready to take but in our haste to get away, all was left behind.

Father and mother and the younger children left in the two-horse carry-all (the older children walking as there was a large family) going about four miles, and camped in a large church called the Manor Church, where many others also were congregated.

On Tuesday evening a friend and I came back to the house, thinking to get some clothing, but found that everything of value had been taken. I then started for Sharpsburg and at the ridge on the field above our house, where the line had formed, General D. H. Hill and some other officers had me brought to them, and questioned me as to whether I was a member of that family. They then asked me about the different roads to the Antietam Creek. I gave them a correct statement although I was a Union boy. After we left, my older brother Daniel came back to the house and went to bed. Toward morning some officers knocked at the door and Daniel being young also, was afraid to open the door and jumped out of the back window, left it up, and spent the remainder of the night in an upper room of a stone building that was once used by slaves. The next day he went to Sharpsburg. That morning the house and barn were burned out but we were told that General Richardson's Battery (a Union General) had shelled the house and barn and burned them.

Our family then went to a friend's house until Spring. In the spring of 1863 we rebuilt our house and had just moved in a few weeks before the Army went to Gettysburg.

As they were passing through to Gettysburg an officer approached me and asked if I knew who had burned that house. I told him that I did not. Then he told me that he and eight other men

186

were detailed by General Ripley to burn the house, and that he picked up a chunk of fire from where they had been cooking and put it in an open window onto a bed. He told me the color of the quilt and the shape of the bedstead.

We lost crops, fencing and everything, all amounting to from $8,000.00 to $10,000.00 and were never recompensed as the Government claimed it was damaged by being right in the heart of the battle.

As well as I can remember, the hospital you spoke of must have been at the home of one Harry Reel, southwest of the old Dunker Church. He had a daughter with black hair. She is now dead and the rest of the family have moved west. That was the nearest hospital that I knew of.

As to your burning our house, we know that in doing so, you were carrying out orders.

Enclosed find a few souvenir postals of the battle.

Hoping that these points will help you in your work, I am,

Sincerely,
Samuel Mumma, Postmaster,
Sharpsburg, Md.

No other farm in the Valley of the Antietam suffered as much as that belonging to Mr. Mumma. The crops were trampled, fruit trees in the orchard stripped of all fruit, fences torn down, personal belongings taken from the house, and the barn and home burned. Part of the springhouse was also damaged.

Mr. Mumma submitted a claim of over $10,000. He listed his home at $2,000, barn $1,250, damage to springhouse and hogpen $100, stock taken by the soldiers $460, grain destroyed or stolen $537.25, and five sleigh blankets at $22.00.[12]

Yet the Mumma claim was about the only one refused by the government. They said the primary damage was done by the Confederates, therefore, the Federal government was not responsible.

The states of Vermont and Connecticut bought land from this farm to erect monuments in honor of their soldiers. Hugh and Hattie Spielman bought the farm in 1924. On December 18, 1961, at 12:13 P.M., they deeded this land to the Park Service.

THE HOFFMAN HOSPITAL

The cannon at Antietam were thundering away early on the morning of the seventeenth, when Charles Carleton Coffin, a New York newspaper correspondent, mounted his horse in Hagerstown and galloped off for the battlefield. The people of the Hub City were aroused by the cannonade. They did not know what to make of the situation. Townspeople were hanging out of windows, asking the meaning of the noise. Small groups were talking excitedly in the streets.

Coffin hoped to gain the left flank of the Army of Northern Virginia, and witness the battle from the Confederate side. This would be a great feat of journalism. However, as he reached the area of Tilghmanton, he met farmers who strongly advised him not to go down the pike, saying, "You will run right into the Rebs. The instant they set eyes on you, they'll see that you are a Yank. They'll gobble you up and take you off to Richmond."

A Confederate prison was the last thing Coffin desired. Thus when he came to the road leading to Keedysville by way of the Upper Bridge, he turned left to gain the right flank of the Army of the Potomac. Ammunition trains were coming up the hill from Keedysville, and were being sent down the Smoketown Road to fill the depleted supplies of the First and Twelfth corps.

To escape the congestion on the road, writer Coffin struck out across the fields. He soon arrived at the Hoffman farm which had been designated as a field hospital. Although it was barely 9:00 A.M., the Hoffman farm presented an appalling sight. The wounded were lying in rows, awaiting an examination by the doctor, or a trip to the operating table. Before the end of the day, the Hoffman home, barn, and carriage house would be pressed into use to serve 800 wounded men.

The hospital would be looked upon as one of Antietam's best. According to the report of the Sanitary Commission, "Buildings, water, shelter, and location were excellent." The operations were quite successful.

AN OLD JOURNAL

Among the items left behind on the field of Antietam was a journal started by an enlisted man in Company B, Nineteenth Regiment, Massachusetts Volunteers. The writer's initials were H. R. D. His last name has faded but research shows it was Dunham. The journal was found in the Hoffman barn, and was loaned to the writer by Fred Scheller, the owner of the journal and the Hoffman farm. He writes of some of his experiences in the following manner (the spelling is his):

Tenallytown Md. Sept 5/63
Dear Brother

This is the first chance that I have had to send you a line. Since I saw you, I have been to Bull Run & back with my Regt. We expect to stop here awhile until we get our rations.

Today is Sunday 7 am but how different from our quiet New England Sunday. Nothing around me to remind one that it is God's day of rest. Much would I give if I could only spend one more Sabbath at home. But that cannot be. It may never be again. But I pray God that it may be. God help me so to live that if I never spend an earthly Sabbath at home with friends I love, that I may meet them all where I can spend an Eternal Sabbath with them in Heaven. O God help me to live aright here that I may reign with Christ in Heaven.

Today my Regt. is on Picket duty bout four miles frm Darnestown.

Sept. 9—Received orders to march at 12. . . . Marched about 8 miles toward the interior of Maryland. It was very warm. Most of us removed our knapsacks yesterday and are pretty well used up. I did not fall out. Corp . . . did because of sun stroke & we had to leave him by the side of the road, to come along with the ambulance train. We halted about 5 pm and commenced to get our suppers. Today for the first time in one month we have had an exchange of clothing and we feel like new men. . . . Every thing stolen out of my knapsack while it was aboard the transport.

Saturday Sept. 13th—All was quiet last night. We had reville at 3 am and were on line to march at sunrise. We marched to Frederick City going through the very pleasant little town of Urbana. We arrived at Frederick about noon. The Rebs left there during the night before after destroying the Telegraph Rail Road, Bridge and depot and other places. The people of the City were very glad to see us. The Stars and Stripes were flying from almost every house. It made me think of Boston as one marched along through it. Sum large numbers of Rebel Prisoners here. The Rebs are now in strong force at the town of Hagerstown about 20 miles from the City. Gen. Burnside is after them. Marched about two miles beyond the City and halted for the night. . . . General Orders read to every Regt, in

189

regard to Straggling. Evry man that straggles or flounders is to be shot down on the spot. . . .

Monday Sept. 15th—All was very quiet with us last night. But the Rebs skedaddled & Hookers Division was sent after them at 2 am. And we had continual skirmishing with them all night & all day.

Rollcall at daylight. About 9 am we were starting after the retreating Rebs. We pushed over the Battlefield of Sunday. The Rebs had a very stong position but they were drove from it with heavy loss. Among them Generall Longstreet & General Reno was killed on our side. Do not know the loss on either side. We were sent after them at noon. We pushed through the town of Boonsborough a very pretty little place about three miles from the Battlefield. Think they are most all Union here. Our troops had a skirmish here. Saw many wounded Rebs, left behind. Our company was consistently bringing in prisoners during the day. About 7 p.m we passed through the town of Keedysville. Halted about 9 pm. . . . Our division have had no fighting to do but plenty of hard marching. Our rations for the last five weeks have been nothing but salt pork & hard bread & coffee. Plenty of that. It was very hot marching and many were compelled to drop behind. In our front we heard the constant booming of our cannon playing on the column of retreating Rebs. We have with us one Battery of 20 pds. and 2 Batteries of Flying Artillery. In the afternoon General Mc Clellan rode along through our lines to the front & the welcome that he Received from his ole Army of the Potomac must have done his heart good. God bless General Mc Clellan. Long may he lead and be . . . to our Country. During the forenoon a flag of truce came in from the Rebs asking for bodys of their dead Generals. They were passed into our lines for that purpose.

H. R. Dunham never made it back to Massachusetts for his New England Sabbath. On October 2 he died from his wounds in the Hoffman barn.

Hollowell Dunham was twenty-four at the time of his death. A native of Littleton, Massachusetts, he joined the army on July 26, 1861, and died in Maryland fifteen months later.

Another patient at the Hoffman Hospital was Sergeant Jonathan P. Stowe, Company G, Fifteenth Massachusetts Infantry. He too kept a diary. These are excerpts from his recordings.

September 17, 1862. Battle Oh horrid battle. What sights I have seen. I am wounded! And am afraid shall be again as shells fly past me every few seconds carrying away limbs from the trees. . . . Am in

190

severe pain. How the shells fly. I do sincerely hope shall not be wounded again.

September 18, 1862. Misery acute, painful misery. How I suffered last night. It was the most painful of anything have ever experienced. My leg must be broken for I cannot help myself scarcely any. I remember talking and groaning all night. Many died in calling for help. . . . Sergt Johnson who lies on the other side of the log is calling for water.

Carried off the field at 10 AM by the Rebs who show much kindness but devote much time to plundering the dead bodies of our men. . . . Water very short. We suffer very much.

September 19, 1862. Rained only little. I had a rubber blanket & overcoat. Rebs retreat. Another painful night.

Oh good good a whole line of our skirmishers are coming. . . . There are lots of us here lain out. . . . By and by our boys come along. What lots of the 15th. Captain comes down to get the names and has coffee furnished us—Twas the best cup I ever tasted. Dr. looks at my wound and calls it a doubtful case. Get me on ambulance at 3 PM but do not get to hospital till nearly dark. Plenty of water which gives us a chance to take down the inflamation. Nurses worn out by fatigue. Placed on straw near the barn

[Note sent home] Near Battlefield September 19/62

Friends at home. I am wounded pretty badly. Have lain 48 hours without dressing. Wound in right knee. I hope to save my leg the ball is still in. Expect to be removed as soon as possible. . . .

J. P. Stowe

September 20, 1862. Fearful it will rain. How cheerful the boys appear. Many must loose their arms or legs but they do not murmur. . . . Leg amputated about noon. What sensations—used chloroform hope to have no bad effects. There are some dozen or more stumps near me. Placed in barn beside J. Hughes. . . .

September 21, 1862—Sunday. Very weak and sore. . . . Hot weather by day cool at night. Hard to get nurses. Men come in and stare at us but detailed men clear out & leave us. How pitiously do they beg for water. People come in from all parts of the country. Stare at us but do not find time to do anything.

September 22, 1862—Monday. Two men died last night. . . . How painful my stump is. I did not know was capable of enduring so much pain. How very meager are accommodations—no chamber pots & nobody to find or rig up one. How ludicrous for 2 score amputated men to help themselves with diarrhea.

September 23, 1862—Tuesday. Oh what long fearful horrid nights. What difficulties we have to contend. . . . Relief can hardly be found. I have at length got my limb dressed by volunteer surgeon. But never was so nearly exhausted for want of refreshment.

September 24, 1862—Wednesday. One week today fought and

191

wounded. Such a week. Suffering all around. . . . Showers this AM and all look for the barn.

September 25, 1862—Thursday. Such nights! Why they seem infinetely longer than days. The nervous pains are killing 2 or 3 every night. All sorts of groans & pleadings. . . . Many patients are leaving daily. Some have gone today to H. Ferry. I watch over J. Hughes nightly. Has had fever. Very cold last night & we are very short for clothing. Sundown just Recd Blankets and beds.

September 26, 1862—Friday. Very cold last night. J. Hughes had shakes again last night. . . . This cold weather may all come for best, certainly maggots do not trouble so much and air is some purer.

4PM J. Hughes died

PM more system day by day. . . . O there comes Mrs. Gray with refreshments. Such a treat. . . . I got tomatoes—just what I wanted most. Have since forgotten when my stump first hemorhage—It was very copious and tho I had stoutly affirmed that I would not use Brandy was now plainly told that if not should be dead in 3 days.

September 27, 1862—Saturday. Commence taking brandy none too soon. Dr. tells me I am dangerously ill and must take his prescription in order to change condition of blood.—He is earnest & too good a man. Mr. L. Sloan a kind hearted chaplain telegraphs for me. Suffer continuously from position in bed. Have to elevate my stump to prevent bleeding and be very still. . . .

September 28, 1862—Sunday. Oh what lengths to the nights. The horrid smell from mortifying limbs is nearly as bad as the whole we have to contend. Mrs. Lee and another lady are here daily dispensing cooked broths. . . . They seem to employ their whole time for us. Moved outdoors in PM. Excessively hot.

September 29, 1862—Monday. Slept little more comfortable last night. Got nice soups and nice light biscuit and tart also nice butter from Mrs. Lee. Also she gets me milk again this morning. How the quinine keeps me parched for water and so sleepy and foolish. Am much better off here than in barn. 10 AM my comrade died from 18th Minn Regt. I recd 4 letters from friends at home but am so boozy it takes the whole AM to read them. My Dr. Kelsey dressed my stump admirably and am quite comfortable if the quinine does not choke me to death. It is far more quiet here but begins to rain.

[At 7:54 on the evening of September 29, Stowe had a telegram sent to J. W. Stowe]

"Dangerously wounded at Hoffmans Hospital near Sharpsburg. Come instantly.

J. P. Stowe

The telegram was too late. Thirty-six hours later on October 1, 1862, Sergeant Stowe expired. His wounds in the West Woods, lying for a day without food or water, taken by the Confederates to apparently the Nicodemus farm, then by

192

his comrades to the Hoffman farm, and going forty-eight hours without medical attention were too much for him. Near the end he was, or so it seems, taken from the Hoffman barn into the house where he died. Certainly "war is hell" and foolish.

In 1914 some of the Antietam veterans returned to the Hoffman home. They told stories of hobbling up to the Smoketown Cemetery to visit the graves of their friends. Some of those recovering at the Hoffman home went almost daily. They would pause for a moment in prayer, and then sing over the graves of their fallen comrades.

Many were treated at the Hoffman farm. Some laid under trees on the front lawn for a week. One of those whose hospital bed was straw on the ground, two blankets, and the sky above, was Edward S. Past from a Minnesota regiment. He later became superintendent of a national cemetery. Once again we wonder what the buildings, trees, and soil would say if they could speak in "the evening dews and damps."

Perhaps the Hoffman barn would tell us of the memories of Jacob Lair, a member of the Twentieth New York who lost an arm in the fighting near the Dunkard Church. The Union soldier said that two rows of wounded were placed on the floor of the Hoffman barn. Daily, according to his memory, one or two would be taken out and buried. He never forgot the kindness of Mrs. Hoffman and her friends. They kept Lair and his comrades supplied with a constant flow of fruits, cakes, and pies.

SAMUEL POFFENBERGER'S

Lovely stone houses dot the landscape of the Valley of the Antietam. They are cool in summer and warm in winter. Thick walls serve as insulation, and in earlier days, as protection from possible Indian raids.

Samuel Poffenberger had a lovely home, off the beaten path with plenty of elbow room when war came to his farm in the memorable September.

On September 17, his farm had the misfortune to be in the rear of the Twelfth Corps' advance, and near the spot where General Mansfield was shot.

193

Samuel Poffenberger's house.

Another view of Samuel Poffenberger's house.

194

Like so many others, Sam had been warned by army authorities to take his family to safer quarters. Thus he took his wife to the home of his father-in-law, Samuel Doub, in Keedysville.

Hurrying back to the farm, the young farmer tried to hide his livestock lest it be carried off by the soldiers. His prize horses he took to the basement of the house, and wrapped their feet in grain bags so those upstairs would not hear their hoofs.

The Poffenberger house, like the Big Spring and many others, was erected over a spring of water. In early days this assured the family of getting water in safety in the event of Indian attack, and it also served as a means of refrigeration. Milk and other items were placed in the cold running water for preservation.

Approximately one hundred and twenty-five wounded soldiers were carried to the Samuel Poffenberger farm. Some were in the house, others in the barn, or wherever shelter could be found.

Sam's beds were all cut up to provide bedding for the soldiers. The straw or feather ticks were simply cut open and the contents spread on the floor or ground.

Piles of arms and legs came off the soldiers carried to the Poffenberger home. These bones were buried in the orchard.

One young officer, a Captain Tayne, died from his wounds in Sam and Catherine's bedroom. Following the war, his widow came to the Poffenberger's and stayed awhile. She painted pictures of the house in which her soldier husband died.

Samuel Poffenberger's farm is important for another reason. After a year of intense research, James Atkinson, formerly the historian at the Antietam National Battlefield Site, has strong evidence to prove that this is the farm where Clara Barton served.

There are many reasons for this. Miss Barton said that she served at the end of Hooker's line of artillery. For years everyone thought this meant the Joseph Poffenberger farm. However, apparently no one thought to check the other end of the line. Miss Barton said the artillery was one-eighth of a mile from where she worked. Pettit's battery, according to the Cope maps, was just that distance from the Samuel Poffenberger house.

She also talked of going into the cellar and finding meal, with the chimney of the house resting on an arch. Historian Atkinson was in the cellar of every 1862 home still standing on the battlefield. Sam Poffenberger's is the only one with an arch.

Miss Barton talks about the fence and wicker gate. As late as the 1920s the Poffenberger farm still had a wicker gate. This was shown in a picture taken by Fred Cross, the great historian from Massachusetts.

Sam's home and some of the fields are in the lee of a hill, protected somewhat from view, and artillery fire. He also had a field of tall corn at the time. In fact, he submitted a bill to the government for damages done to his twenty acres of corn. The home also had a large veranda, again described by Miss Barton.

Thus this house, erected in 1805, according to the Kefauvers who live there now, must have been the site of Miss Barton's work. We hope others who read this book will take the time to do the type of research done by James Atkinson to uncover more of Antietam's secrets.

THE COST HOME

This farm, located on the sharp turn just southeast of the Upper Bridge and across from the Pry Mill, had a long history even before the wounded of the Army of the Potomac were brought to the shelter of its buildings.

Years before this farm had belonged to the Hitts. The Upper Bridge is also known as the Hitt Bridge.

The farm was a favorite stopping place of Bishops Asbury and McKendree of the Methodist Church. In fact, Rev. Daniel Hitt was greatly admired by Bishop Asbury. The Reverend Mr. Hitt spent thirty-seven years in the ministry. During two of these years, he was a traveling companion of the bishop, riding to Maine and other New England states.

Heinrich Kost came to the United States on the ship *Richard and Mary,* arriving in Philadelphia on September 30, 1754.

196

His son, Frederick, who was born in 1772, came to Washington County. Frederick's son Samuel was born in 1794.[13]

Samuel Cost married Barbara Keedy who was born in 1806 and died in 1854. She and her husband were very devout members of the Reformed Church in Keedysville.

They had six children. Two of the sisters married into the Pry family. Mary married Samuel Pry, and Elizabeth Cost, the lady who gave breakfast to President Lincoln on October 2, 1862, married Philip Pry.

Samuel Cost farmed on the Hitt farm on the banks of the Antietam Creek for thirty years.

At 9:00 A.M. on September 17, Dr. Wilcox established a hospital on his premises. Over five hundred soldiers were sheltered in his barn and sheds. Twenty-five wounded soldiers were bedded down in the parlor. Twenty-two of those brought to the Cost farm died there and were buried on Samuel's farmland, and later were moved to Sharpsburg.

On October 4, the wounded on the Cost farm were moved to the Smoketown Hospital. For awhile General Meade had his headquarters in the farm house.

The story of Mr. Cost's kindness to the wounded spread throughout the army units nearby.

HENRY NEIKIRK

The original Henry Neikirk was born in Pennsylvania, probably near Reading in 1782. Early in life he came to the Valley of the Antietam. He took his wife Nancy Furry who was born in 1787. Henry selected a virgin tract of land to homestead, numbering 147 acres. He had to work hard to clear it of timber. With his hands he erected the first buildings on the land. No doubt some of the logs were cut at the nearby Orndorff Mill. They had eleven children, one of whom they named Henry F. He was born on March 19, 1820. On February 20, 1845, young Henry married Mary Miller. About the time of his marriage, he took over the family farm. This seems to have been a custom in the valley. This Henry had eight children, one of whom he named Samuel Henry.[14]

Henry almost lost his life just prior to the Battle of Antietam. It seems as though he had hidden eleven horses.

The Grove House, Public Square, Sharpsburg, Md., Antietam Battle-field. Wartime picture of the Grove House in which General Robert E. Lee, C.S.A., held a counsel of war September 17, 1862. The head-quarters of General Robert E. Lee, C.S.A., with the Army of Northern Virginia were to the west of Sharpsburg on the high ground in what was known as the town woods. Shell marks are still visible in the end of this building.

Somehow the Confederates were aware of the horses, and scouts were sent to obtain them. The horses were safely hidden away behind some huge rocks along the Antietam. Mr. Neikirk was not about to tell the Rebels where they were. In an effort to get the truth, the Rebs threatened to burn the Neikirk barn. This failed, and he was marched into the house to get money for the men in gray. Lizzie, his daughter, hid a purse containing several hundred dollars. The Rebs got but a few pieces of silver. Finally, their patience exhausted, the Rebels took Henry Neikirk out and strung him up by a leather halter. Then they rode off. His son George came to his rescue just in time, cutting him down after part of his body had turned black from lack of circulation.[15]

On the morning of the seventeenth, the Union Second Corps marched through Henry Neikirk's fields, and by noon, his barn and other buildings were filled with Union casualties from Bloody Lane.

Today, the Neikirk farm stands serene and quiet. A lane leads down to the Pry ford from which came the sounds of "drums along the Antietam."

The Pry Mill.

Henry Neikirk's farm.

199

On Monday, September 15, Confederate Generals James Longstreet and D. H. Hill took possession of the Henry Piper farmhouse for their headquarters. The Piper daughters were Union sympathizers. Although they were very frightened by the presence of the men in gray, they wanted to be friendly to the officers. Thus they offered them some wine. Longstreet, being the cautious soul that he was, thought the wine might contain poison. So he refused. Hill was more optimistic and accepted. Seeing that Hill suffered no ill effects, Longstreet had a change of heart, and said, "Ladies, I will thank you for some of that wine."

No doubt the wine was some of the Pipers's home brew, coming perhaps from the old cider press built in 1852.

The Pipers had been in the Valley of the Antietam since the 1790s. About that time Jacob Piper bought a lot across from the old Lutheran Church site from Joseph Chapline, the founder of Sharpsburg. In 1792, Jacob bought 105 acres named "Piles Delight" from Joseph, Jr., and Mary Ann Abigal Chapman. This was near the Potomac River.

The Piper farm which formed the Confederate center was bought by Daniel Piper, Sr., in 1845. The original land grant patent called it "Ellwicks Dwelling," and part of "Mount Pleasant." Daniel farmed the ground for five years, or until 1850. At that time his son Henry took over the farm, and Daniel moved to the large stone house in Sharpsburg, opposite the present Lutheran Church.

When Henry's family fled on September 16 to the shelter of Samuel's farm nearer the river, one of the female slaves carried six-month-old Elmer Piper in her apron. The old slave-house occupied by the Summers family stood beside the well.

Summers said that sometimes the men in blue would kill three or four sheep or hogs, whatever they needed at the time. This apparently continued whenever there was a need.

One hundred bushels of Irish potatoes were taken by the hungry soldiers, as well as thirty bushels of sweet potatoes.

Summers also mentioned the wood and grain taken in the summer of 1863 after Gettysburg. Piper amended his bill to include:

1.	One roan mare	$ 250.00
2.	Eight milk cows, at $30	240.00
3.	Two three-year-old steers, at $30	60.00
4.	Ten head young cattle, at $18	180.00
5.	Four calves, at $5	20.00
6.	Eighteen fat hogs, at $10	180.00
7.	Sixteen head of shoats, at $5	80.00
8.	Six pigs, at $2	12.00
9.	Eighteen head of sheep, at $5	90.00
10.	One hundred bushels of Irish potatoes, at $1	100.00
11.	Thirty bushels sweet potatoes, at $2	60.00
		$1,272.00
	July 1863	
12.	7½ cords of wood, at $3.50	$ 26.25
13.	10 acres grass	45.00
14.	15 shocks wheat, at $1.40	21.00
15.	pasturage of cattle and sheep	10.00
		$1,374.25

Philip Pollard, a first lieutenant in the Third Pennsylvania Cavalry, said in court that the supply trains were delayed in coming from Frederick. The roads were full of moving artillery and ammunition. It was therefore customary for the army to capture and use whatever rations could be found. He remembered taking cattle, sheep, and hogs from the Piper farm after the battle. Pollard said the Third Pennsylvania did not take all the animals. He placed some of the blame on the Fourth Pennsylvania and the Eighth New York Cavalry. Pollard gave the order as he was both commissary officer and quartermaster of the regiment at that time.

The soldiers took six barrels of vinegar, eight hundred pounds of bacon, five sacks of salt, four bushels of onions, pickles, one bushel of dried cherries, two hundred bushels of apples, six gallons of cherry wine, and one hundred and ten jars of fruit. They ate two hundred of Piper's chickens, fifteen geese, along with twenty-four turkeys. They took thirty dollars worth of men's clothing, and sixty dollars worth of lady's clothing. One wonders what in the world they did with the latter.

Henry Piper had other problems during the Maryland campaign. His beloved slave Jerry Summers was carried off by the Union Army. Henry had to make a trip to Frederick to gain his release. When Henry Piper died, Jerry Summers was given a cottage for life, along with a garden plot. This was near the Sunken Road.

On November 17, 1886, Henry Piper, at that time seventy-seven years of age, sued the United States Government for damages to his farm during the Battle of Antietam.

On October 6, 1862, Brigadier General Reynolds, later to be killed on the first day at Gettysburg, had appointed Major Briner, Third Pennsylvania Reserves, Captain McPherson of the Fifth Regiment, and Major Snodgrass, of the Ninth Pennsylvania Reserves, to survey and estimate the damages to the farms of Samuel Mumma, William Rulett, and Henry Piper.

This board of three, with Major Snodgrass acting as president, stated that to the best of their knowledge, the clothing and edibles were taken by the Rebels, while the fences, grain, and hay were destroyed primarily by Union forces. Some of the buildings were damaged by shells, but it was felt the Rebels tried to burn some of them.

The board of survey assessed the damage at Henry Piper's as follows:

Damage to house and barn	$ 25.00
Hay and straw	108.00
Stock	666.00
Vegetables and fruits, etc.	157.00
Grain of different kinds	484.00
Bacon, lard and tallow	117.00
Groceries	78.85
2 bee-hives at $10	20.00
Wines and condiments	72.00
Poultry	39.00
Household, kitchen furniture, clothing, etc.	373.00
Lumber, tools	49.00
Damage to fencing	300.00
	$2,488.85 [16]

The board awarded Mr. Piper that amount. However, at the moment, he did not produce any certificate of loyalty.

His roan mare, eight milk cows, sheep, hogs, and calves were taken after he returned from his brother's farm along the Potomac on September 19, 1862. This was brother Samuel's place about three miles away in a great bend of the Potomac.

On the nineteenth when the Pipers returned home, Union forces were encamped in his fields, as was some of the cavalry. The Hagerstown Road was so congested with soldiers that the civilians found it almost impossible to move.

Jeremiah Summers, testifying in Piper's behalf, said he saw Union soldiers butcher four calves in the orchard, and at least sixteen other cattle on the nineteenth.

Mary Ellen Piper Smith, Henry's daughter who was about twenty-one at the time of the battle, recounts her memories of those September days:

> I remember the battle of Antietam. On Monday, prior to the battle, we all went away from our house to my uncle's, Samuel J. Piper, who resided immediately on the Potomac River about three miles west of my father's house. We left everything as it was on the farm, taking only the horses with us and one carriage. We remained until Friday after the battle, when we returned to the farm. On our return the Union forces were encamped upon the farm and in the vicinity, and the Union cavalry were moving along the Hagerstown pike in great numbers toward Sharpsburg. We had some difficulty in passing across the pike to get to our house. We found the house occupied as a field hospital.* We brought back the horses with us, and they were put in the barn. A large number of cattle, sheep and hogs belonging to father still remained on the place. I saw the Union soldiers butchering some of the cattle, when we came back. . . . The Union forces were encamped in the vicinity for several weeks after the battle—at least some portion of them. During this time . . . all the cattle and sheep on the farm were taken and used by U.S. military forces. The sheep were all taken the day after we returned home. The hogs and cattle were slaughtered at different times. I remember four of the calves were slaughtered in the orchard back of the blacksmith shop.[17]

These words were given in testimony in court in 1886 as she shared her story in an effort to aid her father's cause. We can imagine the difficulties encountered by the farm families in the Valley of the Antietam who lost their food supply to the soldiers.

*Mrs. Smith says the Piper farm was used as a field hospital. If so, it must have been small. It may have been used by the Seventh Maine. However, the Sanitary Commission in its report on Antietam Hospitals, says nothing about a hospital on the Piper farm.

In the early 1960s Webster Piper who supplied the bulk of the material about the Piper farm, sold the land to the Antietam-Sharpsburg Museum, Inc. For a while a very fine historical and educational display was housed in a building across from the National Cemetery. Then on June 25, 1964, the farm was sold to the National Park Service.

THE RULETT FARM

One public official, Washington County Commissioner William Rulett (now spelled Roulette) spent the morning of the battle as a prisoner in the cellar of his own house. He was not confined there by the soldiers, but by the storm of battle. Mr. Rulett felt the basement offered the greatest security. Suddenly the cellar door opened. Rulett looked up to see Chaplain H. S. Stevens of the Fourteenth Connecticut. The good chaplain was bringing some wounded from his unit to the security of the farmhouse.[18]

When the firing died down a little, Stevens stuck his head outside to see what was developing. The Confederates had surrounded the farmhouse. The chaplain thought he'd better surrender everybody before the "Johnnies" took it upon themselves to burn the place. The advance guard of the Rebels came within two rods of Mr. Stevens, "when the operations of a battery brought to bear upon the cornfield and of some infantry throwing a flanking fire into the field started those Johnnies on a retrograde movement of the most lively sort."[19]

When the tide turned, farmer Rulett was out in his fields waving the Union forces on, shaking his fist at the retreating Rebels, and imploring the men in blue to "Give it to them."

During the morning the men of the 132nd Pennsylvania fell victim to Rulett's bees, and as soon as the farm was secure, surgeons ordered the barn prepared for the reception of the wounded.

SADNESS AT ROHRBACK'S

On the morning of September 17, the Ninth Corps of the Army of the Potomac numbered 13,819. Before the end of the day 22 officers and 410 men would be dead upon the field of battle. 96

The burning of the Mumma farm.

The Roulette farm.

officers and 1,645 men would be numbered among the wounded, with 120 missing.

Among gallant men of the Ninth Corps engaged in the fighting at Burnside Bridge and on the hills beyond were Brigadier General Isaac Rodman and Colonel Henry W. Kingsbury.

Isaac P. Rodman was born in South Kingston, Rhode Island on August 18, 1822. His father was a manufacturer. The son was trained to take over the business. As a young man and throughout life, Isaac was distinguished by faithfulness to duty, industry, and integrity.

On June 15, 1847, Isaac Rodman took as his bride Miss Sally Arnold. To this union were born five children, none of whom would be above the early teens when their father died in the home of Henry Rohrback along the Antietam Creek in Maryland.

When the Civil War broke out, Rodman gave up the family business to raise troops, and was given a captaincy in the Second Regiment, Rhode Island Volunteers. At First Bull Run he displayed coolness and valor. In October of 1861 Rodman was promoted to the rank of Colonel and given command of the Fourth Rhode Island. Six months later in April he received the single star of a Brigadier General.

Rodman displayed great executive and administrative ability. His troops were well disciplined. Yet he was well liked by his men. Had his career not been cut short at Antietam, he may have risen to great heights.

On the morning of the 17th, Rodman's command, forded the Antietam and marched up a draw to outflank the Rebel defenders.

Augustus Woodbury, Chaplain of the First Rhode Island, and author of *Burnside and the Ninth Corps,* writes of Rodman:

"Shunning no danger, avoiding no duty, he was everywhere fearless and always faithful. . . . He fell in the front with his face to the foe. . . . a minie ball penetrating his left lung, and knocking him from his horse."[20]

The brave Rhode Island General was carried back to the home of Henry Rohrback. His wife Sally came to nurse him and help him through his last hours. He lingered for twelve very painful days, and on the morning of September 30, quietly breathed his last.

Chaplain Woodbury states that not a complaint or murmur escaped his lips, although at times he suffered intense pain from internal bleeding.

He was a brave and true Christian man. His Bible was his daily companion. After he fell, his Bible was found beneath his uniform stained with blood.

What a shame that war always takes the best. Rodman at age 40 gave his "Last full measure of devotion" to his country and the cause of freedom on the hills overlooking the Antietam.

According to O. T. Reilly, one of the first and most distinguished

Brigadier General Isaac P. Rodman. This distinguished young man from Rhode Island was one of the tragedies of Antietam. He was the father of five, and was but one month past forty when shot in the lung on the hills above Burnside Bridge. A fine Christian man, a brave soldier, loved by his command, he may have risen to great heights had it not been for Antietam.

207

Antietam historians, a Mrs. Ada Thomas of Sharpsburg gained possession of the couch upon which General Rodman died. Where it is now, no one seems to know.

The Lower or Rohrback Bridge was referred to as "The jaws of death." Near the Bridge Colonel Henry W. Kingsbury, Commander of the 11th Connecticut fell at the head of his regiment.

Woodbury describes him as: "a most brave and excellent gentleman and soldier, the pride and flower of the Class of 1861 at the Military Academy at West Point."

Kingsbury was a ward of General Burnside. He was also the brother-in-law of General D. R. Jones, the man entrusted by Robert E. Lee to defend the Lower Bridge. Kingsbury's death was a blow to Jones. The Confederate General almost suffered a nervous breakdown, and asked for a leave of absence for health reasons.

Colonel Kingsbury was also taken back to the Rohrback home where he died.

Here in the Henry Rohrback farmhouse, General Rodman and Colonel Kingsbury breathed their last. Mrs. Rodman came here to nurse her husband until his death on September 30.

Henry Rohrback also lost many of his crops, livestock, and wood to the army. This time it was the Ninth Corps occupying his farm. Henry had cut ten cords of oak wood to heat his house during the coming winter. By the end of September it was gone, used by the soldiers. Near the Middlekauf farm, the soldiers cut two or three acres of standing timber for firewood.

A partial list of Henry's losses include:

Fodder on 31 acres of corn, @ $5 per acre	$155.00
Damage done to barn	20.00
10 head fat cattle, @ $25	250.00
3 Milch Cows, @ $30	90.00
1 Large Bull	30.00
31 Head Sheep, @ $5	155.00
13 Shoats, @ $2	26.00
32 pounds Ham (bacon for wounded), @ 12½¢	4.00
2 Gallons old Grape wine for wounded, @ $2	4.00
200 chickens, @16¢	32.00
15 Turkeys, @ 50¢	7.50
Use of house & 2 barns & outbuildings, 5 days @ $10	50.00
400 bushels of Apples, @ 50¢	200.00

Henry's bill came to $3,097.80.[21] Agent Sallade investigated. He said:

> The corn, wheat and hay were fed to the horses of General Burnside's command at a time when it seems forage could not readily be procured from regular services. . . . Mr. Rohrback owned and cultivated two farms of 120-215 acres situated along the Antietam Creek. . . . After the battle a portion of Maj-Gen. Burnside's command occupied claimants farm, using house and barns, and consuming forage on the farm.

Mr. Rohrback lost eighty-five panels of fencing. In those days a panel of fencing was estimated to consist of six rails and one post. This in itself amounted to a considerable sum of money, as well as time and effort to replace. Henry had to replow twenty damaged acres. One of his best horses was taken by Lieutenant Benjamin for the artillery.

Some of the people had difficulty in collecting their money. Mr. Pry was still trying as late as 1891 to be paid in full. Pry, Rohrback, and Mumma all said "Union supply trains were irregular and often delayed." Thus the army had to rely on the farmers in the Valley of the Antietam. For many such as Samuel Mumma, Pry, and Rohrback, the Battle of the Antietam brought in the words of Mumma, "Great destruction of property, the fruit of a long life of labor, toil and trouble."

CAPTAIN DAVID SMITH

Captain David Smith was born in 1796 and died in 1869. He was the father of G. Finley Smith, a druggist and leading citizen of Sharpsburg.

Early in life, David Smith obtained a 135-acre farm near Antietam Station. He was the captain of a Sharpsburg artillery company. After his death the farm was purchased by the Ottos and is now owned by Miss Ruth Otto.

On the night of September 17, "Stonewall" Jackson had his headquarters "in a grassy enclosure in front of the residence of Captain David Smith, and just across from a field from where the Antietam Station of the Norfolk and Western Railroad now is. I do not think even the General had a tent, the staff rested under the trees on the grass. About midnight General Jeb Stuart made his appearance."[22]

Captain Smith's barn was used as a hospital. In fact, it was one of the largest Confederate hospitals. After the Rebel retreat on the night of the eighteenth, the worst cases were left behind. By the time Union doctors arrived they were in bad shape. The men had been without food, water, or medical attention. Some captured Union wounded were also found. From Friday noon on the nineteenth until Sunday noon, the Sanitary Commission was kept very busy taking care of the Confederate wounded found between Sharpsburg and the Potomac.

Many Confederates died here. At least seventeen were buried in the nearby Smith Orchard. In 1907, the headboard and remains of Lt. A. W. Speight of the Third North Carolina were plowed up by Mr. Otto. His body, along with the others, was taken to the Confederate Cemetery in Hagerstown. Mr. Otto gave the headboard to Fred Cross.

THE GROVE FAMILY

Jacob Groff, the first of the Grove family to come to Washington County, arrived about 1760. "He was the grandson of Hans Groff, who was born in Switzerland in 1661, and who fled to Alsace, Germany, during the persecution of the Mennonites." Hans arrived in Penn's Woods about 1695, and settled along Groff's Run in Lancaster County. Here he estab-

Lieutenant A. W. Speight's marker.

lished a trading post. In time he obtained nearly fifteen hundred acres and established Earl Township on the banks of Groff Run.

Hans's grandson Jacob moved to Sharpsburg and lived in a stone house on one of the side streets. He seemed to have engaged in the practice of medicine. He lived to the ripe old age of eighty-two. The marker in the old Reformed Cemetery reads, "Jacob Grove, born June 4, 1837, died August 15, 1819. His wife Catherine was born on March 3, 1742 and died September 25, 1823. To this union nine children were born."

The second son, Philip, was a leading merchant of early Sharpsburg. He was thrifty, honest, and helpful to those in need. He soon owned several large estates around Sharpsburg. Apparently one of them was Mount Airy. According to family tradition, a daughter of Joseph Chapline and her husband started Mount Airy, but were unable to complete the building. Philip Grove bought it and finished the job. At the time of the battle, Philip's son Stephen P. and his wife, Maria Dillon Robinson, lived on the lovely farm. His son A. Dillon Grove and wife, Julia Katherine Mumma Grove, were to live on the farm in later years. Mrs. A. Dillon Grove still has a tremendous memory, a keen wit, and enjoys life even though she is almost 102. The author is deeply indebted to her, and to her daughter Miss Louise Grove for sharing their memories of days gone by at Mount Airy, the Grove homestead.

MOUNT AIRY

About a mile west of the public square in Sharpsburg, and on the left-hand side of the road, just across from the old Antietam Railroad Station is Mount Airy, or the Civil War home of Stephen Grove.

Louise Grove, the granddaughter of Stephen Grove, tells the following story:

If the old house known throughout Washington County, Maryland, as Mount Airy could talk it would tell of wounded men overflowing the house, barn, and lawns, of soldiers buried in its fields, of Union and Confederate doctors sharing quarters in its attic rooms, of President Lincoln himself visiting its generous hallway. . . . Although

212

it was a few miles distant from the scene of terrible slaughter, it was part of the drama. Commandeered, as a billet for Union officers, it became also an improvised hospital for the wounded. Intended to care for the Blue, it also sheltered the Gray. Major General Fitz John Porter of the Fifth Army Corps was in command and set up his headquarters in what the family called the "old orchard." A Dr. Rocke was head surgeon.

It would seem that the Fifth Corps occupied Mount Airy as they pursued the retreating Confederates on the morning of Friday, September 19. This and other homes near the Potomac River were used to care for Rebel wounded.

Miss Grove who was born at Mount Airy continues her story by saying:

> Situated one mile west of the village of Sharpsburg on the road leading to Shepherdstown, West Virginia, built in the early 1800s, it was at this time the home of grandfather Stephen P. Grove.
>
> The day, September 17, 1862, dawned warm and cloudy. The family, warned of the impending crises, had sent off the young children across the Potomac to stay with relatives. . . . My grandparents were allowed to stay in one room on the ground floor when they refused to leave their house and property. My grandmother repeatedly was urged to go, but she stood her ground.
>
> When the guns were stilled and the wounded could be transported, four hundred soldiers filled the buildings and the tents on the lawn. A great rough hewn table was used for amputations and was offered as a gruesome exhibit for later years.
>
> Arms and legs originally placed at the base of an old stone fence behind the barn were reburied at my grandfather's insistence, in the woods, where the bodies of many dead lay until taken up and placed permanently in the National Cemetery in Sharpsburg, for the Union, and . . . in Hagerstown for the Confederates.
>
> At least one funeral service was held in Mount Airy's hall—that of a Lt. Hobart whose father was understood to be a Bishop of a Southern state and apparently well known at the time. The service was read by the Rev. John A. Adams, the Rector of Sharpsburg's St. Paul's Episcopal Church. Lt. Hobart's body was sent on to his father.
>
> Dr. A. W. Wiseman of Jerusalem, Davis County, North Carolina wrote to my father, Alva D. Grove, on August 20, 1901 describing how the Confederate wounded were housed in tents set up on a side lawn, and how "the medical officers of both armies ate together, slept together, drank together, and had a high old time." Dr. Wiseman was an assistant surgeon with the 7th North Carolina. He shared sleeping quarters in the garret of grandfather's house. For forty days after . . . the Battle, the wounded were cared for at Mount Airy. Dr.

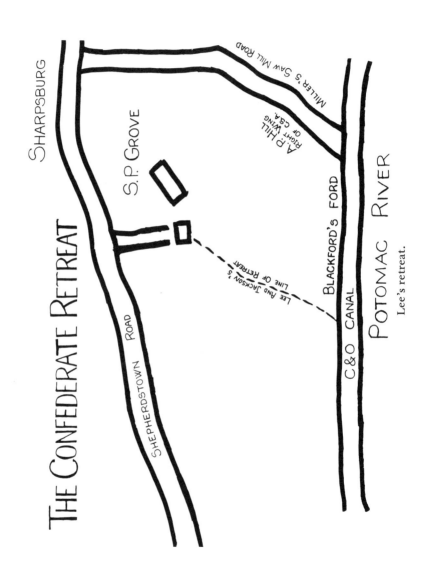

The Confederate Retreat

Sharpsburg

S. P. Grove

Miller's Saw Mill Road

A. P. Hill
Right Wing
of C.S.A.

Blackford's Ford

Potomac River

Shepherdstown Road

Lee and Jackson's
Line of Retreat

C & O Canal

Lee's retreat.

214

The Retreat Glen.

Wiseman's correspondence to my father inquires about Miss Julia Grove, a cousin who "showed great kindness to the soldiers."

Just after the battle, William Blackford came to the Grove home. He found a badly wounded lad from North Carolina lying on the ground near the door of the main house. The boy asked if the lady of the house would permit him to come in. He was so cold. Perhaps he could get warm. He was taken inside. He talked much of home, and expressed the desire to see his mother. This was not to be. The lad died during the night.

As early as the 1920s Fred Cross felt the Grove home was the location of the pictures of Lincoln and McClellan. Mr. Cross also pinpointed the Confederate retreat from Antietam. Francis Miller lived one-half a mile below the Grove farm. "Most of the Confederates seem to have passed through the fields west and southwest of the Miller house, and thence through a glen which led to Blackfords Ford. . . . One can hardly walk down this path without a feeling of pensiveness. To me as I passed this way one September morning in 1922 the glen seemed thronged with ghostly marchers."

Cross feels the artillery and wagons took the roads, while the infantry marched by way of the glen.

Once again, historian Atkinson has done thorough research

on the Lincoln and McClellan pictures. For many years it was thought that these pictures were taken at the Philip Pry

The Honorable
Fred W. Cross.

home. However, McClellan moved his headquarters closer to the Potomac on September 20. About that time he started to date his messages, "Headquarters, Army of the Potomac, near Shepherdstown."

Mr. Atkinson uncovered a picture in the Library of Congress showing a picture of the Pry home from a new angle. This picture had gone unnoticed for many years. Perhaps because the back of it said, "Hooker's headquarters." Hooker was taken to the Pry home to have his wound dressed, but it was not his headquarters.

In the June 1971 issue of *The Civil War Times Illustrated,* historian Atkinson says that the pictures of Lincoln and McClellan were taken at Mount Airy, the home of Stephen P. Grove. He compares pictures of the roofs and chimneys of the Grove and Pry farm. Additionally, eight of the men in the one picture with McClellan and Lincoln were members of Fitz-John Porter's staff. And Porter did have his headquarters at Mount Airy. Thus the latest research would tend to indicate that the famous Lincoln-McClellan Antietam pictures were taken at Mount Airy.

THE SHERRICK FARM

Joseph Sherrick, Sr., bought two hundred acres of land from Henry Orndorff on May 5, 1796. Father Sherrick sold his land to his son, Joseph, on June 30, 1838.

At the time of the battle, the land was farmed by forty-

216

three-year-old Leonard E. Emmert. However, he did not live in the farmhouse. It was vacant when the drums of the Blue and Gray beat along the Antietam. Afterward Emmert submitted a bill for $8,000 to the U.S. Government. His primary claim for damages came from damages done to the house by the artillery of Burnside's Ninth Corps. Emmert also said his corn crop was damaged by wagons and military equipment. The soldiers used twenty to twenty-five loads of his fodder. At the time, fodder was being sold for between five and six dollars a load. Emmert collected but $582 of his $8,000 claim.

Following the battle, the Samuel Mumma family moved into the Sherrick house, and stayed until their own home could be rebuilt.

The Sherrick farm has changed very little since those days of 1862. On May 5, 1964, at 11:47 A.M., the U.S. National Park Service bought the Sherrick farm from Mrs. Abbie Wyand Dorsey.

Wives Search for Husbands

Among the numerous articles written by John P. Smith is one of especial interest which appeared in *The Antietam Valley Record,* a weekly, published in Keedysville, Maryland, dated October 31, 1895.

One of the saddest scenes in my memory is that of a wife whose frantic grief I can never forget. It was that of Mrs. M. H. Fields whose home was in Ravenna, Portage County, Ohio. Her Husband, Myron Hawley Fields, was lying very ill with typhoid fever in the Smoketown Hospital. She received a telegram to come immediately. Gathering together a few delicacies which she thought her husband might relish, she started for Antietam. At midnight of the second day of her starting, she arrived at our hospital where she was kindly cared for by my mother. The next day in the face of a blinding storm I accompanied her on foot to the Smoketown Hospital. We found the Surgeon in charge of General Vanderkief who informed us that her husband had died two days before her arrival and was buried. The kind hearted surgeon accompanied us to his last resting place in the little cemetery a short distance from the hospital. At the sight of the grave she threw herself prostrate upon it and wept in bitter agony.

Returning to the hospital the steward gave her her husband's cap and some other little keepsakes belonging to him among which was a likeness of his wife and two children.

The next day with a weary sad heart, she returned to her Western home to bear the sad news to the fatherless ones.

Smoketown Cemetery

In the little cemetery at Smoketown, neatly enclosed with a paling fence, whitewashed, lay 159 brave hearts, calm in death, each grave with its rounded white head board and rude lettering with the name, Company and Regiment of the dead. In the center of this enclosure was a monument 10 feet in height with the following inscriptions on each of the four sides:

1st side, "Erected in memory of the Union soldiers who died from wounds received in defense of their Country, at the Battle of Antietam, September 17, 1862."

2nd side, "Antietam General Hospital U.S.A., B. A. Vanderkeif, Surgeon in charge."

3rd side, "The land that is not worth our dead is not worth living for."

4th side, "I am the resurrection and the life, he that believeth in me though he were dead, yet shall he live."

The following incident of a sad scene on the Battlefield of Antietam is worthy of notice here. It was related by a Mrs. Holstein. It is as follows:

Among the many who came to visit the Battlefield was a young wife whose frantic grief I can never forget. She came hurriedly as soon as she knew her husband was in the battle, only to find him dead and buried two days before her arrival. Unwilling to believe the facts that strangers told her—how in the early morning they had laid him beside his comrades in the orchard, she still insisted upon seeing him. Accompanying some friends to the spot she could not wait the slow process of removing the body but in her agonizing grief, clutched the earth by handfuls where it lay upon the quiet sleeper's form. And when at length the slight covering was removed and the blanket thrown from off the face, she needed but one glance to assure her it was all too true. Then passive and quiet beneath the stern reality of this crushing sorrow, she came back to the room in our house. The preparations for taking the body to Philadelphia were at once made for her and with his remains she left for her desolate home.

Keedysville Church Hospital

J. A. Miller, a highly respected citizen of Keedysville, Maryland, was editor of a weekly newspaper, *The Antietam Wavelet,* which he published during the Civil War. This paper carried many interesting stories pertaining to the Battle of

Antietam. On March 29, 1890, *The Antietam Wavelet* carried a story written by George A. Allen, Company A, Seventy-sixth New York. After the Battle of Antietam, Allen was a hospital steward in one of the Keedysville hospitals which had been set up in the Reformed Church at the edge of Keedysville, Maryland. Allen's account of his experiences in this hospital follows:

As we had just passed the anniversary of the Battle of Antietam, perhaps a pen sketch of the Keedysville hospital may be interesting to those who were there. While assisting a wounded comrade from the battlefield the writer was detailed to act as Hospital Steward in and about Keedysville. The principle hospital was established in the brick church near the upper end of the town. Boards were laid on top of the seats, then straw and blankets, and most of the worse cases of wounded were taken to this, the headquarters. Comrades with wounds of all conceivable shapes were brought in and placed side by side as thick as they could lay, and the bloody work of amputation commenced. The Surgeons, myself and a corps of nurses with sleeves rolled up, worked with tender care and anxiety to relieve the pain and save the lives of all we could. A pit was dug just under the window at the back of the church and as soon as a limb was amputated I would take it to the window and drop it outside into the pit. The arms, legs, feet and hands that were dropped into that hole would amount to several hundred pounds. On one occasion I had to fish out a hand for its former owner, as he insisted that it was all cramped up and hurt him.

Every morning those that died during the night were taken out and buried in a trench, usually without ceremony. But one morning, as I was directing some North Carolina conscripts that had surrendered, and were set to work digging graves, etc., and while burying a corpse, an officer, I think a Lieutenant, staggered up as drunk as a lord, and prepared to give the remains a send-off; and had I not caught him by the arm, he would have fallen into the trench. With the wave of a hand and a hiccough, he said, "Let the Father take the spirit that gave it." He then braced up and staggered off with a self assurance that he had performed a solemn duty.

Most of the wounded got it into their heads that no one but myself could dress their wounds, change their bandages, etc., so I had to do the most of it, and was kept busy for several weeks, night and day. For three weeks I never realized that I had not slept at all. I was in several battles and on many hard marches, but nothing ever wore me as that did. At night I would drop down upon the sofa in the pulpit, but no sooner had I closed my eyes than some one of the many amputees would call me to change a bandage or something.

When a patient gets it in his head that you can handle his stump more carefully than any one else, you're elected.

Every afternoon I would mix a bucket of aling—whiskey, sugar and water, and pass it around, giving each one a little jugger. But we had one six-footer of an Irishman that belonged to the 69th New York. He was a man of splendid physique; his left arm was gone at the shoulder. He would never taste the toddy that was passed around; he wanted his straight. So I would bring him a big drink of raw commissary, and he would down it with the remark that he was like "shate-iron" inside. Soon he would begin to sing, and he was a fine singer too, with his rich Emerald Isle brogue, and many were the smiles he brought forth from those that were nearer dead than alive. And I believe that more would have died had it not been for the songs of our friend from the 68th, as he had a cheerful word for everyone.

During the day when I could get a few moments to spare, I was writing letters from the pulpit to those dear ones at home, for those who lay there with mangled limbs and bodies. Many of their friends came, but sometimes not until after they had been laid in the trench. Dr. Vanderkief was the boss in taking off a limb. He could snatch a leg or arm off quicker than you could say "Jack Robinson," and it was done right too. No more trouble or second amputation.

Those with lesser wounds were distributed throughout the town, in the school-house, barns and private houses. One day while visiting a barn to see if anything was needed, a German boy complained to me that his back was hurting him. He had been shot in the breast, and on examination I found that the ball was showing itself close to the surface just below the shoulder blade. Just about this time in came three young medical students (contract doctors). They talked Latin over this poor boy for about 15 minutes, and then one of the trio proceeded to take out the ball, which had not exploded but had only blown out in a weak spot in the lead; but it must have been rather hot for the inside of that boy when the powder burned.

These facts, scenes and instances are as fresh in my mind as if it were but yesterday. I can remember few names. I presume that the congregation that now worships God in the brick church at Keedysville, little realize that once upon a time the church was filled with men packed in nearly as thick as sardines in a box, and each minus a limb, while some had five or six dangerous wounds, and that for a while every morning from one to five would be carried out a corpse.

Theresa Kretzer

There are many stories about Theresa Kretzer burying the U.S. Flag in ashes during the battle of Antietam. However, the account the author finds most interesting is the one given by Theresa Kretzer of Sharpsburg to Fred Cross, the Massachusetts State Historian for many years.

Fred Wilder Cross was born on September 15, 1868, and died on March 8, 1950. Among his many visits to Antietam were those made in 1919, 1920, 1922, and 1924. On three of these visits he brought his wife and daughters along. Among his papers there are these quotes; and impressions recorded on his visits:

> I see the dusty blue and gray battalions marching forth to battle. The view from South Mountain is like a huge-lovely theatre.
>
> I have never seen such charming country as that between Braddock Mountain and South Mountain. It surpasses all that I had believed or thought.
>
> Fox's Gap was apparently named for a Mr. Fox who used to live there and worked as a cobbler.
>
> Boonsboro is a neat, prosperous, and attractive little town.
>
> On September 14, 1919, there were gigantic wheat stacks at every barn.
>
> I stayed at the Nicodemus Hotel in Sharpsburg during my 1920 visit.
>
> Mr. Joshua Ford of Boonsboro remembers seeing General Garland's body lying on the porch of the Mountain House before it was removed.

In 1929, Mr. Cross talked with Theresa Kretzer about the flag episode. This is the account of that interview:

> My father, John Kretzer, was a very loyal Union man, and the members of the family all shared his sentiments. We had a large Union flag which, in the early days of the war, we kept strung across the street from our house to a tall pole on the opposite side. There were some Southern sympathizers in town, and on one occasion they cut the halyards which attached the flag to the pole. After that we ceased to use the pole and attached that end of the rope to the roof of a house opposite ours, which I think was occupied by a family named Rohrback.
>
> When it became evident that the Confederates were going to occupy the town I began to fear for the safety of the flag. Finally we took a box, wrapped the flag up, and placed it therein. Then father took the box and buried it in the ash heap which was banked up against the back side of the smoke house in our backyard.
>
> I felt sure that some of the Southern sympathizers in town would tell the Confederates that we had a flag and that the soldiers would be after it. Sure enough, as soon as the Confederates occupied the town a party of soldiers called at the door and demanded the

221

"Yankee Flag." I said, "Gentlemen, there is no Yankee flag in this house."

"O yes there is," was their reply. "We have heard all about that big flag that you have kept strung across the street, and you must give it up."

I then said, "I knew somebody would tell you about that flag, and rather than have it fall into your hands, I laid it in ashes." They thought I had burned it.

Several times during the Confederate occupation of town, a demand was made for the flag. I always gave them the reply, "It is in the ashes."

After the battle was over and the Confederates had left town, we took the box out of the ash heap, unwrapped the flag, and hung it between two of the upper windows on the street side of the house. Some of the Confederate prisoners who were still in the town saw it and cursed me right roundly, and said I had lied to them. I told them, "No, I told you what was absolutely true. The flag was in ashes."

She took Mr. and Mrs. Cross out into the yard, showed them the smokehouse, and the place where the flag had been buried in the ashes.

Help in Time of Need

Dr. John B. Kerfoot, president of Saint James School, located about ten miles north of the fields of Antietam, brought help to many during the long September days in 1862. On Tuesday, September 16, he along with Dr. Falk, and the Reverend Henry Edwards, rector of Saint John's Episcopal Parish, Hagerstown, started for Boonsboro and South Mountain with bandages, spirits, biscuits, and tobacco. At Boonsboro they found four large hospitals caring for those wounded at South Mountain on Sunday. Then they rode on to the crest of South Mountain. The Confederate dead were still not buried, and many seriously wounded men were found at a nearby cabin.

When Dr. Kerfoot heard the booming of the cannon on Wednesday, the seventeenth, he went to the roof to see what he could behold. In the afternoon he took Dr. Falk and together they rode to the Smoketown Hospital just north of the Union lines. Once again they took medical supplies. Again the next day these two men made an errand of mercy.

On Sunday, September 24, Dr. Kerfoot visited the headquarters of Major General Fitz-John Porter at the Stephen Grove home. He read the service and preached a sermon. General Porter's mother had been the matron at Saint James, and one of her grandsons had been on the faculty. Then according to Williams, he went to General McClellan's headquarters, "at the time three miles south of Sharpsburg, and read evening prayers and preached."

Soldiers in the Area

After the battle, Union troops remained in the Sharpsburg-Antietam Furnace vicinity until late October. Some of the medical detachments stayed until late January.

The residents of the valley, to a large extent at least, opened their hearts and homes to the men in Blue. The ladies of Sharpsburg and Keedysville baked cakes, pies, cookies, and homemade bread for the soldiers. Containers of cold milk and baskets of fresh fruits were also taken to the bivouac areas.

The Union Ninth Army Corps encamped for a time near the mouth of the Antietam Creek. Their next move was duty in Pleasant Valley. The Twenty-first Massachusetts had some fine moments near Antietam Furnace. The unit seems to have been a favorite of Clara Barton's. The unit historian wrote:

> On the 19th of September, the 21st went into bivouac near the spot where the Antietam empties into the Potomac. The great event of the 20th was wetting down General Ferrero's star. He had been appointed brigadier-general on the 17th, and on the 20th he furnished the brigade a good supply of whiskey to drink to his health.
>
> The following day, orders from corps and division headquarters were read to the troops congratulating them on carrying the bridge, and lamenting the death of the brave General Reno.
>
> The 21st remained in camp near Antietam Furnace until October 1. Then they marched to Pleasant Valley where they would stay until October 27. That night, the first since August 12, they slept under shelter.
>
> Clara Barton (sometime during the Maryland campaign) kept us well supplied with delicacies in the way of food and articles of clothing, and was a ministering angel to our sick.
>
> This true, noble woman, never sparing herself or failing in her devotion to our suffering men, always maintained her womanly

dignity, and won the lasting respect and love of our officers and men.[23]

Time in Maryland came to an end for the Twenty-first on October 27. That day the regiment crossed the Potomac on pontoon bridges at Berlin, now Brunswick, Maryland. The night was so cold that water froze in the canteens.

Many lifelong friendships were formed between the soldiers from New England, the Midwest, and the East who camped in the fields bordering the Antietam. Many of the men made repeated visits to the area. Some of them stayed at the same home in Sharpsburg on every such occasion. Those who could not return, often wrote to the folks in the valley who had ministered to their wounds, fed their empty stomachs, and gave them friendship in lonely moments. The picture of Burnside's staff at the Lee home in Pleasant Valley depicts some of the happier moments in the fall of 1862.

Union soldiers at the Lee home in Pleasant Valley.

224

Difficulty and Honor for the Twentieth Maine

Camp life brought difficulty for many. In the Civil War disease killed twice as many men as actual combat. The weather in late September and October 1862 turned quite chilly at night. Many men in the Twentieth Maine had not been issued shelter tents. Some were without blankets. Encamped at the mouth of the Antietam Creek, this regiment was forced to sleep on frosty ground without adequate tents and blankets. The chill penetrated their entire body. Exercises were needed in the morning to restore circulation. However, many men in the Twentieth arose before dawn, too cold to sleep.

The diet left much to be desired. The main course was usually salt pork, hardtack, and coffee. The field kitchens such as they were seemed poor. Camp conditions were unsanitary. Diarrhea, measles, fevers, diphtheria, sore throat, and typhoid hit the men of the Twentieth Maine as well as men in other outfits as they camped for six weeks in the Valley of the Antietam.

Among the troops of the Twentieth Maine was a young officer by the name of Joshua Lawrence Chamberlain. He was a graduate of Bowdoin College and the Bangor Theological Seminary. When the war broke out, he was a professor at his college alma mater. Unschooled in military arts, he burned the midnight oil in his Antietam tent, studying military strategy and tactics.

Although he saw little action at Antietam, he participated in twenty-four battles before the end came in 1865. He won the Medal of Honor for bravery at Gettysburg, and six times during the war he was wounded. After an assault on Petersburg, U. S. Grant gave him a field promotion to brigadier general. When Lee surrendered to Grant, Chamberlain was detailed to receive the formal surrender of the Army of Northern Virginia.

From the battlefields of the Civil War, Chamberlain went home to serve three terms as governor of Maine, and then as president of Bowdoin College for thirteen years. When he died in 1914, he was buried in Arlington National Cemetery.

In the fall of 1861 and again after the Battle of Antietam,

the Thirteenth Massachusetts Infantry camped near Sharpsburg while assigned to the task of guarding and patrolling the Chesapeake and Ohio Canal. James Snyder remembered well the imposing sight of the regiment as it formed on the Main Street of Sharpsburg.

On October 7, 1862, the Ninth New York broke camp near the Antietam Iron Works and crossed the mountain into Pleasant Valley. The climb was an arduous one and somewhat tiring for the troops. The way "was rough and steep." Once on top the mountain, the men were repaid for their efforts. Lieutenant Graham described the view in these words:

> A more beautiful and varied panorama than it had been the fortune of many of these city-bred boys to have viewed before. The whole country lay spread below them like a picture, the undulations softened and the land beautified by distance. The villages of Sharpsburg, Keedysville and Boonsboro appeared like collections of toy houses and churches, while the scattered farmhouses, each nestling beside its grove or orchard, assisted in completing a picture of a peaceful pastoral scene, which was so gratifying to the eye of these men so far separate from home and peace. It is hard to realize that only a few days since nearly two hundred thousand men had striven here in mortal combat.

The years pass, and then a New York newspaper, dated September 2, 1921, carried this headline, "Zouaves' Leader Leaves $817,385." General Rush Hawkins, the commander of the Ninth New York, was born on September 14, 1831, and was eighty-nine when he died as the result of an automobile accident on October 25, 1920.

Almost half of the estate, or $400,000 was left to Norwich University in Vermont. Sums amounting to $100,000 each were given to Brown University and the University of Vermont. One hundred thousand dollars was also given to the Society for the Prevention of Cruelty to Animals. Hawkins suggested that the bulk of it be used to "abate the wicked horrors of vivisection."

The Nicodemus Hotel

The Nicodemus Hotel had been the home of Colonel John Miller, an officer in the War of 1812. Colonel Miller was the father of D. R. Miller who owned the "Bloody Cornfield" in

226

Uncle Alec Davis.

Youth and age meet in Sharpsburg.

228

A cold welcome.

1862. After the battle, the hotel became a favorite spot for many veterans, and also for Fred Cross. The walls of this building could certainly tell us many things if they could speak to us in "the evening dews and damps."

Many of those who survived the fighting on the seventeenth were in a state of shock. They were grateful to be alive, but horrified at what they had seen. Years later, Fred Cross heard the distinguished war correspondent Charles Coffin tell how he had gone from campfire to campfire the night of the seventeenth. In most of the bivouac areas the soldiers were singing:

> "Do they miss me at home, do they miss me?
> 'Twould be an assurance most dear
> To know at this moment some loved one
> Were saying, I wish he were here;
> To know that the group at the fireside
> Were thinking of me as I roam.
> O, it would be joy beyond measure
> To know that they miss me at home."

229

Fifty-seven years later in 1919, on the evening of the seventeenth, Fred Cross and others gathered around the piano in the parlor of the Nicodemus Hotel. They sang the song the soldiers had sung by the Antietam campfires in 1862. Once again Cross felt the nearness of those of an earlier day. He said, "I think that a great throng of forms unseen gathered with us there, and that a mighty chorus of voices unheard by mortal ear joined with us in that sacrament of song."[24]

Sad Letters

Sad letters were sent from Sharpsburg to folks at home. This one was sent by a lad from Texas:

My dear afflicted Sister,

It gives me intense pain to tell you of death of my dear brother, your devoted husband Andrew. Oh: how desolate is my sad heart of that brother twice indeared by the hardships and perils we have passed through together. But if my heart is sad, what must yours be my sister, deprived of a husband and a friend. I cannot comfort you, but can only commend you to the tender mercies of our Heavenly Father who hath said he doth not willingly afflict. He has said he will be a Father to the fatherless, a husband to the widow. I pray to him to have mercy on you and your little children. Our dear one suffered no pain in death for he was shot through the temples. He was killed on yesterday morning in the fight at Sharpsburg. Of the conflict being undecided, his body has not yet been recovered, but Mag. George has promised to attend to his interment. I am too badly wounded to return to look after him, having been shot through the left arm and twice, slightly in the side. I cannot write more now, but will do so in a few days. My heart is too sad. To God I commend you my dear sister, Your sorrowing brother,

A. M. Erskine

After the Battle of Antietam, James Weeks traveled from Illinois to Maryland to bury his young brother-in-law, William Cullen Robinson, age twenty-two. In a letter, written September 28, 1862, he said:

Dear Parents & Sister,

It is my sad duty to write you a letter on this fine morning bearing to you the news of the death of our Son and Brother "Cullen." He was wounded in the head on Wednesday, the 17th in the Battle of Antietam, and died on Tuesday evening the 23rd in the School House Hospital at the Village of Keedysville about two miles

230

from the Battlefield. He was unconscious from the time he was found until he died. I arrived at the hospital about an hour after he died. He had by some means, after he was shot gotten to a place near the hospital and was found behind an old house lying asleep. But when awoke he was unconscious.

They took him to the hospital and gave him every care that could be offered him but his wound was mortal and all they could do was to soothe him. He never uttered a sylable after he was found. They said he must have fired a great many rounds as his lips were black from biting the cartridges off. And too, they said he was the favorite of his company and in fact of the regiment. When I got here, the Surgeon had sent his knapsack containing his wallet, letters and his watch and in fact all his effects. I found a match box in his pocket and one of his comrades gave me his knife. I brought with me also some of his hair and the button of his cap which was drawn almost through his head. The surgeon took it out of his head but the ball had gone down into his stomach. I bought a rough coffin (the best I could get) and washed his face and combed his hair smooth and covered him round with a large clean sheet. And they dug a deep grave on a little knoll on the bank of the Antietam Creek, and I buried him there. I marked the place (which was a conspicious one) by a board neatly made at his head with his initials W.C.R. cut deeply into it and one at his feet. I also chipped a tree under which he was buried. It was almost impossible to bring him home with me as I should have had to come way back to Baltimore and purchase a metalic coffin (for him as they won't allow any other to pass over the lines) and by the time I should have got back he would have been so much decayed that they could not keep him for me. So I buried him so that this fall or Winter I can go and get him.

Oh if you could only see the terrible horrible consequences of this unholy war that I have seen during my trip to Maryland. Every house is a hospital full of wounded men. And the whole country is one complete Battlefield. . . . I will write you a more detailed account in a day or two. I am very much fatigued with my journey. . . .

I am truly, but sadly yours,
James

The author feels that Cullen Robinson was buried on a hill overlooking the Little Antietam in Keedysville. The body was supposed to be sent to Palmyra, New York. However, there is no record of the young man's burial in that city.

In the spring of 1971 another James Weeks, the great-great-grandson of the James Weeks who came to Keedysville in 1862, came trying to find the grave of William Cullen Robinson. Thus far his search has been fruitless. There is no record of his burial in the National Cemetery, unless he is one of the unknowns. Most likely, Cullen Robinson who served in the Ninth New York Militia, known as the Eighty-third New York, lies buried overlooking the Little Antietam. Such is the tragedy and horror of war.

James Weeks lives in Birmingham, Michigan, and is still trying to find what happened to the body of Cullen Robinson. The author has printed the story with the permission of Mr. Weeks, and sent him a picture of the Stone School Hospital in Keedysville where Cullen Robinson died of wounds received at Antietam.

Patrick Remembers

Marsena Patrick, who commanded a brigade in the First Corps at Antietam, and who became provost marshal general of the Army of the Potomac, wrote many notes in his diary about the Maryland campaign.

He tells of the Boonsboro-Sharpsburg Pike experiencing a traffic jam of men, wagons, and horses on September 15. Patrick also says that wherever General McClellan went the troops cheered him enthusiastically. This was prior to September 17. According to his records, his brigade had no supper on the sixteenth, and laid in a field in a drizzle with little or no protection from the elements. Patrick was deeply distressed when he learned of the death of Colonel Kingsbury at the Lower Bridge. He wrote, "His poor mother will feel that life is now valueless." During the night of the nineteenth, Patrick prayed much of the time, "I prayed for my country—prayed for my children—prayed for myself. It was a night of wrestling with God."[25]

During the nineteenth and twentieth, details were sent out to bury the dead, in most instances, right where they fell. Patrick said, "The stench arising from the decomposition of the dead is almost intolerable."

On Sunday morning near the camp along the Potomac, Patrick selected a spot for church services in a nearby woods. Toward evening he rode to visit the scene of the Ninth Corps action. He wanted to see where Colonel Kingsbury fell.

Patrick's first camp near the Potomac was called "Oak

232

Grove." Then about the thirtieth, Camp Barnett was established. On October 2 the First Corps was ordered to turn out for a review by President Lincoln. Then men left camp before 2:00 P.M., and by 3:00 or 3:30, all was in readiness. But Patrick says, "We waited, & waited & waited. Reynolds and Meade went to hunt up the President. He was on the Battle Field." The president never made it for the review of the First Corps that afternoon. He went off in an ambulance to Sharpsburg. General Reynolds dismissed the First Corps at 7:00 P.M.

The next day was a repeat performance. This time the president showed up. Patrick's Brigade turned out at 9:30 for the scheduled 11:00 A.M. review. However, the president did not arrive until 3:00 P.M. Patrick, like his men, was "burned up, disgusted & weary." The general's mind wandered during his waiting, or at least during his recording of the day. On that Friday night, October 3, he wrote:

> I want one more good day, to allow the Brigade to wash themselves & their clothes—the latter in boiling water. The Officers and men are without Clothing for Change, are ragged & filthy. Many of them have vermin upon them & cannot get rid of them except by a thorough boiling process. So I purpose to use tomorrow for that purpose. . . . As the President came down the line he shook hands with Meade, Ricketts & myself.

Patrick like many other unit commanders had difficulty in getting tents and other equipment. On October 4 he wrote:

> Our men are poorly prepared for Storms. Their Shelter Tents are worth very little for protection & and they [the men] are getting very weak & unable to endure much exposure. . . . I am sending everywhere for Tents, but do not get them.

The next day Patrick received a note asking if he would accept the appointment of provost marshal of the army. His reply was "Yes." On October 7, army headquarters were moved to the Knoxville area, some fourteen miles from Sharpsburg.

On Sunday, the twelfth, worship services were conducted by an Episcopalian. Mrs. McClellan and Mrs. Marcy were among those attending.

The entry for October 13 is for "Camp between Browns-
233

ville and Burnside." Patrick noted the campgrounds were not especially good, but they were located in "the midst of a beautiful valley, known as 'Pleasant Valley.'"

Writing near Brownsville on Saturday night, October 18, Patrick states:

> Came to Tent & worked until about 10 o'clock, then saw Williams, Marcy & McClellan; then started off for Maryland Heights, with Beckwith. . . . We wound up the Mountain side by a very good horse path & reached the Signal Station in safety. From that point, although the Atmosphere was too smoky to see in the distance, we had a most magnificent view of Pleasant Valley with its thousands upon thousands of snowy tents, its long black lines of soldiery on drill. its endless streams of Waggons & horses.

On the twenty-third, Patrick had to go to Washington on official business. When he arrived back at Knoxville on the twenty-seventh, he was in for a surprise.

> On arriving up here in the Mountain Country I found that the rain storm, which was quiet enough in Washington, was accompanied here with a perfect Gale, blowing down the tents of the Staff & playing very many pranks, to the great annoyance of the General & all the Officers. . . . The Headquarters were to have moved today, but on account of the storm it has been delayed—until tomorrow at ten o'clock.—Then we move to Berlin [Brunswick] where a Pontoon Bridge has been thrown across the Potomac. . . .

Wednesday, the twenty-ninth, Patrick received word of a bad accident at Harpers Ferry. A freight car caught fire. The conductor, instead of detaching the car, permitted the car to run into piles of hay and grain. The result, the derailment of twenty-four freight cars, and the burning of an immense amount of Union forage.

The next few days Patrick had problems with counterfeiters. Several were caught and turned over to U.S. marshals. By the fourth of November, Patrick had moved along with the rest of the Army of the Potomac and was in camp near Waterford in Loudoun County.

Sharpsburg Churches

Although the soldiers left the area, the churches of Sharpsburg retained the scars of battle. The Lutheran Church was damaged so badly that it had to be demolished. The Epis-

234

copal Church also suffered extensive damages. The seats or pews in the Methodist Church were taken from the sanctuary and used as caskets.

The Reformed Church, now the United Church of Christ, served as a hospital. It was hit by at least one shell, and as soon as the Confederates retreated the church was occupied as a hospital.

Boards or planks were placed on top of the pews. On these, straw was scattered and then covered with blankets. As late as the 1950s the floor of the United Church of Christ still showed the bloodstains of Antietam's wounded.

In 1890 the church was remodeled. The front was changed, and two entrances made. Between the two large pillars in front, the Sixteenth Connecticut had a large stained-glass memorial window installed in tribute to their comrades who had fallen at Antietam. On the day the church was rededicated, the survivors of the regiment contributed one hundred dollars toward the liquidation of the remaining debt.

The Sixteenth was a new regiment in September 1862. They had been on active duty but three weeks when they found themselves fighting on the Sherrick farm, and pushing toward the Harpers Ferry Road. Many of the soldiers were young college boys from Hartford. When the news of Antietam reached that city, it cast a gloom over the entire area. All flags were flown from half-mast, and the bells in the city churches were rung in memoriam.

Antietam Farms, Then and Now

1862 Owners	Current Owners
Bishop John Russell, (Locust Spring)	George Line
Philip Pry (Army Headquarters)	Recreational Properties Corporation
The Hoffman Farm, a large hospital	Mrs. Fred Scheller
Samuel Neikirk	Charles Ritchie
Samuel Poffenberger	Millard Kefauver
Joseph Poffenberger	Fred Kramer
Samuel Mumma (burned by the Confederates)	The National Park Service

235

Antietam Farms, Then and Now—*Continued*

1862 Owners	*Current Owners*
William Rulett	Howard Miller
D. R. Miller (Location of Battery B)	Paul Culler
Henry Piper	The National Park Service
Orndorff's or Newcomer's	Charles Ritchie
Sherrick's	The National Park Service
Henry Rohrback's	Rene Burtner
Jacob Miller's	Clifton Churchey
Stephen Grove (Mt. Airy)	Robert Marcum
Captain David Smith	Miss Ruth Otto

XI

HIS RIGHTEOUS SENTENCE

Abraham Lincoln was one of our greatest presidents, yet one of the most criticized. Chief among his critics was Horace Greeley, the erratic, and at times, almost fanatical editor of the *New York Tribune*. He expected the president of the United States to bow to his wishes, and to heed his advice. This was especially true in the issue of slavery.

On August 19, 1862, less than a month before Antietam, Greeley published an open letter in his paper calling it "The Prayer of Twenty Millions." The editorial blasted the president with both barrels. Greeley accused Lincoln of catering to the politicians in the Border States. He berated Lincoln by saying, ". . . that a great proportion of those who triumphed in your election . . . are sorely disappointed and deeply pained by the policy you seem to be pursuing with regard to the slaves of the Rebels."[1] The president was accused of being "strangely and disastrously remiss" in his duties.[2]

Mr. Lincoln could have opened a desk drawer and sent Greeley a copy of a document he had been working on since June. However, he chose not to do so. Lincoln worked on the document daily, very carefully, very deliberately, a page at a time.

In midsummer 1862, Lincoln called a cabinet meeting. He shared with his assistants his plans to free the slaves, permitting Negro men to enlist in the Union Army, noting that such an act would keep England and France from entering the war on the side of the Confederacy. He said, "We must change our tactics or lose the game."

This time as Lincoln discussed his plans, he did not ask

237

their advice. He told them what was on his mind, and what he planned to do. Some suggestions were offered. Secretary Chase desired stronger language in reference to arming the blacks. Secretary Blair felt the plan would cost the administration the fall elections. Mr. Seward brought out a very important point. "Mr. President, I approve of the proclamation, but I question the expediency of the issue at this juncture. The depression of the public mind, consequent upon our repeated reverses, is so great that I fear the effect of so important a step. . . . I suggest, sir, that you postpone its issue, until you can give it to the country supported by military success."[3]

Seward's words made the president stop and think. He realized the significance of the suggestion. Lincoln made the decision to wait for news of a Union victory on the field of battle. Then he would tell the world of his plans to end slavery.

But things would become darker before they became better. The next news from the battlefront was from Bull Run. Once again Union troops had met with reversal. This time it was General Pope running into Jackson at the Second Battle of Bull Run. Hot on the heels of this news, came word that Lee was crossing the Potomac and invading Maryland. The fortunes of the North had reached a low ebb. One more disaster and defeat might cause the end with the South reaping the fruits of victory.

But then came September 17, 1862. At a place called Antietam Creek, George B. McClellan battled Robert E. Lee to a standstill. It was the bloodiest day in American history. The next evening Lee retreated into Virginia. When news from the hills of western Maryland reached the White House, Lincoln opened his desk drawer and put the finishing touches on his proclamation. He sent word to the cabinet officials. There would be a meeting on Monday, September 22. The rest is history.

Monday morning came and with it one of the great moments in the life of the nation. After reading a funny chapter from Artemus Ward's book, the president became very solemn and in slow, deliberate terms said:

Gentlemen, I have, as you are aware, thought a great deal about the relation of this war to slavery; and you all remember that several weeks ago, I read to you an order I had prepared on the subject, which on account of the objects made by some of you, was not issued. Ever since then, my mind has been much occupied with this subject, and I have thought all along that the time for acting on it might very probably come. I think the time has come now. I wish that we were in a better condition. The action of the army against the rebels has not been quite what I should have best liked. But they have been driven out of Maryland, and Pennsylvania is no longer in danger of invasion. When the rebel army was at Frederick, I determined, as soon as it should be driven out of Maryland, to issue a Proclamation of Emancipation such as I thought most likely to be useful. I said nothing to any one; but I made a promise to myself, and (hesitating a little)—to my Maker. The rebel army is now driven out, and I am going to fulfill that promise. I have got you together to hear what I have written down. I do not wish your advice about the main matter—for that I have determined for myself. This I say without anything but respect for any one of you. But I already know the views of each on this question. They have been heretofore expressed, and I have considered them as thoroughly and carefully as I can. What I have written is that which my reflections have determined me to say. If there is anything in the expressions I use, or any other minor matter, which any one of you thinks had best be changed, I shall be glad to receive the suggestions. One other observation I will make. I know very well that many others might, in this matter, as in others, do better than I can; and if I were satisfied that the public confidence was more fully possessed by any one of them than by me, and knew of any Constitutional way in which he could be put in my place, he should have it. I would gladly yield it to him. But though I believe that I have not so much of the confidence of the people as I had some time since, I do not know that, all things considered, any other person has more; and however this may be, there is no way in which I can have any other man put where I am. I must do the best I can, and bear the responsibility of taking the course of action which I feel I ought to take.[4]

President Abraham Lincoln then read a document which would become one of the milestones of America. The document was one which had cost the president "blood, sweat and tears." He felt he had to do it. He promised God that he would do it if given any sign of a military victory, and about a week before Antietam, made his final decision. Who are we to say that the Emancipation Proclamation was not the righteous sentence of God, given to the world through His servant Abraham Lincoln?

Lincoln read:

That, on the first day of January, in the year of our Lord one thousand eight hundred and sixty-three, all persons held as slaves within any State or designated part of a State, the people whereof shall then be in rebellion against the United States, shall—be then, thenceforward, and forever FREE; and the Executive Government of the United States, including the military and naval authority thereof, will recognize the freedom of such persons, and will do no act or acts to repress such persons, or any of them in any efforts they may make in their actual freedom.[5]

Secretary Seward interrupted the president, saying, "I think, Mr. President, that you should insert after the word 'recognize,' in that sentence, the words 'and maintain.' " Lincoln replied that he had already thought of the words, but was not sure he could support them if inserted. Seward insisted, however, and the words were inserted.

On Monday morning, September 24, the preliminary Emancipation Proclamation was published for all the world to see. It seemed for some like God's "Righteous Sentence." Others thought it an act of treason. Serenaders came with a brass band to play in thanksgiving for the act. Mr. Lincoln came out onto a White House balcony and addressed the crowd: "I can only trust in God I have made no mistake. . . . It is now for the country and the world to pass judgment on it, and may be take action upon it."

From now on, the war would have two purposes: One, to reserve the Union, and two, to end slavery.

The President's act had been like a chemist tossing a tiny pinch of a powerful ingredient into a seething and shaking caldron. Colors and currents shifted and deepened. New channels cut their way to the surface. . . . Below the fresh confusion was heaving some deep and irrevocable change.[6]

A new thought was in the words of the president's proclamation. An old way of life was dying. Perhaps it would take a long time to see the ultimate truth of the message, but something was being born in the midst of a terrible war.

Toward the end of September 1862, Mr. Lincoln wrote a riddle. He had given much thought to the question. The riddle was left on his desk, not for publication. John Hay made a copy of it. The president had written:

240

The will of God prevails. In great contests each party claims to act in accordance with the will of God. Both may be, and one must be, wrong. God cannot be for and against the same thing at the same time. In the present civil war it is quite possible that God's purpose is something different from the purpose of either party; and yet the human instrumentalities, working just as they do, are the best adaptation to effect his purpose. I am almost ready to say that this is probably true; that God wills this contest, and wills that it shall not end yet. By his mere great power on the minds of the new contestants, he could have either saved or destroyed the Union without a human contest. Yet the contest began. And having begun, he could not give the final victory to either side any day. Yet the contest proceeds.[7]

And one of the greatest proceedings of the American Civil War was the Emancipation Proclamation, "His Righteous Sentence." After Antietam, the country was on a new course, a course from which there could be no turning back. "Here at last was the sounding forth of the bugle that would never call retreat."[8]

XII

HAIL TO THE CHIEF

After the Battle of Antietam, President Lincoln decided to visit the field of conflict. He had several motives. First of all, he desired to thank the Army of the Potomac for its gallantry in meeting and turning back the Confederate Army of Northern Virginia. His other purpose was the hope that he would be able to inspire McClellan to move against Robert E. Lee. In the summer of 1862, during the Peninsula campaign, Lincoln had taken some of the cabinet and some congressmen to visit McClellan at army headquarters along the James River. This did not work very well. Coldness and hostility filled the air. "Little Mac" was not held in great esteem in the halls of Congress, or in other political circles. The general had little time for politicians. Lincoln felt that taking a group of politicians to Antietam might bring a repeat performance. So he formed a plan to take another group to the hills of Maryland.[1]

One of the traveling companions selected for the Antietam trip was John McClernand, a friend from the days when Lincoln served in the Illinois Legislature, McClernand was a Democrat and ardent supporter of Senator Stephen A. Douglas. He had served eight years in Congress.

Earlier Lincoln had authorized his appointment as brigadier general, then the promotion to major general. McClernand had no real military qualifications or abilities. Lincoln's decision to take him to Antietam was a matter of political expediency.

McClernand was ambitious and boastful. He acted with little tact. He had offended U. S. Grant by claiming that his

242

division was responsible for the Union victory at Shiloh in April of 1862. To make matters worse, he went behind his superior's back and wrote a very critical letter about Grant's leadership ability.

September 1862 found McClernand in Washington seeking to enhance his own career. His goal was permission to recruit new troops in Illinois, thus obtaining a command for himself.

Lincoln, perhaps to get him out of the way for a time and also to promote friendly relations with the Democratic Party, extended an invitation for McClernand to be a traveling companion to Antietam. After all, if a good Democrat, and a supporter of Douglas, toured the battlefield with the president, the public might be led to believe that the Democrats were strongly supporting the Union cause.

Another traveling companion was Ozias M. Hatch, a close personal friend of the president. Hatch had ridden with Lincoln on the inaugural train from Springfield to Indianapolis. Eighteen months had gone by and Lincoln was anxious to spend some time with his good friend. On the way to Antietam the two of them could discuss the political and social events taking place in Springfield since the departure of the Lincoln family.

Hatch had come to Illinois from New Hampshire. He went into business, starting a store in Griggsville. Soon he became clerk of the circuit court. The year 1856 brought the formation of the Republican Party in Illinois and the need for political candidates. Abraham Lincoln was instrumental in placing Hatch's name on ballot as a candidate for secretary of state.

After a victorious election, Hatch's office became the meeting place for young lawyers and politicians. Within the walls of his office, a group of young Illinois attorneys of the Eighth Circuit Court mapped plans designed to gain Lincoln's nomination for the highest office in the land. Hatch was with Lincoln during the nominating convention and also during the hours of that November evening when "the Railsplitter awaited the returns from across the land."

Ward Hill Lamon, another Illinois politician and presidential bodyguard, would also go to Antietam. There would

243

be no dull moments with Hill around. He was lively and gay, quite a singer and banjo player.[2]

Lamon and Lincoln had been law partners. Many times they traveled the Illinois circuit together. Lamon's singing and playing made the trips seem shorter. His music brought cheer to Lincoln in his moments of depression. The Lincoln-Lamon friendship is one of the oddities of history. They were almost exact opposites. Lincoln was no singer. Hill would sing at the drop of a hat. Lincoln loved to read and meditate; Hill was a man of action, a wrestler, fighter, and gambler. Lincoln was slow, deliberate, and cautious; Hill often leaped before he looked and sometimes seemed to be a reckless individual. Lincoln did not care for liquor. Lamon was fond of it. Yet the two were extremely close friends.

When the Lincolns left Springfield for Washington, Lamon was present as the master of ceremonies and as song leader. He came to Washington to serve Mr. Lincoln as marshal of the District of Columbia, and as presidential bodyguard.

Lamon was keenly aware of the possibility of assassination. He frequently cautioned the president to be careful, to watch his step. Many nights, especially in the spring and summer, Lincoln went for an evening stroll before retiring. These walks always caused Lamon great anxiety.

Ward Hill Lamon was one of the few individuals Mary Todd Lincoln trusted. She detested many in Congress and some in the cabinet, and considered them her enemies. But Ward Lamon she trusted. Mary Todd Lincoln was happy that he was going to Antietam to take care of her Abe.

The trip brought happiness to Lamon, too. In a sense it would be going home. You see, his birthplace was near Winchester, and his boyhood was spent near Harpers Ferry. Today the remains of Lincoln's trusted friend rest in the Gerrardstown Cemetery near Martinsburg, West Virginia. We are also indebted to Lamon's account of the Antietam visit. His is the most extensive in existence.

Still another traveling companion was Joseph C. G. Kennedy. Hailing from Pennsylvania, Kennedy was superintendent of the census. He was an authority on statistics and munitions. Lincoln, in the course of the trip, would find much time to compare the manpower and firepower of the North and South with Mr. Kennedy. Little did the two men realize the fate awaiting both of them. Tragedy befell Kennedy in 1887. Like the president who took him along to Antietam, Joseph Kennedy was fanatically murdered by a man from whom he had purchased property.

The plan to go by train to Harpers Ferry, thence by carriage to Antietam, with the return trip by rail from Frederick, was presented to Mr. Lincoln by John W. Garrett, forty-two-year-old president of the Baltimore and Ohio Railroad.

Prior to the Civil War, the Baltimore and Ohio had offered its services to both North and South. However, when the war came, the railroad decided to cast its lot with the North. After all, they had a thirty-million-dollar investment to protect, and the directors felt it was impossible for the South to emerge victorious.

Some questioned Garrett's loyalty, but not Lincoln. He was indebted to the B&O for keeping the Baltimore to Cumberland supply line intact. This was done in the face of great Confederate opposition. The Rebels made many raids, tore up large sections of track, and burned railroad bridges. Yet the trains went through.

Lincoln realized the stature and importance of Garrett and the Baltimore and Ohio. As an act of gratitude he asked the president of the railroad to accompany him to Antietam. Naturally Garrett replied in the affirmative. The list of Lincoln's traveling companions was now complete.

On October 1, 1862, the presidential train left Washington for Harpers Ferry. George B. McClellan came from Sharpsburg to meet Mr. Lincoln. Together they reviewed the troops on Bolivar Heights. This was in the afternoon of the first. McClellan returned to his headquarters at the end of the day. Lincoln stayed in Harpers Ferry, presumably at Storer College, now a part of the Stephen Mather Park Service Training Center.

The next day was spent with General Sumner who took the president to visit and review the troops on Loudoun and Maryland heights. Shortly after the noon hour, Mr. Lincoln started for McClellan's headquarters near Sharpsburg. He arrived in the hills of western Maryland during late afternoon or early evening.

One of the mysteries of Antietam is where Lincoln spent his two nights on the battlefield. Headquarters, Army of the Potomac, was moved from the Pry farm about September 20. McClellan in his official reports lists his headquarters as being near the Potomac and Antietam. The Reverend Mr. Kerfoot, who conducted services for the commanding general on Sunday, September 21, says the location was three miles south of Sharpsburg. The probable location was along the Harpers Ferry Road. The author feels it was at the Keith Meyers farm. Lincoln most likely stayed at army headquarters, but where was headquarters?

During the third, Lincoln was scheduled to review the Third Corps.[3] Actually General Patrick and some of the others had become angry the previous afternoon. Most of the Third Corps, actually renamed and designated the First Corps, just prior to Antietam, was a victim of army hurry-up-and-wait tactics. The corps was assembled on the afternoon of October 2 for the presidential review. However, they stood and stood. The president never did make it.

But on the morning of October 3, Lincoln reviewed the Ninth Army Corps. This unit, commanded by General Burnside, was encamped south of Sharpsburg near Antietam Furnace. This supports the idea that McClellan had his headquarters in the general area, as the Ninth Corps was the first unit to be reviewed on October 3. Most likely it was nearest to the spot where Lincoln spent the night.

Dr. James Oliver, assistant surgeon of the Twenty-first Massachusetts, remembered the historic visit.

At eight o'clock the troops were paraded in a large field for the purpose of being reviewed by the President and Gen's McClellan and Burnside, who made their appearance about ten o'clock, with their usual staff.

I looked with eager eyes upon Lincoln. Had a fine view of him as he paraded along the lines. Oh! he is homely above all description. . . .

I'll pass along to Burnside who rode next to the President point-

246

ing out the troops under his command. There is not a nobler looking man in the service than he is. . . .[4]

After the review, General Burnside accompanied Lincoln to the bridge that bears his name and showed the chief executive the hills above the bridge, stormed by his troops.

However, the general was to meet with great embarrassment. After the Battle of Antietam, the Union Army had a food and supply shortage. On the morning of Lincoln's visit to the Ninth Corps area, a large number of men from Hawkins Zouaves (the Ninth New York), and other soldiers, surrounded a wagon traveling one of the roads near Sharpsburg. The wagon was loaded with bread. Some of the soldiers, accidentally on purpose, slipped a linchpin out of place, and took off a wheel. Consequently the wagon upset. A football-type pileup occurred as the hungry soldiers scrambled for bread.

In the midst of the frolic and robbery, General Burnside came driving up in his carriage, accompanied by the president of the United States. Men flew, running in all directions for the nearest cover. The objective was: Get out of sight as quickly as possible, and hope you would not be recognized.

But Matthew Graham, painting a good picture of the Ninth New York, says his comrades froze in their tracks, came to attention, dropped their rolls and bread, and stiffly saluted. In this manner, so says Graham, they received "the distinguished but unwelcome visitors."

Burnside turned six shades of red. He stood up in the carriage, shouting and shaking with rage. He commanded the Ninth New York, "After them! After them! Bring them back!" Mr. Lincoln must have been amused by the episode. He said not a word, but looked straight ahead.

Some of the soldiers were apprehended. The men received the tongue-lashing of their lives in front of the president of the United States. Burnside's day was ruined. To think that while in the company of Mr. Lincoln, he had to be confronted with such disgraceful behavior. "What did they mean? United States soldiers, robbing a poor peddler? Such conduct was most unbecoming of men in uniform." Finally Burnside cooled down. The carriage and the soldiers went their separate ways. The soldiers going without their fresh bread.

Then the official party went to the home of Stephen P. Grove. There are conflicting stories about the method of travel for the short trip. One source says that Burnside took Lincoln back to McClellan's headquarters, and from there "Little Mac" and the president rode in an army ambulance to the Grove home. This seems more probable than the other account which says the president rode horseback.

Mount Airy, the Grove home, is on the Shepherdstown Road. In 1862 it was the headquarters of Fitz-John Porter, the commander of the Fifth Corps.

Louisa Grove was seven years old in 1862. When war came to the Valley of Antietam, her parents sent her to stay with friends in Shepherdstown. She had returned by early October and was on hand when the president came to Mount Airy. She never forgot the tall, kindly man who placed his great hand of compassion on her head. With his hand on Louisa's head, he spoke to her parents, expressing regret for the damage done to their farm.

Then the president walked down the big hallway. Wounded were stretched out on both sides. A correspondent with the presidential party describes what occurred next.

> The President . . . remarked to the wounded Confederates that if they had no objections he would be glad to take them by the hand. He said the solemn obligations which we owe to our country and prosperity compel the prosecution of this war, and it followed that many were our enemies through uncontrollable circumstances, and he bore them no malice, and could take them by the hand with sympathy and good feeling.
>
> After a short silence, the Confederates came forward, and each silently but fervently shook the hand of the President. Mr. Lincoln and General McClellan then walked forward by the side of those who were wounded too seriously to be able to arise and bid them good cheer, assuring them that every possible care should be bestowed upon them to ameliorate their condition. It was a moving scene, and there was not a dry eye in the building, either among the Nationals or Confederates. Both the President and the General were kind in their remarks and treatment of the rebel suffers during this remarkable interview.

While at Mount Airy Lincoln reviewed some of the Fifth Corps, including the Seventh Michigan Cavalry, bivouacked in one of Mr. Grove's orchards.

The visit to Antietam was not very pleasant for Mr. Lincoln. Not only did he see the devastation of war, and the plight of the wounded, but somewhere near Mount Airy, the president asked Ward Hill Lamon to sing a sad, little song. A presidential favorite was "Twenty Years Ago." Then another member of the group requested "Picayune Butler." This was a lilting comic opera type of song.

Newsmen were nearby and of course heard the music. The dispatches they sent to their home offices carried the news "President Lincoln tours the Antietam Battlefield, and laughs in sight of burial parties." Still others reported the president laughing at the plight of the wounded.

Actually, neither the president nor Lamon saw any burial parties. The battle had been fought two weeks previously and the dead had been buried. Truthfully, the president was very much depressed by the things he saw at Antietam. Years before he had cried when Lamon had sung "Twenty Years Ago." "Picayune Butler" was a harmless effort to cheer the president. The occasion of the singing occurred on the way from Burnside Bridge to Mount Airy.

Of all the criticism Lincoln received during the war years, the account coming from the fields of Antietam hurt him as deeply as any. After the return to Washington, Lincoln and Lamon discussed the possibility of issuing a statement denying the story, and telling the truth of the matter.

Lincoln said:

> There has already been too much said about this falsehood. Let the thing alone. If I have not established character enough to give the lie to this charge, I can only say that I am mistaken in my own estimate of myself. In politics, every man must skin his own skunk. These fellows are welcome to the hide of this one.[5]

A statement was prepared but never released. Once again the man from the prairies showed his stature, and exhibited in person the idea of "with malice toward none."

One cannot help but wonder if the sad event at Antietam might have led to the "few brief remarks" at Gettysburg a year later. Maybe Lincoln would not have gone to the Pennsylvania town had it not been for the sad episode at Antietam. Perhaps the experience near Mount Airy led him to "highly resolve" to say something noble in honor of those "who gave their last full measure of devotion."

Other things troubled Lincoln at Antietam. One of the motives for coming to Antietam was the desire to light an aggressive fire under McClellan. But "Little Mac" told the president he was reluctant to move. He said the army did not have enough blankets or shoes. Very emphatically McClellan told Lincoln, "The army is in no condition to undertake another campaign." Likewise the general expected another Confederate attack at any moment. He seems to have been praying that the rains would come causing the Potomac to rise, thus blocking another Confederate invasion. Naturally, this would also prevent the crossing of the Union Army.

Lincoln, according to Nicolay and Hay, was sick at heart over McClellan's delay. The October visit led Lincoln to believe that with the proper leadership, the Army of the Potomac was ready for any reasonable requested assignment. The one theme present in all the conversations with McClellan was, "General, why don't you cross the Potomac and move on the enemy?"

The night of October 3 was spent somewhere near Sharpsburg. As the roosters were crowing to greet the dawn, Lincoln stood by the cot of his good friend Ozias Hatch. He had a request to make, "Come Hatch, take a walk with me."

Leaving the tent, the two men walked "through the streets of a great tented city." Thousands of soldiers were still sleeping, unaware that the commander-in-chief was walking through the area. For a long time nothing was said. The president was deep in thought. Something was on his mind.

Then the two men reached a commanding hill. In front of them stretched the fields of Antietam and the tents of the Army of the Potomac. Lincoln waved his hand in despair, and said in a dejecting tone, "Hatch, Hatch, what is all of this?" "Why Mr. Lincoln," replied Hatch, "this is the Army of the Potomac." Lincoln thought for a moment, and then in

250

Lincoln at Antietam.

251

Mount Airy.

a loud, clear voice answered, "No, Hatch, no. This is McClellan's bodyguard."

The sadness was shown in Lincoln's face as he reviewed the troops.[6] In fact, it made a deep impression on the men of the Twentieth Maine. This regiment was a part of the Fifth Corps at Antietam and saw little or no action, being stationed in reserve near the Middle Bridge.

After the battle the men went into bivouac near Antietam Furnace. Then came the order to march to Sharpsburg for a presidential review. Although some grumbled about the march and having to wait for the arrival of the president, yet the Twentieth Maine never forgot Mr. Lincoln.

To the men from Maine, Lincoln looked ungainly in the saddle. But there was something in his eyes and on his face that inspired courage and loyalty. There were deep lines in his bearded face, and there were shadows around the president's eyes. He looked as though he was carrying the burdens of the entire country. McClellan was dressed in his finest. But the Twentieth Maine had eyes only for Lincoln. The tall, humble man from the backwoods of Kentucky was like

America at this period of history, a giant emerging from the wilderness. At Antietam a mystical bond developed between the men from Maine and the man from Springfield. He was one of them, and their affection for him was "wonderful in its intensity."[7]

In front of the regiment, Lincoln paused to look at Colonel Chamberlain's horse. He turned to speak to McClellan about the beautiful white animal. Lincoln himself was on a borrowed horse, wearing a tall silk hat. To the men from Maine he looked as though he might be seven feet tall.

Chamberlain wrote:

> We could see the deep sadness in his face, and feel the burden of his heart, thinking of his great commission to save this people, and knowing that he could do this no otherwise than as he had been doing—and by and through the manliness of these men—the valor, the steadfastness, the loyalty, the devotion, the sufferings, and thousand deaths, of those into whose eyes his were looking. How he shrunk from the costly sacrifice we could see; and we took him into our hearts with answering sympathy, and gave him our pity in return.

After the review it was back to the shady glens of the Antietam, the quiet Potomac, and Maryland hills colored by the hand of autumn. That night by their campfires, the men of the Twentieth Maine talked about Mr. Lincoln and the sadness in his face.

Prior to leaving Sharpsburg, Lincoln visited the Dunkard Church. James Peterman, a lad of twelve at the time, recalled the president coming down through Sharpsburg and turning north toward Hagerstown and the church.

In 1937, during the seventy-fifth anniversary program, Harry M. Blanchard wrote to the planning committee saying that he was among the wounded visited by Mr. Lincoln at the Dunkard Church. Blanchard was only sixteen at the time. When he recovered from his wounds, he walked down the canal towpath and rejoined his regiment at Harpers Ferry.

Other wounded were also visited by Lincoln during his last morning at Antietam. Crossing the Middle Bridge, preparing to leave for Frederick, Lincoln asked Frisby Keplinger who lived nearby to get him a drink of water. Mr. Keplinger hurried to his spring to fulfill the request of the president.

McClellan and Lincoln then visited the heroic "Fighting Dick" Richardson hospitalized in an upstairs room at the Pry house. No doubt Lincoln said, "Hurry and get well General, we need more like you." Had time permitted Mrs. Pry would have shown the president the large room where she made fresh pies, cakes, and bread for the soldiers.

But Lincoln had other duties. So it was off to South Mountain; McClellan rode to the summit of the mountain with the president. Then the two parted. McClellan returned to the battlefield, while Lincoln went on to the train awaiting him in Frederick. One wonders if he stopped in Middletown to visit the wounded there.

Lincoln Is Welcomed in Frederick

After visiting the battlefield of South Mountain, President Lincoln and his party occupied two large ambulances in their ride back to Frederick.

At fifteen minutes before the Presidential salute, which was fired by Battery K of the First New York Artillery, announced their approach. Patrick Street was lined with people anxious to see and welcome the President of the United States. Just at this time a smart shower commenced falling, accompanied by a heavy wind, which raised suffocating clouds of dust. But this could not drive in the crowds, who had long and anxiously waiting his approach. The procession was led by Col. Allen, the military governor of Frederick, followed by the ambulances containing the Presidential party, accompanied by a detachment of the First Maine Cavalry. . . . The President was enthusiastically received by the multitude as he rode up Patrick Street to Court Street, where the procession turned off and proceeded to the residence of Mrs. Ramsey, on Record Street, where General Hartsuff was . . . being attended . . . since he was wounded at the battle of Antietam. The President had expressed a desire to pay his respects to this gallant soldier on his way through the city.

Here he remained for a few moments, and upon making his appearance he was again . . . cheered and called upon for a speech. He briefly addressed the assemblage as follows: "In my present position it is hardly proper for me to make speeches. Every word is so closely noted that it will not do to make a foolish one, and I cannot be expected to be prepared to make a sensible one. If I were as I have been most of my life, I might perhaps talk nonsense to you for half an hour, and it wouldn't hurt anyone. As it is, I can only return thanks for the compli-

254

ments paid our cause. Please accept my sincere thanks for the compliment to our common country."

Here repeated cheers were given for the President and Gen. McClellan. Mr. Lincoln then re-entered the ambulance, and was driven to the railroad station, closely followed by the rapidly increasing crowd. The party immediately entered the handsomely fitted up cars, which had been in readiness to receive them for nearly forty-eight hours. The President was again loudly called for by the throng of citizens and soldiers, and upon making his appearance another speech was demanded. He good-naturedly responded: "I am surrounded by soldiers, and a little farther off by the citizens of this good city of Frederick. Nevertheless I can only say, as I did five minutes ago, it is not proper for me to make speeches in my present position. I return thanks to our good soldiers for the services they have rendered, the energy they have shown, the hardships they have endured, and the blood they have shed for this Union of ours; and I also return thanks, not only to the soldiers, but to the good citizens of Frederick, and to the good men, women, and children in this land of ours, for their devotion in the glorious cause, and I say this with no malice in my heart to those who have done otherwise. May our children and children's children for a thousand generations enjoy these benefits conferred upon us by a united country, and have cause yet to rejoice under these glorious institutions, bequeathed to us by Washington and his compeers. Now, my friends, soldiers and citizens, I can only say once more, farewell."[8]

Early in September the Twenty-fourth Michigan, a new regiment, left Wayne County and the Detroit area for Washington. After spending three weeks in the capital, the men from Michigan boarded cattle cars on September 30 and started for Frederick. They detrained near midnight and made camp in the nearest field. The next day, better campsites were selected. The men settled down to the task of drilling, washing clothing, and fishing in the Monocacy River. The bivouac area was between the river and the railroad.

They had a good spot. On October 4, just about a month after leaving Michigan, the soldiers stood near the tracks and greeted the B&O train bearing President Lincoln back to Washington. He was returning from his visit to South Mountain and Antietam. The president stood on the rear platform, looking tired and worn with care. As the train passed, the men of the Twenty-fourth stood up and cheered. They had heard he was coming. And so they had been waiting for some

255

time to catch a glimpse of him. Never did their deep and abiding faith for "Old Abe" diminish.[9]

The next day being Sunday, the regiment visited Frederick, and found every public building filled with wounded from the battlefields visited by the president. On the sixth, the men from Michigan started for Sharpsburg, camping for the night by the Catoctin Creek, and wading in its cool, refreshing waters. They were on their way to become part of the "Iron Brigade," commanded by General Gibbon.

On October 16, after being reviewed, most of the men visited Antietam Battlefield. The mass graves and partially buried dead excited the men. They walked over the ground where the Iron Brigade had fought, and visited the haystacks on the Miller farm where Battery B gave and received great punishment.

From Antietam, the Twenty-fourth went on to fame and glory. They were indeed a valuable addition to the "Iron Brigade." As a tribute to their valor, those who survived the fighting of the Civil War were selected as the "Guard of Honor" for Lincoln's funeral. We wonder how those who cheered the president at Monocacy Junction must have felt in April 1865 when they stood guard over the body of their fallen hero.

Other Presidents Come

Research tends to indicate that George Washington visited the Valley of the Antietam at least twice. The first occasion was in conjunction with Braddock's disastrous expedition. Then in 1789, he returned, this time looking for a suitable site for the capital of the new nation.

Andrew Johnson assumed office when Lincoln was assassinated. On September 17, 1867, Johnson came by train to Keedysville, thence by carriage to Antietam to dedicate the National Cemetery. U. S. Grant, soon to occupy the White House, was with the president.

William B. McKinley fought on the heights above Burnside Bridge and won a battlefield commission. He returned as president of the United States on Memorial Day 1900 to witness the dedication of the Maryland Monument. He also made a few remarks.

President Theodore Roosevelt dedicated the New Jersey State Monument on September 17, 1903. Thirty-four years later, another Roosevelt, Franklin D., would be the main speaker for the seventy-fifth anniversary program.

Dwight D. Eisenhower visited the fields of Antietam while chairman of the Joint Chiefs of Staff. However, he left no written record of his visit.

PRESIDENT JOHN F. KENNEDY

The headlines of the Hagerstown *Morning Herald,* on Monday, April 8, 1963, read "President Visits Antietam Battlefield." The lead story contained the news of the historic visit.

Antietam National Battlefield Site had its most distinguished visitor of the new season Sunday—President John F. Kennedy.

Officials of the battlefield at Sharpsburg got word late Saturday that the President might pay a visit. He arrived in a helicopter at 11:45 a.m. Sunday, landing near the Spong farm at Burnside Bridge.

Robert Lagemann, acting superintendent of the battlefield said that the President showed intense interest in troop movements over the historic sites. He wanted to know about the specific actions of various divisions . . . and how the troops made their way to the scenes of action.

President Kennedy also was asking questions about the high casualty rate that occurred during the conflict and the reason for the greater percentage of killed and wounded men.

In another vehicle, John Bryce, historian at Antietam, served as guide for Senator Edward M. Kennedy, the President's brother, and the Senator's wife.

The President's visit was such a well kept secret that most Sharpsburg residents knew nothing about it until the helicopter was on its way back to Washington. He did not stop in the town itself.

President Kennedy stayed outdoors throughout the tour. He did not visit the new visitors' center . . . or the Antietam National Cemetery.

After the president left, Superintendent Lagemann realized that he had failed to show the president the monument in honor of William B. McKinley.

The previous Sunday, President Kennedy had visited the Gettysburg National Military Park. On the afternoon of the eighth of April, the day after his Antietam visit, the president

257

threw out the first ball of the new baseball season. The Baltimore Orioles proceeded to defeat the Washington Senators three to one.

Some who sought the highest office in the land have also been to Antietam. Most notable is George B. McClellan, commander of the Army of the Potomac during the battle. In the fall of 1864, McClellan ran against Lincoln but failed in his effort to move to the White House.

Winfield Scott Hancock, a hero at Gettysburg, and called "Hancock the Superb," assumed command of Richardson's division when "Fighting Dick" fell at Antietam. In 1868 Hancock received 168 votes at the Democratic Convention. In 1880 he lost a very close race to James A. Garfield. Hancock received 155 electoral votes, while Garfield polled 214. But a shift in New York's thirty-five electoral votes would have given the presidency to Hancock. Garfield won the popular vote count by a slim 7,023 margin.

XIII

THESE HONORED DEAD

After the Battle of Antietam, the fields and lanes were littered with the dead of both armies, debris of all kind, dead horses, and items left behind by men at war.

A Mr. McGraw who lived near Sharpsburg at the time said, "The stench was so terrible. We had to close doors and windows to shut out the nauseating odor of decaying corpses."[1]

Many of those who wore the Blue and Gray were buried in shallow graves in the fields of the farmers where they had fallen. Some were rooted up by hogs, and in other cases, chickens scratched the earth covering away from the bodies buried hastily in army blankets. Those who died in the field hospitals usually received better burials, at least at Smoketown and on the Crystal Spring farm.

Soon after the battle, March of 1865 to be exact, a committee was formed to select the most eligible and most lovely spot possible for the burial of those who fell at Antietam. Augustus A. Biggs, Sharpsburg's doctor and leading citizen, was named president of the four-man trustee body. Thomas A. Boullt of Hagerstown was named secretary-treasurer. The other two members were General Edward Shriver of Frederick and Charles C. Fulton of Baltimore.[2]

The state of Maryland appropriated $7,000 for the committee to purchase and enclose a suitable tract of ground as a final resting place. Those who have visited the Antietam National Cemetery know the committee did an outstanding job. The tract selected and purchased affords a sweeping panoramic view of the fields of conflict. On this ground, General Lee watched the battle unfold on the morning of the seventeenth. From this sacred spot one can view South Mountain where Lee's Maryland campaign received its first jolt. In the distance to the south lies Maryland Heights and the hills around Harpers Ferry. The visitor can also see the Pry farm, headquarters of the Army of the Potomac on that memorable day, as well as the rolling hills around the Dunkard Church to the north, and Burnside Bridge to the south.

On March 23, 1865, just a few days before the end of the Civil War, the Maryland Legislature enacted a bill calling for the expenses incurred in moving the dead from the farms to the National Cemetery, as well as the cost of enclosing and beautifying the place, to be shared by the various states involved on the basis of population.

Money appropriated by the states amounted to $62,229.77. Maryland set aside $7,000 in March of 1865. In January 1866, the legislature voted an additional $8,000.

The committee held its first meeting on May 25, 1865. Aiding the four men in their grim task was the work of Aaron Good, Esq., and Joseph A. Gill. After the battle, these men had made a list of the graves and their locations. This was a labor of love. Good and Gill received nothing for their efforts. Letters, diaries, photographs, Bibles, books, initialed handkerchiefs and cartridge boxes aided Good and Gill in their efforts to identify the fallen.

The task of moving the remains from the fields of conflict and the field hospitals was begun in October 1866 and completed in August 1867.

The local trustees did not confine their efforts to the dead at Antietam. At the suggestion of officials in Washington, they sought to bring the Union dead buried in Frederick, Washington, and Allegany counties to Antietam.

Lt. John W. Shearer of the United States Burial Corps was in charge of the work. The dead were exhumed, placed in coffins, and buried in sections comprising the dead of their state. If unknown, they were buried in the section with others who could not be identified. Most of the men from Maryland, and many from Pennsylvania, killed at Antietam, were moved by family and friends to hometown cemeteries. Usu-

260

ally the bodies were taken by wagon to Hagerstown and there placed on a train for their final destination.

Lieutenant Shearer numbered each coffin. A book with a number corresponding to each grave was used to record the name of the individual, company and state. For instance, after gravestone number one, the following information is listed: Cook, P. E. Private, Company E, 89th New York Infantry. Date of death unknown. Removed from Antietam battlefield.

The records tell of others brought from Middletown, where they died of wounds received at South Mountain. Still others were brought to Antietam from Frederick, Weverton, Burkittsville, Williamsport, Smoketown, Boonsboro, Funkstown and Rohrersville. Frederick Hooker of the Second Connecticut and Nathan Powers of the Seventeenth Michigan are listed as having died at the Big Spring Hospital. Their deaths occurred on October 12 and 24, 1862. Most of the Michigan soldiers buried at Antietam have their hometowns listed in the official record book. George Catlin of the Sixteenth Michigan died of typhoid fever near Sharpsburg on October 26. Private Emory Wood, 104th New York, died at Pry's Mill on October 3. Grave 3,259 is that of Private George C. Drake of the First Wisconsin, killed on July 2, 1861, at Falling Waters. Drake was the first soldier from Wisconsin to be killed in action. On December 22, 1862, Private Charles Ford of the Third Vermont died in the Hagerstown Court House.[3]

A lovely stone wall was erected around the cemetery. Within the confines of the cemetery there is a uniform height of four feet three inches. However, on the outside, due to grading and the slope of the hill, the wall is twelve to sixteen feet high.

For many years the office of the battlefield site as well as a small museum were located just inside the cemetery gates. Now the visitor's center is near the Dunkard Church, north of Sharpsburg.

Dedication ceremonies were held on the fifth anniversary of the battle, September 17, 1867. Special trains brought members of the Masonic Order, Maryland Governor Swann,

An early picture of the National Cemetery.

and President Andrew Johnson to Keedysville. Governors of many northern states and congressmen also came. The trip to Keedysville was made on the train. Then carriages and marching brought the group to Cemetery Hill.

The marshals and those in charge of the dedication program assembled in Keedysville at 9:00 A.M. on September 17, 1867. At 10:30, the military units in the procession formed west of the railroad, and Masons and other civic groups east of the tracks. Promptly at eleven, the head of the column started the march to the National Cemetery. The military was instructed to form in line at the entrance to the cemetery and present arms when the president of the United States passed by.

Among those present on that historic day were General Ambrose Burnside, and a man who would occupy the White House in a few more years, U. S. Grant.

262

After music by the band, and a prayer by the Reverend Hiram Matison, D.D., of New Jersey, Governor Swann of Maryland made a few introductory remarks, saying:

> . . . I extend a cordial welcome to His Excellency the President of the United States and his cabinet, the Governors of our sister States, and the distinguished guests who have come to participate in the ceremonies of this most interesting occasion. . . .
> The flag which floats over us today is the flag of our Union. The sword of battle has been sheathed. The tramp of contending armies, the embittered strife of father against son, and brother against brother, no longer resounds within our borders. The star of this great Republic is again in the ascendant. In the calm sunshine of peace we are here to mingle our tears with the survivors of the illustrious dead who have sacrificed their lives for their country, and are sleeping upon this field.
> May I not, in this solemn hour, invoke the interposition of Almighty God for a speedy restoration of harmony and brotherly love throughout this broad land; and that North, South, East and West, laying aside the animosities of the past, we may stand together hereafter, and in all future time, as one people, having a common origin and bound together by a common destiny? May this Union be perpetual.[4]

After more music and the laying of the cornerstone by the grand master of the Grand Lodge of Masons of Maryland, the Honorable A. W. Bradford, wartime governor of Maryland, made a speech.

Bradford said in his opening and closing remarks:

> We have met here today, my countrymen, on one of the most memorable of the battlefields of our civil war, and we stand upon a site selected from the midst of it as an appropriate resting place for those who here laid down their lives as a sacrifice to the cause of free government and a National Union. We have come . . . to dedicate by some public and official proceeding, on this, the anniversary of the battle, the spot so selected, hallowed as it is already with every hill around it, in the heart of the nation.
> Thus in our heart we would enshrine the memory of the Union soldiers; generations yet unborn shall recount to their offspring the history of their valor; and long after brass and marble have crumbled into dust, shall their names be preserved as the men who perished to perpetuate what their fathers had so struggled to establish—this Heaven-appointed Government of popular freedom.[5]

Next was a hymn composed by the Reverend Edward Meyer of Pennsylvania. It was to the tune of "America."

Hallowed be all around!
This place is holy ground,
    Henceforth, for aye;
Here mountain shadows wave
O'er many a cherished grave,
Where sleep the young and brave,
    Home from the fray!

Here where the flash and roar
Battle and carnage bore
    Over the main,
Soft, on your lowly bed
Rest on your fame laurel'd head,
Our noble patriot dead
    By treason slain.

Grief stricken hearts have throbbed—
Sable clad homes have sobbed
    Far from your rest;
Listen for steps in vain,
That ne'er shall come again,
To swell the victor's train
    From East to West!

Antietam's liquid gem
Murmurs your requiem
    In mournful strain!
Angels unseen stand near,
Bright guard of honor here,
Till Christ our Lord appear,
    Mighty to reign.

Silence and sadness round
No bugle's martial sound
    Your sleep breaks now,
Columbia saved, now sheathes
Her conquering sword; Fame wreathes
Where'er true manhood breathes,
    Your pale, cold brow!

"Glory to God on high,"
Peal through earth, sea and sky,
    "Good Will to Men!"
Blending and rising higher,
Like Pentecostal fire,
Let freedom strains inspire
    All hearts! Amen!

264

Next followed a long, but meaningful poem of dedication, written by Clarence F. Buhler of New York, and read in his absence by G. L. Cranmer, Esq., of West Virginia.

Then the president of the United States, the Honorable Andrew Johnson, spoke to the assembled audience. His remarks were brief:

> I shall not attempt to give utterance to the feelings of emotion inspired by the addresses and prayers which have been made, and the hymns which have been sung. I shall attempt no such thing. I am merely here to give my countenance and aid to the ceremonies on this occasion; but I may be permitted to express the hope that we may follow the example which has been so eloquently alluded to this afternoon, and which has been so clearly set by the illustrious dead. When we look on yon battlefield, I think of these brave men who fell in the fierce struggle of battle, and who sleep silent in their graves. Yes, many of them sleep in silence and peace within this beautiful inclosure after the earnest conflict has ceased. Would to God, we of the living could imitate their example, as they lay sleeping in their tombs, and live together in friendship and peace. [The President was interrupted at this point by applause.]
>
> You, my fellow citizens, have my earnest wishes as you have had my efforts in time gone by, in the earliest and most trying perils, to preserve the Union of these States, to restore peace and harmony to one distracted and divided country; and you shall have my efforts in vindication of the flag of the Republic, and of the Constitution of our forefathers.[6]

Thus concluded the remarks of the president of the United States. The benediction was pronounced, salutes fired, and the presidential party escorted back to Keedysville. There they boarded the train, and left at ten minutes after seven for Washington.

Among the assistant marshals that day was Colonel Leopold Blumenberg. Five years earlier he had been a major in the Fifth Maryland and was severely wounded near Bloody Lane.

When the sun set on that September day in 1867, the president and others had dedicated a final resting place for "the honored dead," and the Masons had laid the cornerstone for an imposing monument. The drums had beaten the last roll call. Another historic day along the Antietam was over.

Eleven years later in 1878, a large soldier, nicknamed "Old Simon" by a Sharpsburg resident, would stand guard over

265

"the bivouac of the dead." The monument was designed and made at James G. Batterson's quarries near Providence, Rhode Island. In 1876, two years before arriving in Sharpsburg, the handsome monument stood to the right of the main entrance at the Centennial Exposition in Philadelphia. When the Centennial closed, the monument was brought to Washington. Next came a long trip up the Chesapeake and Ohio Canal to Snyder's Landing. It was rolled on oak planks to the cemetery which had been turned over to the national government in 1877. The monument stands forty-seven feet high. The soldier is twenty-one feet six inches. He arrived in two pieces and was put together at the belt. The monument weighs 250 tons and cost $30,000.

The Confederate dead at South Mountain and Antietam were buried like many of the men from the North, in gardens, along roads, in fence corners, old caves and wells, and under trees.

Originally, the Union and Confederate dead were to be buried together at Antietam in the new cemetery. However, many states north of the Mason-Dixon Line objected to this, and refused to appropriate money if such a plan was carried out. Therefore, the national cemetery became a Union cemetery.

The Confederate dead remained where they had been hastily buried. But in 1870 the Maryland Legislature made a provision of $5,000 to provide a decent burial for those of the Army of Northern Virginia killed on Maryland soil.

Governor Bowie appointed the Honorable Henry Kyd Douglas of Ferry Hill, George Freaner, and James H. Gambrill to supervise the task. Virginia and West Virginia also contributed money to the effort. Douglas, Freaner, and Gambrill purchased a section of Rose Hill Cemetery in Hagerstown to provide a final resting place for the men in Gray who gave their all in the Maryland campaign. In early 1872 the work of removing the dead Confederates to Rose Hill was begun. Twenty-five hundred skeletons were brought to the area designated as "The Washington Cemetery." Dedication of the site took place on June 15, 1877.[7]

During the one hundredth anniversary of the Maryland

campaign, a service of rededication was held on a Sunday afternoon with former President Dwight D. Eisenhower as guest speaker. Congressman, now senator, Charles Mc. Mathias inserted the story of Hagerstown's Confederate Cemetery in the *Congressional Record.*

In 1868, General John Logan, commander of the Grand Army of the Republic, the forerunner of the American Legion, issued the directive that the GAR posts should observe May 30 as a day to strew flowers upon or otherwise decorate the graves of their fallen comrades. This was the beginning of Decoration or Memorial Day. Across the country parades were held with the theme of God, country, and brotherhood. Bands played patriotic and martial music. Great orations were given in town parks and in cemeteries.

The year 1868 marked the beginning of the annual observances in Sharpsburg. Memorial Day as well as September 17 would play an important role in the life of the town for many years. Annually, until the men of the Blue and Gray started to answer the last roll call, those who had fought at Antietam tried to return on either Memorial Day or Anniversary Day. Many of them stayed in the local hotels, the Nicodemus Hotel being a favorite.

These men usually marched or rode in the Memorial Day Parade, and often occupied places of honor. Local historians stress that the avenue of trees near the Antietam station were planted to provide shade for the aging veterans as they returned to Sharpsburg.

The Memorial Day observances provide enough material for a book. In *Drums Along the Antietam* we simply stress the fact that Sharpsburg had one of the first Memorial Day programs, and still provides a meaningful display of remembrance and patriotism on May 30. On that day, thousands come to Sharpsburg to see little children, school bands, civic groups, and military organizations march up Cemetery Hill. Then within the walls, the visitors hear hymns of faith, and inspiring speeches.

In 1885, George B. McClellan was invited to Sharpsburg to be the featured speaker at the Memorial Day Services in the National Cemetery. Douglas says this was his only return trip

Parade honors dead.

to Antietam. However, the 1867 program for the dedication of the National Cemetery lists McClellan as a participant.

But in 1885, Henry Kyd Douglas invited McClellan to be his guest in Hagerstown. The former commander of the Army of the Potomac came with his son, his brother, and Colonel Wright who had served on his staff during the war.

George B. McClellan, Jr., fared better politically than his father. The younger McClellan, born in late 1865, was elected a Democratic member of Congress in 1895 and served until 1903. At that time he resigned to become mayor of New York City, a position he held until 1910. From 1912 to 1931, with time out for overseas duty in WW I, he served as professor of history at Union Seminary.

Writing of Memorial Day, 1885, Douglas says:

> We had a most interesting day on the field. It was much of a reunion, and for the first time a large delegation of men who wore the grey came over the Potomac and marched in review past the Federal General, as he stood on the rostrum at the Cemetery, hat in hand, greeting them and responding to their salutes with all the frankness and ease which distinguished him as a soldier and gentleman. He made an admirable address and his reference to "that splendid man and soldier Robert E. Lee," with whom he had served "in the land of the Montezumas," made the old Confederates uncover in memory of their great leader and filled them with personal liking for his manly and chivalric opponent.[8]

On Memorial Day, 1885, George B. McClellan made his last visit to Antietam. For the final time in his life, soldiers marched by as he stood, watched and took their salutes.

C. W. Rohrer was in the crowd that day. Years later he related his memories of seeing General McClellan in 1885.

> I was greatly impressed by General McClellan's eloquent address. I shall never forget the tremendous ovation which he received when he arose and walked to the front of the rostrum, clad in the same faded blue uniform which he had worn when he commanded at the Battle of Antietam, twenty-three years before. He was warmly applauded at intervals during his speech and at its close the applause was almost deafening. I recall also the vast throngs of Grand Army men who were present.

On that Decoration Day, General McClellan said:

> When I last stood upon this historic field, the smoke of battle still wreathed these hills and filled the valleys. These rocks still echoed

the harsh sounds of strife. The ground was all too thickly strewn with the forms of the quiet dead, and of those still in agony. . . .

We are here with a common purpose. We are here to testify our reverence for the valiant dead. In these too numerous graves, stretching so far and wide around us, let us bury all animosity, all bitter recollections of the past, remembering only that on Antietam's hills brave men gave their lives for what they thought the right, and proved that the heroism of our ancestors still reigned in the hearts of Americans on that day. . . .

I pray that this fair land of ours may never again be the scene of such carnage as some of us beheld long years ago on these blood stained heights. . . .

Let us not forget a prayer that our great Union may never again be endangered. . . . [but] whatever danger may threaten the land in ages to come, the people may rest secure if such armies arise for its defense as the two which fought on this very field.

Burials at Antietam National Cemetery

	Known	Unknown	Total
Connecticut	80	5	85
Delaware	28		28
Illinois	28	1	29
Indiana	138	8	146
Iowa	2		2
Maine	88	8	96
Maryland	87	6	93
Massachusetts	130	62	192
Michigan	100	37	137
Minnesota	10		10
New Hampshire	24	1	25
New Jersey	65	5	70
New York	730	137	867
Officers-Commissioned	31	7	38
Ohio	320	29	349
Pennsylvania	550	92	642
Rhode Island	22	1	23
West Virginia	171	2	173
Wisconsin	130	12	142
United States Regulars	79	7	86
Vermont	56	9	65
Unknown Soldiers		1,436	1,436
Total	2,869	1,865	4,734

The preceding list was compiled by George Hess, Battlefield Superintendent in 1889. Bodies were interred from the battlefields of Antietam and South Mountain. Others who died from their wounds or in cavalry skirmishes were brought to Antietam from Keedysville, Boonsboro, Frederick, Middletown, Hagerstown, Smoketown, Clarysville, Hancock, Weverton, and Burkittsville.

Memorial Day, 1900

On May 30, 1900, the Maryland Monument was dedicated opposite the Dunkard Church. The next day the Hagerstown paper carried this story:

Another link in the chain which binds together the once warring factions of the North and South was forged Wednesday by the dedication of a monument erected to the memory of men who wore the Gray as well as those who wore the Blue and who died in mortal combat on the bloody field of Antietam. This event which is probably without parallel in the History of the world, was graced by the presence of the President of the United States William McKinley, accompanied by many members of Congress, the Governor of Maryland, and prominent men from all parts of the country. There were also present hundreds of veterans who fought the "lost cause" and thousands who fought for the side that proved victorious. Side by side and shoulder to shoulder they stood with uncovered heads throughout the ceremony which marked the conveyance of the monument from the State of Maryland to the National Government.

Governor Smith of Maryland turned the monument over to the Honorable Elihu Root, Secretary of War, as the representative of the National Government. Secretary Root responded. He told how President McKinley—38 years ago on September 17, 1862—while yet a boy of 18 years, won his commission on Antietam's field. At that time President McKinley was a commissary Sergeant in charge of wagon trains some distance back from where the fighting was going on. Without receiving orders from his superior officers, and entirely on his own responsibility, he directed the drivers of the wagons to proceed to the front in order that the hunger of the men of the 23rd Ohio Regiment might be appeased. It was for this gallant act that he was made a commissioned officer.

President McKinley then, amid the strains of "Dixie" and "Yankee Doodle," arose to speak. . . .

"My fellow citizens, I appear here only for the moment that I may make acknowledgement for your courteous greeting. I am glad to meet on this field the followers of Lee, Jackson, Longstreet, and Johnson, with the followers of McClellan, Grant, Sherman, and Sheridan, greeting each other, not with arms at their hands but with affection in every heart. One reflection and only one crowds my

271

mind. It is the difference between this scene and the scene 38 years ago when the men wearing the blue and the men wearing the gray visiting in shot and shell, death on each other. This meeting after these many years has but one sentiment, love for Nation and flag."[9]

The New York Monument

In the Army of the Potomac at Antietam were sixty-seven infantry regiments, five cavalry regiments, fourteen batteries of artillery, and two engineer regiments from New York. On May 4, 1908, the New York Monuments Commission purchased seven acres of ground from Rezin and Emma Fisher for the purpose of erecting a monument to the more than twenty-seven thousand New York troops who participated in the Battle of Antietam. The cost of the land near the Dunkard Church was $1,402.[10]

The lovely monument was made by the Swenson Granite Company of Concord, New Hampshire, and dedicated on September 17, 1920. Each New York unit participating at Antietam was permitted to send three men to the dedication ceremonies. Nearly three hundred of the thinning Blue line came for the program.

The procession formed near the Dunkard Church and then walked to the hill where the New York Monument is located. Through the courtesy of the War Department a battery of artillery and a troop of cavalry came from Fort Myer for escort duty and to fire the customary salutes. Music was provided by the Rohrersville band.

The Reverend William T. Pray, a member of the 102nd New York in 1862, gave the invocation, praying:

> We bow before Thee to give Thee thanks and praise for Thy guidance, protection and care during the past, which enables us who are but a remnant of those who fought on this field fifty-eight years ago, to gather here and in Thy presence join hearts and hands to dedicate this monument to the memory of the brave men from our great Empire State, who, on that never-to-be-forgotten seventeenth day of September 1862, made the supreme sacrifice of life itself so that our Union should be preserved.[11]

The featured speaker was Lt. General Nelson A. Miles, U.S. Army Retired. Colonel Lewis Stegman, chairman of the event, introduced the general in glowing terms:

272

Comrades, ladies and gentlemen, we have here with us one of the most glorious of American commanders; one of the finest soldiers . . . the world has ever known; and one who upon this field, and upon many other fields, achieved feats of skill and valor that go down through the war record of the Army of the Potomac. Starting as a young fellow in the ranks, he went through the various stages of promotion, until finally we see him as a lieutenant-colonel in the Sixty-first New York Infantry. . . . On this great field of Antietam . . . he fought a calm, grim, and unyielding fight at the Bloody Lane and Piper House. . . .

Then in the days succeeding the war, no name upon the historical records of our country bears a more magnificent impress of what we call "the settling of the West," between the Mississippi and the Pacific. A great Indian fighter and one of the greatest fighters the United States ever produced . . . Lieutenant-General Nelson A. Miles.[12]

Nelson A. Miles

When Colonel Francis Barlow, commanding the Sixty-first and Sixty-fourth New York regiments, fell severely wounded near Bloody Lane, the leadership of the two regiments fell upon a young lieutenant colonel by the name of Nelson A. Miles. At Antietam he stepped into command and "inscribed on the annals of American military history a record seldom if ever equaled by a volunteer soldier."[13] Wounded four times during the war, he won the Medal of Honor for gallantry at Chancellorsville.

In 1868 he married a niece of General William T. Sherman. Then it was off to duty in the West. He had come a long way. Only twenty-three when he assumed command at Antietam, he was brevetted major general of volunteers before the end of the war.

Miles had the ability to look over a field of battle and evaluate the terrain at a glance. At Antietam, as always, his command was "Advance." He was greatly depressed by McClellan's failure to follow the Confederates. In his writings, Miles tells of piling fence rails and brush on the swollen carcasses of the horses and burning them after the graves of the soldiers were completed.

Miles succeeded against the Indians after just about everybody else failed. In Texas in 1874 he put an end to the raids of the Kiowas and Comanches. After the Custer massacre, he drove Sitting Bull into the hills of Canada. This was done by marching through blizzards and zero weather. Miles broke the power of Chief Crazy Horse at Wolf Mountain, and finally captured Chief Joseph of the Nez Perces after the brilliant Indian leader had outwitted everybody sent against him. In 1891 he captured Geronimo after campaigns in Arizona and New Mexico. The Indians called him "Bear Coat." Miles always respected the Indians, and called for their fair treatment. However, his advocation of fair treatment for the Indians earned him many political enemies.

In September of 1895, the young lieutenant colonel who led the Sixty-first and Sixty-fourth New York at Antietam received the following order: "By direction of the President, Major-General Nelson A. Miles is assigned to the command of the Army of the United States."[14]

Thus the New England farm boy and storekeeper moved into a position once held by George Washington, U. S. Grant, Sherman and Sheridan.

His job was not easy. He fought many battles with the politicians, and differed with the administration over the Spanish-American War. He was opposed to sending untrained troops to Cuba. McKinley and the secretary of war tried to put him on the shelf. But after many troubles in the field, Miles was ordered to Puerto Rico and captured the place without loss. He won a major victory by strategy and maneuver.

In 1903 President Theodore Roosevelt believed there were too many Civil War veterans on active duty. He, therefore, issued an order that all officers would prove their physical fitness by a cross-country ride of ninety miles in three days. Although nearly sixty-four, Miles accepted the challenge. At five o'clock on a July morning, Miles set out from Fort Sill, Oklahoma. Relay points with fresh mounts were established at ten-mile intervals. Miles made the first thirty-four miles in two and one-half hours. By eight o'clock it was ninety in the shade, and by noon the temperature had risen to one hundred. Miles, who always stayed in tip-top shape, rode the ninety miles in nine and one-half hours, a remarkable feat indeed.

But a month later, Miles reached the mandatory retirement age and stepped down as a lieutenant general. The rest of his life was devoted to traveling, speaking, and writing. In many respects he was a man like Douglas MacArthur.

General Miles lived until May 1925. He was eighty-five then. But the Ringling Brothers Circus was coming to town and he wanted to see the circus. He often remarked that something happened to him whenever the National Anthem was played. Perhaps it brought back memories of advancing on Bloody Lane, or withstanding repeated Confederate assaults at Chancellorsville, or leading the crack Fifth Infantry across the Plains, or talking with Sherman, Sitting Bull, Chief Joseph, and Geronimo.

Something did happen to Nelson Miles on that day in May 1925. As the National Anthem was being played, he collapsed and was carried from the tent.

The next day newspapers across the nation carried stories of the passing of Nelson A. Miles, the last combat general of the Civil War, and a veteran of the Civil, Indian, and Spanish-American wars. President Coolidge attended the rites for the old soldier at Saint John's Church. Then the veteran fighter was laid to rest in Arlington National Cemetery.

Seventy-five Years Later

In August 1937, heavy rains came to the Valley of the Antietam. In fact, according to the September 1 issue of the *Morning Herald,* Mr. Miller, the Keedysville weatherman, reported 8.98 inches of rain in August, a new record. The previous high was 8.70 inches in 1911. Rain fell on sixteen of the thirty-one days in August 1937. However, not even a record rainfall could dampen the spirits of those working on the seventy-fifth anniversary of the Battle of Antietam.

A month earlier, on August 1, the *New York Herald Tribune* printed a feature story with this subtitle "McClellan's Son and Lee's Grandson to See Event Recalling Their Crucial Civil War Struggle." The article's concluding paragraph read:

The Antietam Commemoration . . . will include a re-enactment of the crucial struggle at Burnside's Bridge, in which 4,000 troops from Maryland, Virginia and Pennsylvania will take part. It will be witnessed by President Roosevelt and William Ruhe, commander in chief of the Grand Army of the Republic and his staff, as well as a large delegation of Confederate veterans. A feature will be the presence of Colonel George B. McClellan, former Mayor of New York City and son of General McClellan, and Dr. Charles Bolling Lee, grandson of the Confederate leader. Senator Millard E. Tydings is chairman of the National Antietam Commission.

These plans had been in the making for a long time. On January 16, 1936, a group of Hagerstown men and state officials met to plan a fitting observance for the 200th anniversary of the settling of Washington County, the 175th anniversary of the settling of Hagerstown, and the 75th anniversary of the Battle of Antietam, all occurring in 1937.

More than two hundred men and women met to discuss the need for careful planning. "Particular stress was placed upon the fact that seldom, if ever, is there afforded the opportunity for the simultaneous celebration of three so far-reaching events." The Washington County Historical Society was designated as the sponsoring agency for the observance, with the task of planning, preparing, and carrying through to completion plans to be proposed in various subcommittees. The historical society said:

It . . . seems fitting and logical that the descendants of those who fought in the sixties, in both the uniform of the Blue and that of the Gray, should be brought together in commemorative observance on Maryland soil.

The story of Antietam and Washington County was to be printed, and a program prepared depicting the life of the early settlers, farming, the development of towns and villages, the establishment of government, wars, and rumors of war, conservation of wildlife, the growth and development of transportation, religion, and education. The hope of the planners was reported to the Seventy-fourth Congress on June 17, 1936, in a document bearing the number 3016:

Therefore in moulding the character of the observance, the objective has not been the momentary display of patriotism through the medium of oratory and parades but rather the development of an educational theme, the imprint of which may be a lasting one for posterity.

It is therefore proposed that while oratory, civilian and military

276

parades and martial music will find their logical places on the program through exhibits, replicas, restorations, and pageantry, there will be re-created for visual review in concrete form much of the life and customs of the early settlers in the development of this State, and the building of a Nation.

On June 9, Maryland Senator George L. Radcliffe wrote a letter to Colonel Marvin H. McIntyre, assistant secretary to the president, saying:

> Dear Mac:
> As you doubtless know, elaborate preparations are being made to celebrate the Seventy-fifth Anniversary of the Battle of Antietam. This was the most important battle ever fought on Maryland soil, and is certainly one of the most outstanding ones in the history of the nation. . . .
> The members of the Commission are desirous of extending an invitation to the President to be present on some day during the celebration. . . . The members of the Commission would indeed be grateful if the President could spare us a moment or two for the purpose of extending the invitation and indicating briefly the scope of our plans.

Secretary McIntyre received another letter concerning Antietam on July 26, 1937. This one came from Congressman David J. Lewis of the Sixth Congressional District of Maryland. The letter read:

> Anent my visit with you the other day at which time I urged that the President accept an invitation to participate in the celebration of the 75th Anniversary of the Battle of Antietam. . . .
> . . . The climax will be the exercises on September 17, . . . and this is the day it is hoped the President may be present. I know this is also the anniversary day of the Constitution, but the Committee thinks there could not be a more appropriate place for the President to give an address in commemoration of the Constitution; for the Battle of Antietam was the crucial test as to whether the Union was going to survive. . . .

The committee composed of Maryland Senators Tydings and Radcliffe, Senator Byrd of Virginia, Congressman Lewis, and Park Loy of Hagerstown gained an audience with the president who decided to make the trip to Antietam on the anniversary of the Constitution, as well as the anniversary of the battle which changed the course of the war.

The official invitation read:

Dear Mr. President:

The sponsoring and advisory agencies for the National Commemoration of the 75th Anniversary of the Battle of Antietam
herein present a memorandum of the backgrounds, objectives, facts
and planning in connection with that historically famous conflict of
arms and the proposed anniversary observance.

On behalf of the countless thousands interested in the proposed
commemoration, these agencies solicit your endorsement and most
cordially invite your participation, at least on the climatic day, as
the honor guest and speaker.

Respectfully submitted,
The Washington County Historical Society,
The United States Antietam Celebration Commission,
The Maryland State Advisory Committee,
The Hagerstown Chamber of Commerce

When he learned the president had responded favorably, L.
F. Staub, superintendent of the Shepherdstown Ferry, sent a
note to the White House inviting Mr. Roosevelt to use the
ferry. However, the secretary to the president sent a note
declining the kind offer. The route selected was from Washington to Frederick, Maryland, Frederick to Boonsboro,
Maryland, and Boonsboro to Sharpsburg, Maryland.

As the summer of 1937 passed all the pieces of a stirring
program started to fall into line. A great pageant, *On the
Wings of Time,* was to be presented nightly at the Hagerstown
Fairgrounds. During the seventy-fifth anniversary, these
grounds were known as the "Exposition Grounds." Curtain
time was listed as 7:15 and 9:00 from September 3 through
September 16.

On Saturday, September 11, Washington County honored
her sister cities. Mayors and city officials from nearby towns
in the tri-state area were given the red-carpet treatment, plus
a tour of the battlefield. In the evening, the Waynesboro High
School Band presented a concert.

Sunday, September 12, massed choirs from Sharpsburg,
Boonsboro, Keedysville, Williamsport, and Shepherdstown
gave a sacred concert as a memorial to those who wore the
Blue and the Gray. The very picturesque service, starting at
4:00 P.M. was described by the *Morning Herald* on September 7:

278

The processional through the National Cemetery of the vested choirs will be a scene of impressive beauty, possibly never equalled by any outdoor service in this section of the country.

Julia Brandt as Miss Antietam presided over the activities. Monday, the thirteenth, was dedicated to Baltimore and designated "National Anthem Day." Tuesday an old fashioned family picnic was held at the Exposition Grounds. The day was dedicated to agriculture, and featured a livestock parade. The Boonsboro and Myersville bands gave concerts. Wednesday was proclaimed aviation and areoplane day. Trips were offered by air over the battlefield. The next day governors of the states involved at Antietam arrived. They visited the battlefield, and were welcomed by the governor of Maryland. A Memorial Bench was dedicated in the National Cemetery. In the evening, a big dinner was held at the Hotel Alexander. Notable state and national figures were in attendance. After the final presentation of *On the Wings of Time*, a ball was held at the State Armory in honor of those visiting Washington County from other states.

Excitement was building. It was the eve of the seventy-fifth anniversary of the Battle of Antietam. In Frederick County, Winchester, Virginia, Chambersburg, Pennsylvania, and other places, families were preparing picnic lunches, and checking the car. Tomorrow they would leave bright and early for the Antietam Creek and Sharpsburg.

The papers had carried stories released earlier that Franklin Delano Roosevelt was coming to Antietam. On September 3, the *Baltimore Sun* released this interesting story:

> A.P. Wirephoto Service plans to use this new service for the first time for practicable purposes . . . to take its station on Antietam Battlefield on September 17, there to transmit photographs of the battle re-enacted like a flash across the continent.
> . . . the occasion will add extreme magnificence to the re-enactment of the Battle of Antietam—because it will be the first time employed, to go down in history as another invention with the President of the United States playing the leading role.

Franklin D. Roosevelt, president of the United States, drove from Pennsylvania Avenue to South Mountain in a steady rain on September 17, 1937. By the time he reached the Mountain House there was a break in the clouds. And by

President Franklin D. Roosevelt at Antietam.

the time he reached the area near Bloody Lane, the weather
was beginning to clear.

Between thirty and forty thousand persons had gathered
to hear the president. He sat in the car and waited while
nearby artillery pieces fired a twenty-one-gun salute. The
United States Army Band played the National Anthem.

Then accompanied by Senator Millard Tydings of Maryland, Senator Harry Byrd of Virginia, and Congressman
Lewis, he went to the rostrum. On the way, Miss Josephine
Remsburg and Miss Orpha Renner gave President Roosevelt a
piece of wood from a tree near Burnside Bridge.

His original manuscript fluttered off the stand at the close
of his speech. It is now the proud possession of one of the
natives of Sharpsburg. Other copies had been released to the
press. His message on Constitution Day as well as Anniversary
Day stressed unity and harmony. President Roosevelt said:

It is too soon to define the history of the present generation, but I venture the belief that it was not until the World War of twenty years ago that we acted once more as a nation of restored unity. . . .

Deeply we appreciate that the distress or difficulty of any one part of the Union adversely affects each and every other part. We stand ready in all parts of the land to lend a helping hand to those Americans who need it most.

In the presence of the spirits of those who fell on this field—Union soldiers and Confederate soldiers—we can believe that they rejoice with us in the unity of understanding which is so increasingly ours today. They urge us on in all we do to foster that unity in the spirit of tolerance, of willingness to help our neighbor, and of faith in the destiny of the United States.

In my own case, though I came into the world seventeen years after the close of the War Between the States, the results of that war and of the difficult years that followed it do not make me think of it as history.

And today, seventy-five years after the critical Battle of Antietam, there are still many among us who can remember it. It is therefore an American battle which thousands of Americans, middle-aged and old, can still visualize as bearing some relationship to their own lives.

We know that Antietam was one of the decisive engagements of the Civil War because it marked the first effort of the Confederacy to invade the North—tactically a drawn battle, but actually a factor of vital importance to the final result because it spelled the failure of an attempt.

Whether we be old or young, it serves us little to discuss again the rights and the wrongs of the long four-year War Between the States. We can but wish that the war had never been. We can and we do revere the memory of the brave men who fought on both sides—we can and we do honor those who fell on this and other fields.

But we know today that it was best for the generations of Americans who fought the war and for the generations of Americans who have come after them that the conflict did not end in a division of our land into two nations. I like to think that it was the will of God that we remain one people.

Today old and young alike are saddened by the knowledge of the bitter years that followed the war—years bitter to the South because of economic destruction and the denial to its population of the normal rights of free Americans—years bitter to the North because victory engendered among many the baser passions of revenge and tyranny.

We must not deny that the effects of the so-called "era of reconstruction" made themselves felt in many evil ways for half a century. They encouraged sectionalism, they led to misunderstanding and they greatly retarded the unity of the nation.[15]

281

Before he left to return to the White House, President Roosevelt shook hands with the surviving Union and Confederate veterans present. One of them, William Lovell, a member of Phillips's Georgia Legion, was indeed fortunate to be on hand. Seventy-five years earlier he had been with his comrades guarding the approaches to Burnside Bridge. About 4:00 P.M. Lovell fell severely wounded. In fact, he was left for dead, and like many others spent the night on the battlefield with little water or cover. Finally at 9:00 A.M. on the eighteenth, Lovell was picked up and given treatment.

No history of Sharpsburg would be complete without the mention of two of its physicians, Augustus Asbury Biggs and Walter Hal Shealy. Dr. Biggs first saw the light of day on December 27, 1812, near Pipe Creek in Carroll County, Maryland. As a lad he lived and worked on his father's farm. He was always interested in what made animals and frogs work. Like many other children of his day, he obtained his early education in the one-room schools dotting the countryside. Many times he walked in his barefeet to school, often reading as he walked. Being interested in medicine, he studied under the direction of a nearby doctor until he went to Jefferson Medical College. In 1836, Augustus Biggs was granted his M.D. degree.

Returning from Philadelphia, Dr. Biggs commenced practice in Carroll County. However, he soon moved to Sharpsburg where he remained to practice medicine for fifty-three years. In those years he delivered more than three thousand babies, most of them at home. His trusty horse carried him from Sharpsburg to the edge of Hagerstown to the north, and over the hills to Rohrersville to the south. East and west his practice extended from Boonsboro to the Potomac River.

Dr. Biggs was a gentle and reserved individual. Yet, he took an active part in every program aimed at community betterment. He served his town as burgess on numerous occasions. Being anti-slavery, he became a Republican and a staunch Unionist.

There is some indication that his home might have served as a hospital during the Battle of Antietam. Other records

282

indicate that he had charge of the hospitals located on Sharpsburg's Main Street. During the battle a shell entered one of the rooms in his house and destroyed just about all the contents. Another shell hit the gabled end of the house and displaced some of the stone. A sick Confederate was sitting in the doorway of the Biggs home when a stray bullet hit him and ended his life.

Dr. Biggs was named by the Maryland General Assembly as one of the incorporators of the Antietam National Cemetery. He was the first president of the board. He formulated the plan of burial by states in plots, which was adopted, and to a degree, followed in other national cemeteries. Those of us who embrace the beauty and reverence of the Antietam National Cemetery today, owe much to Dr. Biggs. Although there were others on the board, he was instrumental in selecting and obtaining the site of the cemetery. He also helped to supervise the construction and upkeep until the site was turned over to the United States Government.

Williams in his history says of Dr. Biggs, "His patriotism and unselfishness enabled him to link his name for all time with one of the most beautiful of our national cemeteries."

The Sharpsburg doctor was a member of the Methodist Episcopal Church. In fact his middle name was given him in honor of Bishop Francis Asbury. The bishop learning of this, later gave him a Bible.

In 1971 the doctor's fine residence is still maintained much as it was in 1862. The house still shows the mark of an artillery shell. The proud owners are Mr. and Mrs. John McCullom who work for WHAG-TV in Hagerstown, and who led the effort to get Paul Cunningham of NBC-TV to feature Sharpsburg on the May 30, 1971, "Today Show."

Walter Hal Shealy was a dedicated physician, and a warm, public-spirited citizen. He loved the people of the Valley of the Antietam, and they loved him. Often as he talked with them, they found balm for the soul, as well as help for their physical ailments.

A native of South Carolina, Dr. Shealy moved to Sharpsburg in 1928. Immediately he took an intense interest in the history of the area. He sought to learn about it, and also to preserve the beauty and history of Sharpsburg and vicinity. He was a man who loved Sharpsburg, Washington County, and his adopted state of Maryland. He served as president of the Washington County Historical Society for many years. During his presidency, and largely due to his leadership, the historical society purchased the Spong farm and the site of the Dunkard Church. These tracts were in turn given to the National Park Service.

Dr. Shealy endeavored to master history as he had mastered medicine. In 1937 he was appointed chairman of the Antietam Division of the Seventy-fifth Anniversary of the Battle of Antietam. Greater tasks faced him in 1962 when he served as general chairman of the centennial observance. His efforts led to the restoration of Burnside Bridge and the reconstruction of the Dunkard Church.

Joining the American Legion just after World War II, having served in the Marine Corps in World War I, Dr. Shealy worked with the Antietam post and the state American Legion in a program to get Congress to study the importance of Antietam, and at the same time adopt a program to preserve it. Many of the present-day improvements are due to his efforts. He along with others urged Congress to acquire additional land to preserve Antietam for future generations.

For many years Dr. Shealy worked almost as a committee of one, planning and promoting the annual Sharpsburg Memorial Day observances. In 1948 the Sharpsburg American Legion Post assumed the task. In their *99th Annual Memorial Day Booklet,* his comrades wrote, "Dr. Shealy has joined the ranks in Post Everlasting."

The year 1971 finds many of the Civil War battlefields in the East threatened by commercialism and development. Some have already lost large portions of ground. Manassas was saved the tragedy of an interstate highway cutting through the battlefield by mass protests. Civil War round tables were able to keep a power line from going through Antietam. But Fredericksburg, Petersburg, and Richmond, Virginia, are in great danger of losing land that in the 1860s

284

was the scene of history in the making. Even the remote areas such as the Wilderness of Spotsylvania have not been spared. Golf courses and summer homes have taken large tracts of land which had remained almost untouched since the days of the Blue and Gray.

Gettysburg is out of this world. Name the type of restaurant, motel, or museum you wish to visit, and you will most likely find it at Gettysburg. J. Robert Dunphy speaking of Gettysburg, stated in *The New York Times* on May 30, 1971, that:

> It seems as though Americans are not so much consecrating the tragic sacrifice of the 51,000 men in Blue and Gray who fell here as they are cashing in on it.
>
> At least that's the view of National Park Service officials, many historians, Civil War buffs, concerned tourists and other Americans.

Thus far, Antietam has been spared the blight of commercialism and development. But the park service owns only 800 acres, whereas another 1,000 acres are needed to preserve the historical heritage and scenic beauty of Antietam.

Key sections of land are in the hands of developers. At the spot where A. P. Hill came with his "terrible swift sword" to hit the Union flank, one developer wants to sell farmettes. Yet, at this point, the Confederate Army of Northern Virginia almost met its Waterloo in September 1862. If the plans go through, the monument erected at the spot where General Isaac P. Rodman was mortally wounded, and the monument to Hawkins's Zouaves could very well be in someone's backyard.

There are many opinions as to what are the best solutions. However, reality must be faced. Once the bulldozer and backhoe have gone to work and houses erected, something is gone forever.

With all the talk today about environmental controls, saving nature, and having elbow room for the city people, this writer sincerely hopes that the battlefields of the Civil War, and other historic spots, will be spared for future generations to see, to enjoy, and to study.

XIV

TO MAKE MEN FREE

On February 22, 1851, Samuel Mumma and his wife Elizabeth deeded to seven deacons, Joseph Wolfe, John S. Rowland, Samuel Fahrney, Jacob Reichard, Samuel Emmert, John W. Stouffer, and Valentine Reichard of the German Baptist Brethren, a plot of ground on a hill north of Sharpsburg. Two years later, the congregation completed the building of a house of worship.

The members of the church were at worship on Sunday, September 14, 1862, when suddenly they heard the booming of the cannon in the nearby passes of South Mountain. We can imagine that some of the younger children started to cry, frightened by the strange noises. No doubt the women became alarmed and anxious. All present must have wondered what the next days would bring. We can almost picture these godly people kneeling in prayer, asking for the Almighty to protect them and their farms. No doubt church was dismissed early so the congregation could get home and take steps to protect their crops and animals.

Next Sunday the little white brick church would present an entirely different picture. On Wednesday, it would be the objective of the attack by the Union First and Twelfth corps on "Stonewall" Jackson's position. The fields and trees around the church witnessed some of the bloodiest fighting in the history of mankind. Bloody and wounded men were placed upon the church floor. Dead horses lay near the main entrance. Shell holes made large openings at numerous places in the building as the opposing forces traded blow for blow.

The land upon which the Dunkard Church stands was a

part of "Anderson's Delight," a component of the Samuel Mumma, Sr., farmstead, traced back to 1785.[1]

The last regular minister at the Dunkard Church was the Reverend John Otto, the father of Miss Ruth Otto who still lives in Sharpsburg. He died in 1916. Occasional services were held in the building until it was destroyed by a violent wind and hail storm on May 23, 1921.

During the next few years the heirs of Samuel Mumma made efforts to reclaim the land. The original agreement was that the German Baptist Brethren should erect a church and establish a cemetery on the land. With no cemetery, and no church standing, the Mumma heirs rightfully felt the land should come back to them.

The Washington County Court directed Omer Kaylor to sell the property at public auction. The proceeds were to be divided among the fifty-six Mumma heirs. The directive was carried out by Attorney Kaylor, and on May 13, 1924, the Dunkard Church site was sold to Elmer and Daisy Boyer of Sharpsburg for $800. Two years later the Boyers sold it to Charles and Ora Turner. The Boyer-Turner transaction occurred on November 19, 1926, the anniversary of Lincoln's "Gettysburg Address." Before Mr. Boyer sold the land, he took many of the bricks, doors, window frames, and flooring from the ruins of the church to Sharpsburg. He showed these items to Louis Tuckerman, ranger-historian, and Superintendent Doust at the Antietam National Battlefield Site on July 11, 1951. Some materials had been carried off by souvenir hunters before Mr. Boyer was able to haul them to his Sharpsburg home. Historian Tuckerman and Superintendent Doust were amazed to find many of the wooden benches, joists, door locks, keys, and even window frames with the initials of soldiers carved in them.

These men along with Dr. Shealy and others sought to purchase the site and restore the church. Earlier in 1951, Dr. Shealy with the assistance of the Washington County Historical Society purchased the ground where the white brick church stood in 1862. The cost was $4,000. As a part of the Memorial Day program in 1951, Dr. Shealy presented a symbolic deed for this historic property to Ronald E. Lee, assistant director of the National Park Service.

Today the reconstructed "Dunker" Church stands on its original foundation. Visiting this historic shrine turns the mind backward to September 1862. The visitor can almost visualize the members of the church sitting and listening to Elder David Long's sermon on Sunday morning, September 14, 1862. If any fell asleep he was rudely awakened by a booming noise which sounded like thunder. But it was a clear day. And it wasn't thunder. It was the booming of cannon over at Fox's Gap.

Little could the folks imagine the things that would happen to them during the week. After the service, many of them went as was the custom to one of the neighboring farms for food and fellowship. On this Sabbath day they went to Sam Mumma's. Large tables were set up. The Dunkards prayed and ate. The children played on the lawn. With every noise, anxious eyes were turned toward the mountains. As the moments ticked by, and they prepared to go home to do the evening chores, these folks had the uneasy feeling that they were in for a big storm. Within hours, men in Gray would be encamped in their fields and orchards. And soon, the bloodiest battle of the war would rage around their beloved white brick church, and across Sam Mumma's fields and lawn.

On September 15 and 16 the men of "Stonewall" Jackson's Confederate command assumed their positions in the woods around the church. The dawn of the seventeenth brought the Yankee advance down the Hagerstown Pike to the high ground about the church. The destination of Hooker's men, marching from Joe Poffenberger's fields, where some say the original bricks were made for the church, was a house of peace, the Dunkard Church.

A plaque at the foundation, prior to reconstruction, said: "During the battle the wounded of both armies sought and found sanctuary within its walls. The church was seriously injured by the fire of Union batteries."

Martin Snavely, who lived at Belinda Springs, hauled dead bodies to Hagerstown following the battle. Many of these he obtained at the Dunkard Church, which, after service as a hospital, was used as a morgue. Hagerstown was the nearest major train station to the North. Families anxious to have the remains of their loved ones brought home, hired the farmers in the Valley of the Antietam to haul the coffins to Hagerstown. Mr. Snavely told many of his friends about seeing the pile of arms and legs by the one window at the Dunkard Church. An operating table was just inside the window. A veteran of the battle says he was detailed to haul the arms and legs away, and dispose of them by burning or burial.[2]

Bloodstains remained on some of the church furniture for over one hundred years. Dead horses lay on the lawn of the church, and Mr. Mumma had to drag fifty-five dead horses from his fields to the East Woods where they were burned. Several Union batteries had over a dozen horses killed near the church.

Soldiers have always liked to gather mementos of war. One of these, Sgt. Nathan Dykeman, Company H, 107th New York Volunteers, took as his souvenir the large leather-bound Dunkard Church pulpit Bible. From the hills of Antietam the Bible was taken on September 28, 1862, and moved to the hills of southern New York.

But God works in mysterious ways His wonders to perform. Antietam marked a new beginning along the way to Negro freedom. A member of that race, John T. Lewis, was born on January 10, 1835, in Carroll County, Maryland. He grew up among Dunkard people and joined the Pipe Creek congregation when he reached the age of eighteen.[3]

Being a free man, he went from Maryland to Gettysburg, to Elmira, New York. Arriving in 1862, he became a small farmer, much like the truck farmers of today.

Many folks fear a new day, because they fear what may happen. However, each new day may bring good things, new experiences, new friends, and events which may change the course of life in a wonderful new manner. Such was the experience of Mr. Lewis. Early one afternoon he was returning home from Elmira after taking his vegetables to market. Suddenly he saw a carriage coming directly at him. It was out of control. The three women passengers were unable to manage the horse. Lewis pulled to the side of the road, waited, and at the proper moment jumped. He seized the bridle of the horse, and finally brought the animal to a halt. Neither he nor the three women were injured. Mr. Lewis was profoundly thanked by the three women who turned out to be Mrs. Charles Langdon, her daughter Julia, and a nurse. General Langdon was not at home on that day. But upon his return, he rewarded John Lewis with a check for $1,000. Samuel Clemens, better known as Mark Twain, was at the Langdon home, as they were his in-laws. Mr. Clemens to show his gratitude gave Lewis fifty dollars and a set of autographed books. Mr. Crane in whose home the Langdons had been visiting gave John $400. Mrs. Langdon, thankful for her rescue gave a gold watch with the following inscription:

John T. Lewis, who saved three lives at the
deadly peril of his own, August 23, 1877.
This in grateful remembrance from
Mrs. Charles J. Langdon.

The brave Mr. Lewis was able to buy his sixty-four-acre farm. He became Mr. Langdon's coachman. He and Mark Twain became great friends and spent much time together. In fact, they were often photographed together. Writing of Lewis he said:

John T. Lewis, a friend of mine. These many years—thirty-four in fact. He was my father-in-law's coachman forty years ago; was many years a farmer of Quarry Farm, and is still my neighbor. I have not known an honester man nor a more respect-worthy one. Twenty-seven years ago, by the prompt and intelligent exercise of his courage, presence of mind and extraordinary strength, he saved the lives of three relatives of mine, whom a runaway horse was hurrying to destruction. Naturally I hold him in high and grateful regard.

The years were rolling by. Sergeant Dykeman had answered the last roll call. The Antietam Bible which he carried to New York was given to a widowed and needy sister. To her credit, she wanted to return the Bible to the church on the battlefield. When the 107th New York met for a reunion, the matter was discussed. Dykeman's comrades in arms raised ten dollars and purchased the Bible.

The sister had the much needed money. The old soldiers had the Bible. But how were they to get it back to the Valley of the Antietam? Then someone remembered that John T. Lewis belonged to the Brethren Church. He was the only one of that faith living in the Elmira area. Being an informed church member, he was able to tell the men that the church was still standing, and was being served by Elder John E. Otto of Sharpsburg. The men of the 107th then asked Lewis to return the Bible to the white brick church.

Elder Otto received the express package with joy. At last the Bible was home. He pasted a note inside the front cover of the Bible.

Sharpsburg, Dec. 4th, 1903

This Bible was taken from the Church after the Battle of Antietam by Sergeant Nathan F. Dykeman, September 28, 1862, Regt. 107 Co. H. N.Y.S.V. He is now dead and it fell into the hands of his afflicted sister. She presented it to the Company at their reunion this fall 1903 for which they gave her ten dollars.

Their desire was to send it back to its home in the Brethren Church at Antietam Battlefield if it was still in existence. Through the kindness of Brother John T. Lewis, Elmira, New York, they received my name and address. They wrote me, I answered. The Bible is here after an absence of 41 years, 2 months, 6 days. It is supposed to have been placed in the church by Daniel Miller.

John E. Otto[4]

Daniel Miller was the father-in-law of John Otto, and the great-grandfather of Miss Ruth Otto who still lives in Sharpsburg.

The Bible rested on the Dunkard Church pulpit until 1914. A new church had been erected in Sharpsburg and the old church was being used less and less. Hungry souvenir hunters kept carrying away loose bricks from the rear of the church. Finally, the congregation decided to place the historic Bible in the vault at the denominational home for the aged near Boonsboro. When the Dunkard Church was rebuilt and rededicated in September of 1962, Mr. and Mrs. Newton Long of Baltimore, Mr. Long being a grandson of Elder Long, the preacher at the time of the battle, loaned the Bible to the National Park Service to be placed and preserved in the Dunkard Church.

John T. Lewis had done his job well. In 1906 he died. His obituary, prepared by his own hand, describes his faith and stature: "I have tried to be faithful to the New Testament and order of the Brethren. Though separated from them here, I hope to meet them above where parting is no more."

Four years later, his friend Mark Twain was laid to rest in another section of Woodlawn Cemetery, Elmira, New York.

From the hands of a man whose brothers had been set free by Lincoln after the Battle of Antietam, the Book of Books came back to the little white church.

Lincoln is supposed to have visited the church in October 1862. Jacob Cox, a Union general, says he was with the presidential party. Cox claims the group started from McClellan's headquarters. This poses an interesting question as according to new research, army headquarters had been moved from the Pry farm nearer Shepherdstown. However, Cox says the party followed the route taken by Sumner's Second Corps over the Antietam, through the East Woods, the Miller Cornfield to the church, thence to Bloody Lane and back to army headquarters.[5]

In 1895, a Major Parker who commanded a Confederate artillery battery near the Dunkard Church returned to visit the battlefield. Traveling from the Antietam station down through town, Major Parker pointed out the Moses Poffenberger home as the place where he and some others had been given white bread and apple butter in 1862. Four other veterans were with Parker. When they reached the Dunkard Church they went to the position of their batteries, and knelt down to pray in the shade of the big walnut trees. O. T. Reilly says this was the first and only time any group he led did this in the thirty-five years he served as guide.

When the church was rebuilt in 1962, the first visitor was Miss Ruth Otto of Sharpsburg.[6] As a girl she had worshipped in the church many times, and her father was the last regular minister. "Miss Ruth," as she is known in Sharpsburg, always wanted to be a missionary. However, due to a crippled foot, she never got to the mission field. But those who know her in the Valley of the Antietam and in Church of the Brethren circles realize that her mission in life has been fulfilled in one of America's loveliest spots. She has indeed been a missionary at home. People come to her with their problems and for prayer. Just to be in the presence of her radiant countenance lifts the spirit and sends the visitor on his way inspired to meet the challenges of the day. Of her it can be said, "The world is better by far because she lived and shared her faith in this part of God's vineyard."

On a rainy Sunday afternoon, September 2, 1962, the reconstructed Dunkard Church was dedicated. Miss Ruth Otto was there, representing the past and the present. Her great-uncle, Samuel Mumma, had provided the land for the original church. Her forefathers built the church, her father served for five years as minister, and she worshipped within the walls for twenty-nine years.

The Sunday afternoon service marked the culmination of over thirty years of work. Finally, in 1960, the state of Maryland gave the National Park Service $35,000 to rebuild the church. Prior to that, the Sharpsburg American Legion Post, the "Sharpsburg Rifles," and the Washington County Historical Society had talked and worked to get the land, and then money for the reconstruction of the church.

Hundreds of cars parked in the fields east of the Maryland and New York monuments. At 1:30 P.M. the Rohrersville Band, an organization participating in most of the Sharpsburg Memorial Day parades, commenced the program. The Reverend Austin Cooper, a noted Church of the Brethren historian, gave the invocation and made some remarks about the historic occasion. Conrad L. Wirth, the director of the National Park Service, was introduced and then spoke to the crowd. Dr. Shealy presented the original Dunkard Church Bible to the National Park Service. Next on the program was an address by the Honorable J. Millard Tawes, governor of the state of Maryland.

A Service of Commemoration followed. Folks from many Washington and Frederick County churches comprised a large choir. Dr. Harry K. Zeller, Jr., moderator of the Church of the Brethren, gave the message of the afternoon. Then those present united in a Litany of Dedication, written especially for the occasion by Dr. DeWitt P. Miller of Hagerstown.

293

Visitors to Antietam can almost visualize President Lincoln standing on the big stone step at the Dunkard Church. The president seems to have been very fond of those embracing the Dunkard faith. The Reverend Austin Cooper and the Reverend Freeman Ankrum have evidence which tends to prove that Lincoln was baptized by a Dunkard preacher. In their writings they tell of a Mrs. Anna Wagner of Indiana who, on October 22, 1936, made the following statement:

Elder Isaac Billheimer, at one time a resident of Heath, Indiana, and an Elder in the Fairview Church of Southern Indiana, told my father he was acquainted with the minister that baptized Lincoln. Father had forgotten the name of the minister, but he was a member of the German Baptist Church, sometimes nicknamed "Dunkard." Lincoln sent this minister word to come to Springfield on a certain train which arrived there at night.

Lincoln met him and they went to the river where Lincoln was baptized yet that night. Lincoln had brought extra clothes needed for both, and having changed clothes they went and waited for the train to arrive, and the minister left after midnight. . . . Lincoln promised that after his term of office expired he would conform to the church.[7]

The Wagners were known as good and honest people in Indiana. There is at least one other source which points to the truth of the story. Some of course doubt it because of lack of information. However, Lincoln may have indeed been baptized by a Dunkard preacher.

Mr. Lincoln was a close personal friend of Elder Daniel P. Sayler who lived in Detour, close to the Frederick-Carroll County line. Elder Sayler had lived in the Midwest, and spent much time in Lincoln's Springfield home. Later he moved to Maryland, and during the days of the Civil War was a frequent visitor at the White House.[8] Mr. Sayler is buried in the Rocky Ridge Church of the Brethren Cemetery near Thurmont.

Years ago, E. Russell Hicks, a leading Washington County historian, and a member of the Church of the Brethren, wrote about the Dunkard Church in these words:

I am the Church of the bloodiest battlefield in all American history. I had my conception in the minds of a group of pious, zealous

294

folks, who were among the first settlers to make their homes on the banks of the Antietam.

They called themselves Brethren because brotherhood was the main objective of their devotion.... Their associates in the neighborhood called them Dunkers or Dunkards, ... a corruption of the German word tunker which means plunger or the word tunken, to dip. Immersion was their form of baptism.

At first the Dunkers held their meetings in large rooms of ... houses or sometimes in barns. Their church architecture was barn like in style. They conducted their services in the German tongue.

I drew my first breath of life, February 22, 1851. Samuel Mumma gave a corner of his woodland along the Hagerstown Pike as a plot for my permanent home. This woodland is now the "West Woods" of battle fame. On the farm of another member, John Otto, the Brethren made the bricks, kiln-baked them. I was begun in 1852 and completed in 1853. For nearly a decade there was peace in the community I represented.

Early before daylight, on the 17th of September 1862, the bloodiest single day battle of all American history began. I was the objective of the Federal forces....

I was pierced with cannon balls and bullets—my rafters studded with metal. I was used first as a bulwark for both armies. Then I became a hospital. I heard shrieks, moans, groans, and cries that stayed with me all my life. My furniture was all splattered with blood.... As soon as it could be done, I was remodeled and worship was resumed within my walls. A severe hailstorm swept the Antietam Valley, May 21, 1921, and it totally demolished me....

But I still exist as the little white church of the Antietam Battlefield. I live in the hearts of all who ever knew me. I am still a symbol of peace and brotherhood. Antietam was the battle that emancipated the slaves; I am a symbol of spiritual emancipation.... I represent unity, ... the Brotherhood of Man under the Fatherhood of a loving, kind God. ...

> There is a charm in footing slow
> Across the silent plain,
> Where patriot battle has been fought,
> Where glory had the gain.
> Keats

Of all those who have written about Antietam, this writer appreciates most of all the work of Fred Cross. During his lifetime he wrote no books, but he had a love of people, places, and historic spots. He was a true historian, going beyond the scenes looking for all the facts, and the little unknown stories. He specialized in the human interest approach to history. He kept scrapbooks and pictures for his own enlightenment and memories. Mr. Cross was drawn to Antietam like a magnet. The creek, hills, and fields spoke to him as they speak to me. In the 1920s Fred Cross wrote:

Reader, I shall have to confess to you at the outstart that I have a passion for battlefields. As the patriarch of old in a wonderful dream of which the Scriptures tell saw a ladder stretching from Earth to Heaven with the Angels of God ascending and descending upon it, so my own mind, pictures a shining way over which the spirits of the hero dead are ascending and descending between the scenes of their service and suffering and the heaven of their rest. If they still live, as our faith teaches us, I cannot but feel they still love the spot which witnessed their supreme sacrifice. And I love to stand at the foot of their shining Way.

Of all the many fields I have visited no other has quite the charm for me that has Antietam. Situated in Western Maryland in a beautiful rolling agricultural area . . . it has a delightful location. . . .

Commanded by the imagination . . . contending lines reappear, the ripple of the silken banners, the spiteful crack of the muskets, the chaos of struggling columns, the hoarse yells of the combatants—how like a flood they come.

Massachusetts was here—the 2nd under Andrews, the 12th under Burbank, the 13th under Gould. Across these selfsame fields from east to west in Sedgwick's column swept the 15th under Kimball, the 19th under Hinks, and the 20th under Lee. And hundreds came here to find their eternal rest.

We gaze and tremble and wonder and recall,—when suddenly the tumult dies,—a burst of light appears surpassing the glory of the rising sun, and countless hero forms in Gray and Blue—boys from Texas and from Massachusetts arm in arm—ascend and descend along the Great White Way.

On the 57th anniversary of the battle, starting out long before breakfast, I took a morning walk, reaching Cornfield Avenue at almost the exact hour of Hooker's attack. Were I to attempt it, I should be unable to describe the emotions awakened by the surroundings of that hour. As I lingered near the Massachusetts Monument, . . . birds . . . were pouring forth their morning carols. The friendly sun shot its first warm rays over the summits to the eastward, and the fertile fields and well kept avenues around told of the healing touch that the intervening years of peace had brought. . . .

For me every field over which the contending lines have swept, every wall or bony ridge that once afforded shelter from the bullets of the foe, every ancient tree that saw and heard and felt the whirlwind of the fight has its own eloquent story.[9]

These were the reasons why Cross was so impressed with Antietam. Here history was made. The tide of the war turned. Brave men gave their all for the cause in which they believed. Fred Cross was a better citizen, a better American because on the fields of Antietam he came to the realization that our heritage and our freedom have been bought with a great price, the lifeblood of thousands of young, middle-aged, and older Americans.

Every time I visit the National Cemetery, the little white headstones seem to say, "I died to make you free. I died to preserve the American way. What are you doing to make men free?"

Young men, Americans all, gave their all at Antietam, dying not for themselves, but for the cause in which they believed. They call to us, "Live for God, live for others, live to make this a better world, a world where someday men will beat their swords of war into farming instruments."

Save Antietam

Nineteen years have passed since I wrote my first article on Antietam. That was in September 1951 when as a high school student I prepared a full page about the Maryland campaign for the *Frederick News-Post.*

Much of the information was gathered from a day of hiking over the battlefield. My folks took me to Burnside Bridge at 7:00 A.M. and then went on to work. I was equipped with notebook, thermos bottle and sandwiches. Lunch was eaten at the Mansfield Monument. At the end of the day my folks found a tired young man sitting on the wall at the National Cemetery. However, a nice picnic supper at Taylor Park in Keedysville soon brought refreshment. A highlight of the day was meeting Superintendent Doust. He was very kind and helpful and gave the young, aspiring writer one of the large Cope maps.

Nine years later *September Echoes* came off the press. This was the first work of any size on Antietam in over fifty years, or so I have been told. It is now in its third printing.

Ten more years went by. Then in the summer of 1970, *The Sharpsburg Echo* was published. The first volume was printed as a Sharpsburg paper might have looked two days after the Battle of Antietam.

Next came *Antietam Hospitals,* containing some of the first research done on the homes, barns, schools, and churches which served as hospitals in 1862. In the process, the writer had the opportunity to meet many fine folks in the Sharpsburg-Keedysville area. Many items seen by few individuals, and never appearing in print before were shared.

Why do I write about Antietam? Well first of all, I have fallen in love with the area. The natural beauty and historical heritage have long held an almost mystical attraction for me.

Some of my finest religious and inspirational moments have come as I have walked along the Antietam Creek and through the fields surrounding Sharpsburg.

These walks and moments of meditation have been in the rain, snow, sunshine, and moonlight.

Every time, I get the feeling that Antietam was indeed a pivotal point in American history, a hinge of history upon which one door closed, and a great new door opened.

The door was closed forever on the prospect of a divided nation as after the Confederate withdrawal, England and France decided not to enter the war on the side of the South. The door was closed on slavery, as President Lincoln used Antietam to announce to the world that he was freeing the slaves. The door was opened to the humane care of the wounded as Clara Barton was led to think of an organization which would help the sick and needy in moments of disaster.

Antietam marked the beginning of a new birth of freedom in our country, and the beginning of a new America. As far as I am concerned, the high tide of the Confederacy was reached at Antietam.

In and around the battlefield are many other shrines. Not only do we find the Dunkard Church and the other churches which were used as hospitals in Sharpsburg and Keedysville, but we find the home of George Adam Geeting, a teacher and a bishop. We find the site of the old Geeting Meeting House which was the first building in our country used exclusively for worship by members of the Church of the United Brethren in Christ, the first American-born denomination.

We find the Hitt home which was used as a resting place by Francis Asbury, the "Methodist Prophet of the Long Road," and the man acclaimed by many to be the founder of Methodism in the United States.

Across the field from the Pry farm is the Geeting or Bishop John Russell farm. Bishop Russell was one of the first publishers of the Church of the United Brethren. He wanted the denominational printing press to be situated on his farm. He also desired the seminary to be established on his land. Five of his fourteen rooms were used for that purpose. In fact, his five students worked part of the day in the fields, and studied the rest of the day.

In the Keedysville and Sharpsburg cemeteries are the graves of the Costs, the Prys, the Geetings, Chaplines, Millers, and others who came to this valley as pioneers.

Yes, the Valley of the Antietam is rich in natural beauty and historical heritage. May this beauty always be used for future generations to cherish. It is my hope and prayer that this beautiful valley will be spared from the bulldozer and not be desecrated by the urban sprawl.

In this day and age, we need places where we can get away from the hustle and bustle so God can speak to us, and where we can find the restoration of the soul. The Valley of the Antietam is such a place. In its beauty and quietness, in the majesty of the hills, the tranquility of the Antietam, and from hallowed ground, God speaks and the soul is uplifted and inspired. This is why I write about Antietam, this is why I love the Valley of the Antietam, and this is why I hope its beauty and history will be preserved.

Since that September day in 1862, many eloquent speeches have been delivered at Antietam. However, President Theodore Roosevelt, speaking on the occasion of the dedication of the New Jersey Monument on September 17, 1903, summarized the importance of Antietam to world and American history:

Governor Murphy [he had fought at Antietam as a lad], Veterans of New Jersey, men of the Grand Army: I thank you for the monument to the troops of New Jersey who fought at Antietam, and on behalf of the nation. I accept this gift. We meet today on one of the great battlefields of the Civil War. No other battle of the Civil War lasting but one day shows as great a percentage of loss as that which occurred here—upon the day on which Antietam was fought. Moreover, in its ultimate effects, this battle was of momentous and even decisive importance; for when it had ended and Lee had retreated south of the Potomac, Lincoln forthwith published that immortal paper, the preliminary declaration of emancipation; the paper which decided that the Civil War, besides being a war for the preservation of the Union, should be a war for the emancipation of the slave, so that from that time onward the causes of Union and of Freedom, of national greatness and individual liberty were one and the same. . . .

If the issue at Antietam had been other than it was, it is probable that at least two great European powers would have recognized the independence of the Confederacy; so that you who fought here forty-one years ago have the profound satisfaction of feeling that you played well your part in one of those crises big with the fate of mankind. You men of the Grand Army by your victory not only rendered all Americans your debtors forevermore, but you rendered all humanity your debtors. If the Union had been dissolved, if the great edifice built with blood and sweat and tears by mighty Washington and his compeers had gone down in wreck and ruin, the result would have been an incalculable calamity, not only for our people . . . but for all mankind. . . .

We take just pride in the great deeds of the men of 1776, but we must keep in mind that the Revolutionary War would have been shorn of well nigh all its results had the side of union and liberty been defeated in the Civil War. In such case we should merely have been added to the lamentably long list of cases in which the peoples have shown that after winning their liberty they are wholly unable to make good use of it. . . .

There are many qualities which we need alike in private citizen and in public man, but three above all,—three for the lack of which no brilliancy and no genius can atone,—and these three are courage, honesty, and common sense.[10]

With this we end the story of *Drums Along the Antietam.*

"Lest We Forget."

A Prayer

Father, we remember the days of old, and consider the years of many generations. We give thanks for the religious heritage handed down to us by men like Geeting, Asbury, Hitt, and Russell.

We give thanks that we have met You in the beauty and quietness of the Valley of the Antietam. In the majesty of its hills, in the tranquility of the Antietam Creek, and from hallowed ground, You have spoken our Father, and our soul has been uplifted and inspired.

We give thanks that from Antietam came one nation—the end of slavery, and the humane care of the wounded.

May we who live today, dedicate ourselves to the unfinished task before us—the task of making this world a little better place because we have passed this way.

We ask that the day will soon come when men shall beat their swords into instruments of peace and brotherhood. Hasten the day Father, when there shall be peace in the human heart, and peace in your world. Amen.

"Let There Be Peace on Earth."

NOTES

CHAPTER I (Pages 1-13)

1. J. Thomas Scharf, *History of Western Maryland* (Philadelphia: Louis H. Everts, 1882), vol. 2, p. 986.
2. Thomas J. C. Williams, *A History of Washington County, Maryland: From the Earliest Settlements to the Present Time, Including a History of Hagerstown* (n.p., John M. Runk and E. R. Titsworth, 1906), vol. 1, p. 19.
3. Helen Ashe Hays, *The Antietam and Its Bridges* (New York: G. P. Putnam's Sons, 1910), p. 10.
4. Interview with Austin Flook, present owner of Felfoot. See also, Lee McCardell, *Braddock of the Coldstream Guards.*
5. Scharf, *History of Western Maryland,* vol. 1, p. 81.

CHAPTER II (Pages 14-52)

1. A. Vera Foster, *Your Maryland* (Lanham, Md.: n.p., 1965), pp. 11-13.
2. Rogers, Adams, and Brown, *Story of Nations* (New York: Henry Holt and Company, 1952), p. 209.
3. Rogers, Adams, and Brown, *Story of Nations.*
4. Dieter Cunz, *The Maryland Germans* (Princeton, N.J.: Princeton University Press, 1948), p. 11.
5. Cunz, *Maryland Germans.*
6. *Ibid.*
7. *Archives of Maryland* (published by the authority of the state, under the direction of the Maryland Historical Society, Baltimore), vol. 28, pp. 25-26.
8. *Ibid.*
9. J. Thomas Scharf, *History of Western Maryland* (Philadelphia: Louis H. Everts, 1882), vol. 2, p. 978.
10. *Jefferson County Sesqui-Centennial, 1801-1951* (Charleston, W. Va.), p. 9.
11. Maryland Hall of Records.
12. Will of Joseph Chapline, dated Jan. 27, 1768, recorded in *Wills,* Washington County Courthouse, Hagerstown, Md., Book D, p. 345.
13. Deed, Joseph Chapline to Christopher Cruss and others, vestrymen and church wardens of the Lutheran Church in the town of Sharpsburg, March 5, 1768.
14. Deed, Joseph Chapline to Abraham Lingenfelter, March 3, 1768.
15. John P. Smith, "Reminiscences of Sharpsburg from July 9, 1763, to January 1, 1912." This is a copy of the notebook or scrapbook kept by Sharpsburg's distinguished teacher and historian during the last half of the 1800s and the early 1900s. A copy is in the Western Maryland Room at the Washington County

Library in Hagerstown. The author also had access to some of Mr. Smith's private papers.

16. *Ibid.*

17. *Ibid.*

18. Thomas J. C. Williams, *A History of Washington County, Maryland: From the Earliest Settlements to the Present Time, Including a History of Hagerstown* (n.p., John M. Runk and E. R. Titsworth, 1906), vol. 2, p. 1302.

19. Williams, *History of Washington County.*

20. *Ibid.*

21. *Ibid.,* p. 1304.

22. *Ibid.,* p. 1305.

23. *Ibid.,* v. 1, pp. 101-2.

24. Julia A. Drake and James R. Orndorff, *From Millwheel to Plowshare* (Cedar Rapids, Iowa: The Torch Press, 1938), p. 4.

25. *Ibid.,* p. 21.

26. *Ibid.,* p. 32.

27. *Ibid.,* p. 58; Scharf, vol. 2, p. 1013.

28. John Blackford, *Ferry Hill Plantation Journal, January 4, 1838-January 15, 1839,* ed. Fletcher M. Green (Chapel Hill: The University of North Carolina Press, 1961), p. xi.

29. Henry K. Douglas, *I Rode With Stonewall* (Chapel Hill: The University of North Carolina, 1940), p. 1.

30. *Ibid.,* p. 160.

31. *Ibid.,* p. 167.

32. *Ibid.,* p. 181.

33. *Ibid.,* p. 181.

34. *Ibid.,* p. 243.

35. *Ibid.,* p. 168.

CHAPTER III (Pages 53-83)

1. In his will, dated Sept. 19, 1811, George Adam Geeting spells his name several different ways. The will is on file at the Washington County Courthouse, Hagerstown, Md.

2. H. A. Thompson, *Our Bishops* (Dayton, Ohio: The United Brethren Publishing House, 1903), p. 104.

3. Paul E. Holdcraft, *A History of the Pennsylvania Conference of the United Brethren Church* (Fayetteville, Pa.: The Craft Press, 1938), p. 28. Dr. Holdcraft was the pastor of Salem Church, Keedysville, and did much research on Geeting and the Geeting Meeting House. He was a noted church historian, and the author of many books.

4. W. J. Hinke, *Ministers of the German Reformed Congregations in Pennsylvania and Other Colonies in the Eighteenth Century* (Lancaster: Rudisill and Company, Inc., 1951), p. 39.

5. Paul R. Koontz and Walter E. Roush, *The Bishops of the Church of the United Brethren in Christ* (Dayton, Ohio: Otterbein Press, 1950), vol. 1, p. 39.

6. Henry G. Spayth, *History of the Church of the United Brethren in Christ* (Circleville, Ohio: The United Brethren Publishing House, 1857), p. 21.

7. Hinke, *Ministers of the German Reformed Congregations,* p. 72.

8. Holdcraft, *History of the Pennsylvania Conference,* p. 21.

9. John H. Ness, Jr., "The Life of George Adam Geeting" (Thesis submitted at Bonebrake now United Theological Seminary, Dayton, Ohio, May 1945), p. 4. Dr. Ness is now historian of the United Methodist Church.

10. Thompson, *Our Bishops,* pp. 104-5.

11. A. W. Drury, *The Life of Philip William Otterbein* (Dayton, Ohio: The United Brethren Publishing House, 1902), pp. 151-52.

12. A. W. Drury, *History of the Church of the United Brethren in Christ* (Dayton, Ohio: Otterbein Press, 1924), p. 108.

13. *Ibid.,* p. 110.

14. Drury, *History of the Church.*

15. Christian Newcomer, *The Life and Journal of Revd. Christian Newcomer, Late Bishop of the Church of the United Brethren in Christ, Containing His Travels and Labors in the Gospel from 1795-1830,* transcribed, corrected, and translated by John Hildt (Hagerstown, Md.: F. W. Kapp, 1834; reprint ed., Dayton, Ohio: Otterbein Press, 1941), p. 13.

16. Holdcraft, *History of the Pennsylvania Conference,* p. 25.

17. Newcomer, *Journal,* p. 8.

18. Holdcraft, *History of the Pennsylvania Conference,* p. 18.

19. *Ibid.,* p. 148.

20. Drury, *History of the Church,* p. 40.

21. *Ibid.,* p. 109.

22. "Pipe Creek Minutes of the United Ministers."

23. *The Religious Telescope* (Dayton, Ohio), March 25, 1944, p. 10.

24. William Warren Sweet, *The Story of Religion in America* (New York: Harper and Brothers, 1930), p. 133.

25. Spayth, *History of the Church,* pp. 60-61.

26. Spayth, *History of the Church.*

27. *Ibid.,* pp. 82-83.

28. Holdcraft, *History of the Pennsylvania Conference,* p. 38. From the protocol of the United Brethren in Christ. The original German written by Geeting.

29. Drury, *History of the Church,* p. 281.

30. Spayth, *History of the Church,* p. 129.

31. Thompson, *Our Bishops,* p. 115.

32. Thomas J. C. Williams, *A History of Washington County, Maryland: From the Earliest Settlements to the Present Time, Including a History of Hagerstown* (n.p., John M. Runk and E. R. Titsworth, 1906), vol. 2, p. 127. Article written by John Miller who married a direct descendant of George Adam Geeting.

33. D. Homer Kendall, "Geeting Meeting House," mimeographed paper. Pastor Kendall served as minister of Salem Church, Keedysville. He has taken a leading role in the preservation of the Mount Hebron site.

34. *Ibid.* Once again we are indebted to the invaluable research conducted by Mr. Kendall.

35. Newcomer, *Journal,* p. 8.

36. *Ibid.,* p. 9.

37. *Ibid.,* p. 20.

38. *Ibid.,* p. 13.

39. *Ibid.*

40. *Ibid.,* pp. 1-2.

41. *Ibid.,* p. 15.

42. Koontz and Roush, *Bishops of the Church,* p. 275.

43. Thompson, *Our Bishops,* p. 288.

44. *Ibid.,* p. 290.

45. Koontz and Roush, *Bishops of the Church,* pp. 278-79.

46. *Ibid.,* p. 288.

47. Drury, *Otterbein,* p. 429.
48. Williams, *History of Washington County,* vol. 1, p. 1299.
49. *Francis Asbury Journal.*

CHAPTER IV (Pages 84-100)

1. Laurence Greene, *The Raid* (New York: Henry Holt and Company, 1953), p. 82.
2. *Ibid.,* p. 91.
3. Oswald Garrison Villard, *John Brown: A Biography Fifty Years After* (New York: Alfred A. Knopf, 1909).
4. *Ibid.*
5. Thomas J. C. Williams, *A History of Washington County, Maryland: From the Earliest Settlements to the Present Time, Including a History of Hagerstown* (n.p., John M. Runk and E. R. Titsworth, 1906), vol. 1, p. 290.
6. *Ibid.,* p. 293.
7. Bruce Catton, *The Coming Fury* (Garden City, N.Y.: Doubleday and Company, 1961.) An excellent book on the political struggles of 1860.

CHAPTER V (Pages 101-8)

1. *War of the Rebellion, Official Records of the Union and Confederate Armies* (Washington, D.C.: Government Printing Office, 1880-1891). Cited hereafter as *O.R.* See Robert E. Lee's report in vol. 19, pt. 1, p. 147.
2. *O.R.,* p. 839. Longstreet's report.
3. Robert U. Johnson and Clarence C. Buel, eds., *Battles and Leaders of the Civil War* (New York: The Century Company, 1884-1887), vol. 2, p. 667 (hereafter cited as *B. and L.*).
4. *O.R.,* pp. 53-54. George B. McClellan's report.
5. *O.R.,* p. 819. James E. B. Stuart's report.
6. Francis W. Palfrey, *The Antietam and Fredericksburg* (New York: Charles Scribner's Sons, 1882), p. 46.
7. *Ibid.,* p. 47.
8. *O.R.,* p. 54. McClellan's report.
9. Palfrey, *The Antietam,* p. 56.
10. James Longstreet, "Antietam or Sharpsburg," *The Photographic History of the Civil War* (New York: Review of Reviews Company, 1911), vol. 2, p. 66.
11. *O.R.,* p. 55. McClellan's report.
12. G. F. R. Henderson, *Stonewall Jackson and the American Civil War* (New York: Longmans, Green and Company, 1906), vol. 2, p. 234.
13. *O.R.,* p. 967. Jubal A. Early's report.
14. Palfrey, *The Antietam,* p. 56.
15. *Ibid.,* p. 59.
16. *O.R.,* p. 217. McClellan's report.
17. *Ibid.*
18. Palfrey, *The Antietam,* p. 62.
19. On this drizzly night, Hooker took shelter in the Poffenberger home.
20. Jacob L. Cox, "Battle of Antietam," *B. and L.,* pp. 635-36.
21. Miles C. Huyette, *The Maryland Campaign and the Battle of Antietam* (Buffalo: The Hammond Press, 1915), pp. 27-28.

CHAPTER VI (Pages 109-22)

1. Francis A. Lord and Arthur Wise, *Bands and Drummer Boys of the Civil War* (New York: Thomas Yoseloff, 1966), p. 83.
2. *Ibid.*, p. 84.
3. *O.R.*, p. 218. Hooker's report.
4. *Ibid.*
5. Francis W. Palfrey, *The Antietam and Fredericksburg* (New York: Charles Scribner's Sons, 1882), p. 82.
6. From the official reports of Gorman and Dana, brigade commanders in Sedgwick's division.

CHAPTER VII (Pages 123-31)

1. "Pennsylvania at Antietam," *Report of the Antietam Battlefield Memorial Commission* (Harrisburg, 1906), p. 190.
2. John B. Gordon, *Reminiscences of the Civil War* (New York, 1907), pp. 84-87.
3. *Ibid.*
4. Bruce Catton, *Mr. Lincoln's Army* (New York: Doubleday and Company, 1951), p. 306.
5. Otto Eisenschiml and Ralph Newman, *The Civil War and the American Iliad, as Told by Those Who Lived It* (New York, 1956), vol. 1, p. 262.
6. The fighting at the Sunken Road started around 9:30 A.M. and continued until 1:00 P.M.
7. Thomas L. Livermore, *Days and Events, 1860-1865* (Boston, 1920), p. 146.
8. *Ibid.*, p. 138.
9. Gordon, *Reminiscences*, p. 90.
10. *Ibid.*
11. *O.R.*, vol. 19, pt. 1, pp. 285-86.
12. The high ground upon which the National Cemetery is located offers a commanding view of the field of battle.
13. *O.R.*, p. 1024. Hill.
14. *B. and L.*, vol. 2, p. 669. Longstreet.
15. Edwin P. Alexander, *Military Memoirs of a Confederate* (New York: Charles Scribner's Sons, 1907), p. 263.
16. Livermore, *Days and Events*, p. 143.
17. *The Photographic History of the Civil War* (New York: Review of Reviews Company, 1911), vol. 2, p. 69.
18. Livermore, *Days and Events*, p. 149.
19. The lady has never been identified.

CHAPTER VIII (Pages 132-38)

1. *O.R.*, p. 890. Toombs's report.
2. *O.R.*, p. 425. Cox's report.
3. *O.R.*, p. 444. Sturgis's report.
4. *Ibid.*
5. *O.R.*, p. 981. Hill's report.
6. *Ibid.*
7. Douglas S. Freeman, *Lee's Lieutenants* (New York: Charles Scribner's Sons, 1934), vol. 2, p. 221.

8. Edwin P. Alexander, *Military Memoirs of a Confederate* (New York: Charles Scribner's Sons, 1907), p. 266.

9. *O.R.*, p. 981. Hill's report.

10. Henry K. Douglas, *I Rode With Stonewall* (Chapel Hill: The University of North Carolina Press, 1940), p. 173.

11. *B. and L.*, vol. 2, p. 629.

12. *O.R.*, p. 426. Cox's report.

13. *O.R.*, p. 981. Hill's report.

14. Douglas, *I Rode With Stonewall*, p. 178.

15. James Longstreet, "Antietam or Sharpsburg," *The Photographic History of the Civil War* (New York: Review of Reviews Company, 1911), vol. 2, p. 76.

16. Freeman, *Lee's Lieutenants*, p. 224.

17. *Ibid.*

18. Francis W. Palfrey, *The Antietam and Fredericksburg* (New York: Charles Scribner's Sons, 1882), p. 126.

19. *O.R.*, p. 151. Lee's report.

20. *Ibid.*, p. 929.

21. G. F. R. Henderson, *Stonewall Jackson and the American Civil War* (New York: Longmans, Green and Company, 1906), p. 262.

22. *B. and L.*, vol. 2, p. 672.

23. *B. and L.*, vol. 2, p. 681. Walker.

24. *B. and L.*, vol. 2, p. 685. Coffin.

CHAPTER IX (Pages 139-70)

1. Mary A. Livermore, *My Story of the War: A Woman's Narrative of Four Years of Personal Experience as a Nurse in the Union Army* (Hartford, Conn.: A. D. Worthington and Sons, 1889), p. 126. An excellent book.

2. Livermore, *My Story of the War.*

3. *The Photographic History of the Civil War* (New York: Review of Reviews Company, 1911), vol. 7, p. 330. This volume on prisons and hospitals is very informative.

4. Livermore, *My Story of the War*, p. 131.

5. *Ibid.*, p. 137.

6. Livermore, *My Story of the War.*

7. *Ibid.*, p. 138.

8. *Ibid.*, p. 139.

9. Livermore, *My Story of the War.*

10. *Ibid.*, p. 133.

11. *O.R.*, pp. 107-10. Letterman's report.

12. *O.R.*

13. *O.R.*

14. *O.R.*

15. Journal of James Oliver.

16. Fred Cross Papers.

17. Matthew Graham, *The Ninth Regiment, New York Volunteers (Hawkins' Zouaves)* (New York: E. P. Coby and Company, 1900), p. 300.

18. *Ibid.*, p. 350.

19. Journal of Dr. Theodore Dimon.

20. The United States Sanitary Commission Map of Antietam Hospitals and descriptions of the hospitals.

21. *O.R.*, p. 110. Letterman's report.

22. *Photographic History of the Civil War*, vol. 7, p. 219.

CHAPTER X (Pages 171-236)

1. Fred Cross Papers.
2. Oliver T. Reilly, *The Battlefield of Antietam* (Hagerstown, Md., 1906), p. 26.
3. From an interview with Hazel Pry Moreno.
4. War Damage Claims in the National Archives. Philip Pry.
5. War Damage Claims in the National Archives.
6. Thomas J. C. Williams, *A History of Washington County, Maryland: From the Earliest Settlements to the Present Time, Including a History of Hagerstown* (n.p., John M. Runk and E. R. Titsworth, 1906), vol. 2, p. 934.
7. George Washington Cullom, *Biographical Register of the Officers and Graduates of the United States Military Academy* (New York, 1879), vol. 2, pp. 100-101.
8. William Warren Hassler, *Colonel John Pelham: Lee's Boy Artillerist* (Richmond: Garrett and Massie, 1960), pp. 89-96.
9. *O.R.,* p. 821. Stuart.
10. A copy of Captain Hallowell's description of Antietam was loaned to the author by Fred Remsburg.
11. Fred Cross Papers.
12. War Damage Claims in the National Archives. Samuel Mumma.
13. Williams, *History of Western Maryland* (Philadelphia: Louis H. Everts, 1882), vol. 2, p. 933.
14. Williams, *History of Washington County.* See his description of the Neikirk family.
15. Reilly, *Battlefield of Antietam,* p. 25.
16. War Damage Claims in the National Archives. Henry Piper.
17. *Ibid.*
18. *Souvenir of Excursion to Battlefield by the Society of the Fourteenth Connecticut Regiment* (Washington, D.C., 1893), pp. 51, 56-57.
19. *Ibid.*
20. Augustus Woodbury, *Burnside and the Ninth Army Corps* (Providence, 1867).
21. War Damage Claims in the National Archives. Henry Rohrback.
22. Henry K. Douglas, *I Rode With Stonewall* (Chapel Hill: The University of North Carolina Press, 1940), p. 174.
23. Woodbury, *Burnside and the Ninth Army Corps.*
24. Fred Cross Papers.
25. David S. Sparks, *Inside Mr. Lincoln's Army: The Diary of General Marsena Patrick, Provost Marshal General, Army of the Potomac* (New York, 1964). Remarks concerning Antietam and movement to Pleasant Valley are interesting.

CHAPTER XI (Pages 237-41)

1. *The New York Tribune,* Aug. 19, 1962. Horace Greeley.
2. *Ibid.*
3. F. B. Carpenter, *Six Months at the White House* (New York, 1867), pp. 20-22.
4. This account is found in the monumental work on Lincoln by Nicolay and Hay.
5. Abraham Lincoln, "The Emancipation Proclamation."
6. Carl Sandburg, *Abraham Lincoln—The War Years* (New York: Dell Publishing Co., 1959), p. 210.

311

7. *Ibid.,* p. 211.

8. Bruce Catton, *Mr. Lincoln's Army* (New York: Doubleday and Company, 1951), p. 336.

CHAPTER XII (Pages 242-58)

1. Judge Edward S. Delaplaine, *Lincoln's Companions on the Trip to Antietam* (Harrogate, Tenn.: Lincoln Memorial University Press, 1954). This is an excellent little book detailing the selection of the presidential party.

2. Ward Hill Lamon, *Recollections of Abraham Lincoln, 1847-1865* (Washington, 1911). Pages 141-54 give a fine, detailed account of President Lincoln's visit to Antietam.

3. From notes of Miss Louise Grove.

4. John Hay and John G. Nicolay, *Abraham Lincoln—A History* (New York: The Century Company, 1900), vol. 6, p. 174.

5. Lamon, *Recollections of Abraham Lincoln,* p. 151.

6. Journal of Dr. Oliver

7. Thomas Pullen, *The Twentieth Maine* (Philadelphia: J. B. Lippincott, n.d.).

8. *The Baltimore Sun,* Oct. 7, 1862.

9. Donald L. Smith, *The Twentieth: The Twenty-Fourth Michigan* (Harrisburg: The Stackpole Company, 1962), pp. 27-28.

CHAPTER XIII (Pages 259-85)

1. Fred Cross Papers.

2. Antietam National Cemetery Records, Sharpsburg, Md.

3. *Ibid.*

4. Speech of Maryland Governor Bradford on Sept. 17, 1867, at the dedication of the Antietam National Cemetery.

5. *Ibid.*

6. *Ibid.*

7. Henry Kyd Douglas Papers.

8. *Ibid.*

9. *The Morning Herald,* Hagerstown, Md., May 31, 1900.

10. *New York at Antietam* (Albany: J. B. Lyon Company, 1903), pp. 11-13.

11. *Ibid.,* p. 24.

12. *Ibid.,* p. 30.

13. Ezra J. Warner, *Generals in Blue* (Baton Rouge: The Louisiana State University Press, 1964), p. 322.

14. Nelson A. Miles, *Serving the Republic* (New York: Harper, 1911).

15. A copy of the presidential address on Sept. 17, 1937, was also obtained from the Franklin D. Roosevelt Memorial Library, Hyde Park, N.Y.

CHAPTER XIV (Pages 286-303)

1. An excellent history of the Dunkard Church was prepared by Louis Tuckerman while he was historian at the Antietam National Battlefield site. The study is in the file at the park office. It contains a wealth of information.

2. O. T. Reilly records Snavely's experience at the Dunkard Church as well as a wealth of other human interest stories.

3. Freeman Ankrum, *Sidelights on Brethren History* (Elgin: The Brethren Press, 1962). See the chapter "John Lewis and the Antietam Bible," pp. 116-22.

4. Much of the information about the Dunkard Church came from Miss Ruth Otto, daughter of the last preacher at the little white brick church.

5. Jacob D. Cox, *Military Reminiscences of the Civil War* (New York, 1900).
6. *The Morning Herald,* Hagerstown, Md., July 13, 1962, p. 12.
7. Ankrum, *Brethren History,* p. 140.
8. *Ibid.,* p. 141.
9. Fred W. Cross Papers.
10. *Addresses and Presidential Messages of Theodore Roosevelt 1902-1904* (New York: G. P. Putnam's Son, 1904), pp. 245-49.

Although we constantly refer to the little white brick church as the Dunkard Church, officials in the Church of the Brethren say it should read "Dunker Church." This word comes from the German "tunker" or "dunker" which means one who dips or dunks, especially in baptism. The early Dunkers were called Dunkards, but Dunker is the correct word.

BIBLIOGRAPHY

Primary Sources

Records of the United States Sanitary Commission, found in the Maryland Historical Society and in the National Archives.

War Damage Claims in the National Archives involving the Middlekauf, Mumma, Piper, Pry, Joseph Poffenberger, Rohrback and Sherrick farms.

War of the Rebellion: A Compilation of the Official Records of the Union and Confederate Armies, series 1, vol. 19. Washington, D.C., 1880-1901.

Antietam National Cemetery

Antietam National Cemetery Records, Antietam National Battlefield Site Office, Sharpsburg, Md.

Existing Sources on the Valley of the Antietam

Drake, Julia A., and Orndorff, James R. *From Millwheel to Plowshare.* Cedar Rapids, 1938. Reprinted by the Maryland Historical Society, 1971.

Hays, Helen Ashe. *The Antietam and Its Bridges.* New York, 1910.

Scharf, Thomas J. *A History of Western Maryland.* Vols. 1 and 2. Philadelphia, 1882.

Williams, Thomas J. C. *History of Washington County, Maryland.* Hagerstown, 1906.

Manuscripts, Letters, Diaries, and Documents

John Blackford. "Ferry Hill Plantation." University of North Carolina Library.

Fred Cross. Antietam papers, pictures, and scrapbooks. Middletown, Md.

Dr. Theodore Dimon. "Memories of Antietam."

Henry Kyd Douglas Papers. Boonsboro, Md.

H. R. Dunham. Diary, August-September 1862.

Dr. T. L. Dunn. Letters to his wife, 1856-1906. The University of Virginia Library, Charlottesville, Va.

Louise and Julia Mumma Grove Papers. Hagerstown, Md.

Norwood Penrose Hallowell. "Remarks Written for My Children at the Request of Their Mother."

Christian Newcomer. Life and Journal.

Dr. James Oliver. Journal.

John P. Smith. Sharpsburg Papers. Hagerstown, Md.

Jonathan Stowe. Antietam Journal. Sharpsburg, Md.

James Weeks. Letter to the family of William Cullen Robinson.

Personal Reminiscences and Unit Histories

Alexander, Edwin P. *Military Memoirs of a Confederate*. New York, 1907.

Cox, Jacob D. *Military Reminiscences of the Civil War*. Vol. 1. New York, 1900.

Dawes, Rufus R. *Service With the Sixth Wisconsin*. Marietta, Ohio, 1800.

Douglas, Henry K. *I Rode With Stonewall*. Chapel Hill, N.C., 1940.

Gibbon, John B. *Personal Recollections of the Civil War*. New York, 1928.

Gordon, John B. *Reminiscences of the Civil War*. New York, 1904.

Graham, Matthew. *The Ninth Regiment, New York Volunteers*. New York, 1900.

Huyette, Miles C. *The Maryland Campaign and the Battle of Antietam*. Buffalo, 1915.

Lamon, Ward Hill. *Recollections of Abraham Lincoln, 1847-1865*. 1895.

Livermore, Mary. *My Story of the War: A Woman's Narrative of Four Years of Personal Experience as a Nurse in the Union Army*. Hartford, 1889.

Livermore, Thomas L. *Days and Events, 1860-1865*. Boston, 1920.

McClellan, George B. *McClellan's Own Story*. New York, 1887.

New York Monuments Commission. *New York, at Antietam*. Albany.

Nolan, Alan T. *The Iron Brigade*. New York, 1961.

"Pennsylvania at Antietam." *Report of the Antietam Battlefield Memorial Commission of Pennsylvania*. Harrisburg, 1906.

Pullen, Thomas. *The Twentieth Maine*. Philadelphia, 1957.

Smith, Donald. *The Twenty-Fourth Michigan*. Harrisburg, 1962.

Sparks, David S. *Inside Mr. Lincoln's Army: The Diary of General Marsena Patrick, Provost Marshal General, Army of the Potomac*. New York, 1964.

Walcott, Charles F. *History of the Twenty-First Regiment, Massachusetts Volunteers*. Boston, 1882.

Woodbury, Augustus. *Burnside and the Ninth Army Corps*. Providence, 1867.

General Works

Ankrum, Rev. Freeman. *Maryland and Pennsylvania Historical Sketches.* West Newton, Pa., 1947.

Battles and Leaders of the Civil War, Vol. 2. New York, 1884-1887.

Catton, Bruce. *The Coming Fury.* New York, 1961.

———. *Mr. Lincoln's Army.* New York, 1951.

Cullum, George Washington. *Biographical—Register of the Officers and Graduates of the United States Military Academy.* Vol. 2. New York, 1879.

Cunz, Dieter. *The Maryland Germans.* Princeton, 1948.

Delaplaine, Edward. *Lincoln and His Companions to Antietam.* Harrogate, Tenn.

Drury, A. W. *The Life of Philip William Otterbein.* Dayton, Ohio, 1902.

———. *History of the Church of the United Brethren in Christ.* Dayton, Ohio, 1924.

Eisenschiml, Otto, and Newman, Ralph. *The Civil War: The American Iliad, as Told by Those Who Lived It.* Vol. 1. New York, 1956.

Foster, A. Vera. *Your Maryland.* Lanham, Md., 1965.

Freeman, Douglas Southall. *Lee's Lieutentants.* Vol. 2. New York, 1942-1944.

Greene, Laurence. *The Raid.* New York, 1953.

Hassler, William W. *A. P. Hill, Lee's Forgotten General.* Richmond, 1957.

———. *Colonel John Pelham: Lee's Boy Artillerist.* Richmond, 1960.

Hinke, W. J. *Ministers of the German Reformed Congregations in Pennsylvania and other Colonies in the Eighteenth Century.* Lancaster, 1951.

Holdcraft, Paul E. *A History of the Pennsylvania Conference of the Church of the United Brethren in Christ.* Fayetteville, Pa., 1938.

Lord, Francis A., and Wise, Arthur. *Bands and Drummer Boys of the Civil War.* New York, 1966.

Miles, Nelson. *Serving the Republic.* New York, 1911.

Murfin, James. *The Gleam of Bayonets.* New York, 1965.

Ness, Dr. John H., Jr. *The Life of George Adam Geeting.* Dayton, 1945.

Nicolay, John G., and Hay, John. *Abraham Lincoln: A History.* Vols. 4, 6. New York, 1890.

Palfrey, Francis W. *The Army in the Civil War, The Antietam and Fredericksburg.* New York, 1881.

Photographic History of the Civil War. New York, 1911.

Reilly, Oliver T. *The Battlefield of Antietam.* Sharpsburg, 1906.

Rogers, Adams, and Brown. *Story of Nations.* New York, 1952.

Sandburg, Carl. *Abraham Lincoln, The War Years.* Vol. 1. New York, 1939.

Spayth, Henry G. *History of the Church of the United Brethren in Christ.* Circleville, Ohio, 1857.

Sweet, William W. *The Story of Religion in America.* New York, 1930.

317

Thompson, H. A. *Our Bishops.* Dayton, Ohio, 1903.

Villard, Oswald Harrison. *John Brown: A Biography Fifty Years After.* New York, 1909.

Warner, Ezra. *Generals in Blue.* Baton Rouge, 1964.

Williams, T. Harry. *Lincoln and His Generals.* New York, 1952.

Interviews

Interviews were held with many people in the Valley of the Antietam. Without their aid, the sharing of memories, family items, and records, this book could not have been written. I wish to thank the following wonderful people:

James Atkinson, former historian at the Antietam National Battlefield Site, a man who has done invaluable research on Clara Barton and Lincoln's visit to Antietam.

Howard Beckinbaugh, a nephew of Henry Kyd Douglas, who permitted the use of the Douglas journals and scrapbooks.

Mrs. Emma Burtner, a descendant of George Adam Geeting and Bishop John Russell.

Rene Burtner gave information about the Rohrback farm which he owns.

Mrs. Madge Carter, Sharpsburg historian and schoolteacher. Mrs. Carter lived on the Joseph Poffenberger farm as a child.

Austin Flook, the owner of Felfoot, provided many helpful insights into the growth and development of Felfoot and Mount Hebron.

John Frye, chairman of the Washington County Historical Advisory Commission, constantly provided new leads and contacts.

Russell Geeting and Mrs. Rachel Scheller shared memories and records of the Geeting and Russell families.

John Grayson shared boyhood memories of ten Union soldiers staying with the family when they returned for reunions.

Mrs. Julia Mumma Grove, now 102 years old, shared memories of living at the Sherrick farm where she was born, and later at Mount Airy. Her daughter Louise shared the written family record of Lincoln's visit to the Grove home.

Virginia Mumma Hildebrand shared many records of the Mumma farm and family.

Mr. and Mrs. Millard Kefauver permitted the author to visit the Samuel Poffenberger farm, the lovely place which they own.

The Reverend D. Homer Kendall helped with the research on Bishop Geeting and the Geeting Meeting House.

Mr. and Mrs. George Line, current owners of the Locust Spring farm, always opened their hearts and home to the author.

Mrs. Park Loy shared her husband's papers relating to the seventy-fifth and one hundredth anniversary observances at Antietam.

Mr. and Mrs. John McCullom, owners of the Dr. Biggs house in Sharpsburg, helped me with the research on the doctor's life. The McCullom's work for WHAG-TV and were instrumental in getting Paul Cunningham of NBC-TV to do a special on Antietam on May 30, 1971.

Hazel Pry Moreno shared items of interest relating to the Pry family.

Mr. and Mrs. Leon Morgan gave information on the Chaplines at Mount Pleasant.

Dr. John H. Ness, Jr., curator and historian of the United Methodist Church, shared his wealth of information about the early days of the church of the United Brethren in Christ.

Miss Ruth Otto, a granddaughter of one of the founders of the Dunkard Church and daughter of the last minister of the church, assisted in the research on the historic congregation and building.

Webster Piper, former owner of the Piper farm, genealogist, and collector of Antietam materials, loaned his records of the Piper family.

Mr. and Mrs. Edgar Remsburg shared some of the John Smith Papers and related items about the old Nicodemus Hotel.

Fred Remsburg loaned his materials about Oliver Wendell Holmes at the Nicodemus farm.

Charles Ritchie gave information about the Samuel Neikirk farm.

The late Fred Scheller gave an account of the Hoffman farm and loaned the author the journal of H. R. Dunham who died in the Hoffman barn.

Louis Tuckerman, college professor and former historian at Antietam, shared his knowledge and vast research on the Dunkard Church.

John Winters, personal friend of Fred Cross and an outstanding historian in his own right, was a constant source of inspiration and information.

The Leo Wyands, who owned the Pry farm for thirty years, were always helpful.

These people are co-authors of *Drums Along the Antietam*. I just put on paper what they shared. My life is richer because of their sharing, and because of the moments spent in their homes, and in their fields along the Antietam.

INDEX

321